STRATEGIC PUBLIC PERSONNEL
ADMINISTRATION

STRATEGIC PUBLIC PERSONNEL ADMINISTRATION

Building and Managing Human Capital for the 21st Century

VOLUME 1

EDITED by ALI FARAZMAND

Westport, Connecticut
London

Library of Congress Cataloging-in-Publication Data

Strategic public personnel administration : building and managing human capital for the 21st century / edited by Ali Farazmand.

    p. cm.

    Includes bibliographical references and index.

    ISBN–0–275–96536–8 (set: alk. paper)—ISBN–0–275–99378–7 (vol 1 ; alk. paper)—ISBN–0–275–99380–9 (vol 2 : alk. paper)—1. Public administration. 2. Manpower planning. 3. Strategic planning. 4. Policy sciences. 5. Globalization. 6. Public administration—United States. 7. Civil service—United States—Personnel management. I. Farazmand, Ali.

    JF1351.S856 2007

    352.6′234—dc22   2006029132

British Library Cataloguing in Publication Data is available.

Library of Congress Catalog Card Number: 2006029132
ISBN: 0–275–96536–8 (set)
    0–275–99378–7 (v.1)
    0–275–99380–9 (v.2)

First published in 2007

Praeger Publishers, 88 Post Road West, Westport, CT 06881
An imprint of Greenwood Publishing Group, Inc.
www.praeger.com

Printed in the United States of America

The paper used in this book complies with the Permanent Paper Standard issued by the National Information Standards Organization (Z39.48–1984).

10 9 8 7 6 5 4 3 2 1

CONTENTS

PART IV. ISSUES AND TRENDS IN PUBLIC
PERSONNEL ADMINISTRATION

PREFACE

The history of public personnel administration is as old as human civilizations. Indeed, strategic public personnel administration has been in practice for at least 2500 years, if not longer, with planning, recruitment, and development of long-term career professional experts for key strategic positions in government and public administration leadership. Several great ancient civilizations—for example, Persia, China, Assyria, Egypt, and Rome—practiced strategic personnel management systems, some systematically and others unsystematically. An example of a systematic and elaborate strategic public management is what was practiced by the ancient Persian Empire, so famous for its highly efficient and effective public bureaucracy that managed the largest empire the world has ever known.

This was evident in the planning for, and development of, political and administrative leadership elites as well as key professional experts in the ancient world-state Achaemenid Persian Empire that governed virtually the entire known world of the time. In building the historic structure of the palace city complex of Persepolis in the 5th century B.C. that employed hundreds of thousands of workers and technical professionals and engineers, educated women also played a major role as "compensation managers and supervisors" many of whom also occupied key managerial positions in the huge bureaucracy.

Similar strategic positions and personnel were managed in all other areas of the meritorious Persian bureaucracy—from building and running the Continental Royal Highway that extended from Persepolis and Persian Gulf to Sardis, capital of the Lydian Satrapy in the eastern Mediterranean area; to building and managing hundreds of miles long underground irrigation canal systems, *Qanats*; to the construction and management of the Suez Canal (circa 500 B.C.) under Darius the Great. Although the centralized professional bureaucracy of Persia was pushed into a temporary backseat during the decentralized and yet powerful Parthian Empire for almost half a millennium, meritocracy and professionalism were immediately revived during the successive centralized and mighty Empire of Sasanid Persia that lasted till its fall to Islamic forces in the 7th century A.D.

Throughout these periods, goal-oriented strategic thinking and management characterized the Persian administrative systems and their public personnel administration for over a millennium. The legacies of the Persian strategic administrative system can be easily traced in the impacts and influences they have had on the governance and administrative systems of not only the regional governments of the east but also of the countries of the West such as Rome and Greeks that have inherited lessons learned from the knowledge on ancient Persia.

Ancient Assyria, Babylon, and Egypt prior to being conquered by Persia by Cyrus the Great in the 6th century B.C., as well as China and Rome later, also exercised various forms and degrees of practice in strategic thinking and management in governance and administration. These empires did practice strategic personnel administration, albeit unsystematically at times, and their interest in building managerial capacity through strategic personnel development was instrumental in managing major enterprises with success.

Notwithstanding the historical practice of strategic public personnel administration, the systematic study of strategy and strategic personnel administration is a fairly new development in the modern world. Indeed, such a study is only about 50 years or so old if we include the military strategic personnel administration. The more comprehensive and systematic study and teaching of strategic personnel management should be traced in the strategic management and systems theory literatures that have come to the forefront of management in public and private or business administration curricula. We also have to add the military systems in the United States and abroad in the post-World War II era. Indeed, one may argue that strategic thinking and administration has always been a key component of military planning and execution throughout the history. Thus, strategic public personnel administration has been and will continue to be a central function of strategic public administration, governance, and leadership, especially in the changing and uncertain environment of rapid globalization.

The 21st century will be characterized by rapid environmental, technological, demographic, economic, political, and cultural changes that pose serious challenges to governments and public personnel management worldwide. These challenges include growth of the knowledge societies, technological knowhows, transworld and transborder migrations of capital and labor, cyber employments and virtual workplaces, and relentless global pressures for results-oriented performance through outsourcing, networked organizations, and temporary-based human resources loosely joined by virtual places and institutions. Coping with and managing these challenges require new capacity building and development in human capital as a key asset of modern governments and private organizations. There is no escape from these global challenges of the 21st century if governments are to survive and thrive. Failure to address these and other strategic challenges of the 21st century will only result in disasters and demises.

This book was conceived initially a few years ago, when the world had began experiencing the massive fallouts of rapid globalization of corporate capitalism worldwide, with profound structural and process impacts of privatization, outsourcing, downsizing, and contracting out of public service and administration. The need for strategic thinking in public personnel administration and human capital development has never been so urgent. Today, strategic public personnel management is a central component of strategic governance and administration in public and nonprofit organizations. Although not a panacea, strategic personnel administration aims to lead organizations into the right directions with needed right people to achieve strategic goals and objectives in modern governance and public administration.

Aside from the above rationale that led to the initial conception of this important book, another impetus served as a major motivation: lack of few or inadequate textbooks with a focus on strategic thinking, development, and management of public personnel administration in the 21st-century governments. This book intends to fill in this major gap, and to hopefully serve as a key textbook that addresses the history, knowledge, policy, management, process, and culture of public personnel administration with a strategic perspective. Without such as strategic perspective, we cannot have a full analysis of the development and function of the field, and gain a clearly balanced picture of public personnel administration in both theory and practice.

This book is not a "how to do strategic personnel management." Rather, it advances knowledge on the concept, history, organization, management, policy, and politics of strategic public personnel administration and its institutional settings such as civil service and bureaucracy, patronage and career systems. It also addresses a host of other issues that affect the function, behavior, performance, and value or culture of governance and public administration. As such, the book is also an important policy tool for political executives and public administrators in running the machinery of government. It is, moreover, a major primary and secondary textbook in graduate and upper undergraduate public personnel administration/HRM courses in public administration and policy programs worldwide.

This book could not have been accomplished without the genuine cooperation of its contributors. Their preparation, revisions, and last-minute updating of their manuscripts made this book a fresh and most up-to-date textbook on strategic public personnel administration or HRM. My special thanks go to all the contributors. I would also like to thank the publisher Greenwood and its senior editor, Nicholas Philipson, whose patience and cooperation made the book a success. Moreover, I would like my former doctoral student, Jocelyn Fernandez, who provided some assistance in the initial stage of the project. Finally, my appreciation also goes to another of my doctoral students, Rafiqul Islam, who assisted me in the final work of completing and sending the book to the publisher. His assistance is very much appreciated. May I also thank the production people at Greenwood Press for their timely work and quality production of the book?

Ali Farazmand
Florida Atlantic University
March 2006

PART I

STRATEGIC PUBLIC PERSONNEL ADMINISTRATION/HRM: HISTORY, DEVELOPMENT, AND TRANSFORMATION

1

Strategic Public Personnel Administration: A Conceptual Framework for Building and Managing Human Capital in the 21st Century

ALI FARAZMAND

HISTORY, CONCEPTS, AND PERSPECTIVES

History

Public personnel administration is a historical component of public administration. As such, it is also as old as human civilization, dating back to several millennia, when mass scale public administration projects were carried out. The advent of agriculture and rise of slavery required, and facilitated, the practice of personnel management with different scales. Construction of large-scale public works projects in the ancient time required slaves, semi slaves, mercenaries, volunteers, obligatory laborers, and paid workers, all of whom had to be organized, coordinated, and managed. Selection of different workers, skilled and unskilled, and professional artisans such as carpenters, blacksmiths, accountants, record keepers, inspectors, planners, stone cutters, artists, and the like was not an arbitrary function; it was mostly calculated with instrumental rationality as well as political loyalty.

Construction of the Pyramids in Egypt, of the Suez Canal in Egypt under the Persian rule circa 500 B.C., of the gigantic Persepolis ceremonial capital-city structure in 5th century B.C. Persia, the great Wall of China about the same time, as well as many other huge public projects in Rome, Persia, and elsewhere indicate how human labor and skills were organized, selected, retained, coordinated, and managed to achieve planned and unplanned goals throughout the history of human civilizations. Similarly, the early Sumerian elaborate city planning, the early

Iranian Elamite Empire's strategic planning and construction of underground canal systems, the Persian bureaucracy and administrative system, and the Roman army regimentation demonstrate how human activities were elaborately selected, developed, mastered, and managed with efficiency and effectiveness on a large scale. Recent discoveries show evidence of "women supervisors" serving as managers of the compensation system during the 90-year-period construction process of the gigantic Persepolis superstructure as the ceremonial capital of the first World-State Achaemenid Persian Empire in the 5th century B.C. Thousands of skilled workers, professionals, and functionaries were selected from around the vast corners of the empire to perform the project; their compensation system was a challenging task. The women bureaucrats performed an efficient job of personnel management, many of whom must have served in strategic positions of public administration.

Thus, the history of public personnel administration goes as far back as early human civilizations. Continuity in civil and military public personnel administration is also manifest in the landmark public projects—roads, highways, buildings, bridges, fortifications, palaces, castles, and others—built around the world during the last two millennia.

What is more significant about the history of public personnel is the "strategic" feature of this undeclared and understudied profession within public administration throughout its long history. While supervisory personnel management is very common throughout the history, strategic personnel management has played a key function in recruitment, selection, development, and retention of strategic personnel for key positions or tasks. Thus appears the role of strategic personnel management in the history of public administration. But what does the concept "strategic" mean?

Concepts and Perspectives

By "strategic," I mean at least two principal perspectives: One is the long-term, capital building and development perspective that guides today and tomorrow's preparation through education and training in human resources management for a long-term and results-oriented future performance and organizational behavior. This strategic perspective must be congruent with the overall strategic mission, vision, and plans for building and managing human capital to meet the challenges of the 21st century. It requires broad-based, holistic thinking with visions that consider all sorts of challenges as well as opportunities in the age of accelerated globalization of capital, labor, management, organizational diversity, and virtual as well as space-oriented organizations worldwide.

The second meaning of strategic public personnel administration refers to instrumentally key positions as well as functions and tasks that link the nerve system of operation of an organization in government and nonprofit organizations. All positions and functions or tasks are important to organizations. However, high-performing organizational managers and leaders know—and should know—well that certain positions and functions or tasks are instrumental to linking strategic performance points of an organization, and this is where preparation for human capital building and management is absolutely essential to manage the highly demanding organizations with increasingly complex and challenging environments in the age of rapid globalization of the 21st century.

In this new volatile environment, every manager and administrator must learn how to ride the high waves of change, develop and pursue vision, manage his/her employees and coworkers, and coordinate human performance activities with skilled leadership, motivation, and equitable compensation. Building and developing such a human capital or asset also requires capacity building in retention and promotion, without which organizational waste and productivity loss are almost guaranteed.

Key to understanding and implementation of these strategic perspectives in building and managing human capital is innovations in flexible structuration concerning organizational authority and decision-making systems, communication networks, coordination, job and position classifications, virtual as well as space-based workplaces, planning and recruitment, and promotion, compensation, and motivation systems. The age of structural rigidity to maintain stability is over, and the new age of the 21st century requires massive "flexibilization." However, like everything else, flixibilization offers its own negative as well as positive effects to public personnel administration systems; it offers opportunities to both management and labor, but it also carries drawbacks and problems to employees and workers.

DIMENSIONS OF STRATEGIC PUBLIC PERSONNEL ADMINISTRATION

There are several dimensions to strategic public personnel administration in modern organizations of governments and nonprofit sectors, as well as private sector corporations. While these dimensions are rather universal across sectors and organizations, there are key features unique to public organizations. These features include partisan politics and patronage systems, parliamentary versus presidential systems, or a combination of the two that define the environmental parameters of personnel systems in governments; legislative and other legal or constitutional requirements or constraints that public personnel managers are conditioned by; and a host of such other issues as gender, race and color, representation, diversity, fairness, and equality, among others. The following briefly outlines some of the key dimensions of strategic public personnel administration in the 21st century.

Strategic Planning Dimension

Strategic planning is a key component of the systems approach to public personnel administration. A systems approach requires several key components, such as advance identification of a vision as well as mission statements, strategic and operational goals and objectives, and strategies to achieve those goals and missions. Obviously, these coherent ideas are recent formulations and conceptualizations, but the history of strategic management is as old as civilizations and it goes back to the ancient time.

As a key component of strategic public administration, strategic personnel administration was viewed highly for recruitment and development of key leadership and supervisory positions under, for example, the first World-State Achaemenid Empire of Persia during King Darius the Great, who initiated long-term strategic planning and administration as part of his "administrative reforms" around 520 B.C. The reforms were aimed at building and developing administrative capacity suitable to the management of the vast Empire that covered virtually the entire known world of the ancient time for well over 220 years, extending at times from India and Central Asia in the East to North Africa and Southern Europe in the West (Cook, 1983; Frye, 1975).

Gender played a major role in the efficient bureaucracy, and women served as significant compensation system managers during the 80+ years of the construction of the gigantic ceremonial capital of the Persian Empire, Persepolis, involving over 100,000 professionals, artisans, and laborers, not slaves. Persians did not practice slavery since the time of their Founding Father Cyrus the Great, who abolished slavery forever in his 526 B.C. Declaration of the "Universal Charter of Human Rights," the first in human history. The bureaucracy was staffed on the basis of merit and professionalization of the civil service and personnel system expanded by advance planning and training schools attached to the bureaucracy and public enterprise organizations throughout the Empire (Cook, 1983; Farazmand, 2001; Ghirshman, 1954). We may find similar strategic planning dimension in other parts of the ancient world, such as China and Rome.

Strategic planning envisions a long term plan of reaching where the personnel system desires to be in 10, 15, or 20 years, while outlining clear goals, objectives, and programs by which to accomplish its mission. Strategic public personnel administration of the 21st century must envision a period of at least 25 to 30 years in advance and plan for a sound system of management that has the capacity to anticipate and respond to the needs of a fast changing knowledge society in the age of globalization. This is a big challenge of strategic planning and development. No country in the current world has such a full capacity, and it will be a daunting task that challenges all public managers in the new century. Strategic public personnel planning and management must answer the big questions of "what" and "when" in governance and administration.

Structural Dimensions

Structural dimensions must address the big question of "*where*," meaning several things that point to the "*locus*" and "*focus*" of modern strategic public personnel administration. First, it means the "location" of the strategic positions in an organization. This is fairly identified by the organizational chart, but not necessarily always the case, as some positions outside the formal organizational chart gain prominence over time and become central to organizations without being emphasized in their formal structure. Second is the *"focus"* of the subjects or departments and programs that an organizational leadership or legal authority gives them in different times. Focus may change as time and external environmental changes demand; here, flexibility and adaptation become key words in strategic public personnel management.

Third is the structural *"locus"* question of centralization or decentralization of public personnel administration. This is a key strategic question to all governments. Under the traditional systems of administration, a centralized system of personnel management was a universal rule. Many governments still practice this system through a centralized personnel agency in charge of handling all personnel matters for the entire government agencies. It provides coherence, fairness, and a high degree of professionalism, but its disadvantages such as red tape, delay, and poor or lack of timely adaptation to changing environment cannot be overlooked. Very often, highly talented recruits are lost to the labor market due to delays in processing and inability to hire qualified people in time.

The recent worldwide waves of reforms have emphasized "agencification"— not to be confused with my earlier terms of "chainification and outsourcing" —and decentralization of public personnel administration by individual agencies and organizations with great deal of flexibility and managerial discretion to respond to rapid changes and organizational needs. While offering great advantages of adaptability and flexibility, decentralization has a tendency to promote nepotism, conflicts of interests, and patronage of personalism in civil service and personnel systems; it can also promote potential administrative abuse and corruption, and thus hurting the long-term strategic performance of an organization. Centralization or decentralization is an old snake-and-ladder issue, and these two terms have taken their turn over time, as the snake gets tired of staying either on the ground or at the top of the ladder.

Process Dimension

The process dimension must answer the key question of "how" in strategic public personnel administration. This dimension addresses the processes of personnel functions and behaviors leading to expected performance results or outcomes. It include software, hardware, techniques, methods, approaches, systems, procedures, rules and regulations, and many other issues that are central to the "process" of public personnel administration system—processing and transforming inputs into desired outputs. However, the real process of personnel system is dynamic and goes beyond mechanical transformation of inputs into outputs; the process becomes much more synergetic and holistic with dynamic changes of its own.

Value and Cultural Dimensions

Viewing organizations as systems, we find a powerful institutional dimension of cognition, that is the normative value feature that tends to mold and modify the structural and process dimensions of an organization. The value dimension is formed by a multitude of elements such as people, religion, belief, perception, formal policy, and informal habit that never stay stagnant; rather they change and transform dynamically, and by so doing, these attributes form and reform organizational cultures by defining and redefining the basic assumptions organizations live on. The normative values helping shape organizational culture tend to institutionalize as they progress and transform; they give, and take away, legitimacy to policy and administrative actions, hence a powerful institutional dimension of organizations.

Public personnel systems operate in such an environment and carry within themselves the powerful value or cognitive dimension that is extremely important to organizational change, adaptation, and strategic functions of modern governance and administration. Once institutionalized, organization culture is the hardest to change and alter. That is why building and developing a professional, strategic oriented, and representative public personnel system of administration is extremely important to capacity building for national development and long-term modernization programs.

Functional Performance Dimension

This is where action and actual behavior of performance count. Strategic public personnel administration is expected to respond to organizational, institutional, managerial, citizen-driven service expectations and needs at local, national, and now global levels, as most governments are becoming players of the globalization processes one way or the other and must develop capacity to function in this world of increasing globalization.

Strategic personnel administration is tested by its functional behaviors, that is, delivery of expected or desired results and outcomes, from planning and forecast analysis to recruitment, development and compensation, and motivation. Every step in the process of functional performance, whether decentralized or centralized, must be taken with competence, professional criteria, and democratic representation as well as responsiveness, not to particularistic interests but to the broad-based public interests of citizens. This is a functional challenge strategic personnel system must meet in the age of rapid change and globalization.

A key feature of this functional performance challenge is delivery of quality personnel, from operational to managerial, who are expected to perform and produce high quality outcomes and results. As governments are challenged increasingly to perform more like private market organizations in an increasingly volatile and changing environment, "quality" becomes more and more a top priority to compete and progress or decline and wither away through downsizing, outsourcing, contracting out, and eventual privatization.

Organizational Dimension

Organizational dimension presents an interesting yet challenging task to strategic public personnel administration. Traditional organizations of government were structurally stable and defined goals and environmental predictability. Personnel administration was similarly stable operating in a stable environment full of predictability suitable for forecasting, planning, and recruitment. Personnel systems of modern public organizations in the 21st century is significantly different and more challenging as it is more difficult. Public service delivery organizational systems have become pluralized and their structural features reconfigured toward multiorganizational and network structures with rapidly changing and adaptive capabilities or requirements that must deal with transient and temporary workforces.

To operate in this environment of networked and multiorganizational structure capacity system, modern public personnel administration must be prepared to strategically develop and adapt to rapid changes, yet not lose sight of immediate tasks of operational capacity to deliver effectively and efficiently. One way to build and manage new capacity is to integrate personnel functions system-wide throughout an organization; every department of organizational unit needs to be developed with a strategic human resource capacity management. Every supervisor and manager must be viewed as a strategic human resource or personnel manager regardless of what the departmental or locus is in the organization. Spreading personnel capacity system-wide builds organizational capacity in all areas of personnel and performance. Yet the key strategic function of public personnel administration does not diminish. On the contrary, it becomes a part of the organizational central nerve system that must read the short- and long-term environmental conditions of organizational domains. It must respond accordingly with maximum adaptation and capacity in forecasting, labor market analysis, and more exactly the environment of temporary labor force, "flexibilization" criterion, and other requirements that drive public organizations to act more like private business corporations.

Leadership and Managerial Dimensions

Key to strategic public personnel administration is a sound leadership to manage not only the human capital, but also the entire organization. Leadership is the glue of an organization, and strategic personnel administration is a key part of sound leadership. No organization can exist or operate without a competent cadre of personnel, and managerial soundness requires understanding, appreciation, and proper utilization of valuable human resources that constitute the human capital of the organization, especially in the knowledge society of the 21st century.

The leadership dimension of public personnel administration presents three distinct sub-dimensions: One consists of the two groups of political and career appointees. Political executives' appointment as heads and leaders of public organizations are on the basis of partisan, personal, and political criteria. They are political managers in charge of organizational leadership. Right below them are a cadre of highly experienced, professional civil servants whose longevity in service, expertise, and professionalism afford them invaluable institutional memory so vital to organizational leadership that they become the highest valued assets of public organizations. These two groups of politicians and top bureaucrats are often in conflict due to political and partisan preferences, but their cooperation and teamwork are key to organizational success.

The second subdimension deals with the civil service system, and as an extension of the first, it has to do with the machinery of government. Civil service systems can vary from the American model to its close cousin of the British elitism, to the French bureaucratic and other parliamentary systems with a strong bureaucracy under control of the ruling political party in government. Civil service system is generally on career personnel administration with laws, rules, and regulations protecting public employees from partisan abuse and affording them a degree of independence in policy implementation as well as initiation and formulation. The higher civil servants play a key role in the management of a bureaucracy in government.

The third subdimension of the leadership dimension in strategic public personnel administration is the policy matter that plays as a guiding lever in organizational performance by its personnel. Personnel policy in recruitment, planning, development and training, compensation, promotion, and other functions sets the tone of organizational formal culture and signals values of fairness or unfairness, discrimination or equality, merit or patronage and arbitrary behavior, and representation or exclusivity in public management. It also reflects the priorities and preferences of the governing political leadership of the time.

Labor-Management Dimension

Labor movements and labor organizations have been around for thousands of years. However, officially recognized or legally established employee and worker organizations have gained the status during the long struggles of the last two centuries. Yet, their progress and development has always been marred by employer organized violence, firing, and legislative pressure under probusiness governments of capitalism.

The labor-management dimension of public personnel administration is a very significant part of governance in all societies, as without employees and workers nothing gets done. And wherever there are workers and managers, there are potential conflicts and differences between the two groups. Managers always seek unrestrained absolute discretion in dealing with employees and workers. Workers and employees, however, have their own interests to protect and promote, interests that range from pay and working conditions to job security and health and retirement benefits.

Without a union organization to deal with the power of management, workers and employees are subject to abuse, manipulation, and exploitation. Thus, public sector management-labor relations presents a strong challenge in personnel administration. This is a more serious challenge when governments are under the pressures of corporate globalization, with massive downsizing, workforce restructuring, and conversion to temporary labor at the expense of a career-oriented workforce.

Environmental Dimension

This dimension of strategic public personnel administration reflects the environmental conditions the system operates in. These conditions include a multitude of religious, political, cultural, economic, financial, and geographical factors and values that influence and affect the shaping and reshaping of organizational and personnel system culture, values, performance, and effectiveness. Public personnel systems operate under local, regional, national, and now global or international environments, each of which presents significant challenges to its structure, process, and capacity to perform.

In today's environment of rapid globalization, changes come fast and challenge personnel systems to adapt to new realities of labor out-migration, immigration, job and capital flight to overseas, technological innovations, and changing knowledge and skill requirements. The world is becoming more uncertain in many ways, and managing human resources in this environment requires strategic vision, ideas, and skills.

Technological Dimension

Technology is a tool to get things done with higher efficiency and accuracy. Technological innovation is key to adaptation and modernization of public personnel administration. Changing technology demands changing structural and process flexibility, with a culture that can welcome new changes. Technological changes also force public personnel managers to abandon traditional routine ways of performance and demand new techniques, methods, soft and hardware systems, and knowledge and skills in managing organizational functions. The Internet system, e-mail systems, and a multitude of other fast advancing forms of technological innovations allow managers and employees to perform with efficiency and effectiveness, while providing them with many opportunities for personal and professional growth and development. Yet, like any technology, personnel administration technologies have their own downsides. Notwithstanding these drawbacks, technological advancements are defining and redefining the environments of organizations worldwide, and e-governance and e-personnel administration systems are developing rapidly around the world.

ISSUES IN STRATEGIC PUBLIC PERSONEL ADMINISTRATION

Key issues in strategic public administration are many and subjects of multiple volumes of book presentations. They range from social and economic to managerial, political, and legal or constitutional, local and national or global, as well as professional and labor, and the like. Following is a brief account of some of these broad issues.

Socioeconomic Issues

Social issues in strategic pubic personnel administration raise several important concerns that range from social equity and fairness to class and social mobility and organizational representation to economic status and development. For example, "public" employment of middle and lower class as well as racially and ethically diverse or disadvantage groups brings into society an element of inclusion and integration that contributes to social mobility. Social mobility in turn promotes potential for raising standards of living, higher income level and tax revenues pouring into government treasury, leading to more resources for economic and social programs of development, progress, and advancement.

The advantages of strategic employment further advances causes for social equity and fairness by contributing to the abridgement of the social and economic gaps that exist in society. An example is the U.S. Postal Service that was established to promote public employment, social equity, and economic development. Creation and operation of most public enterprise organizations (government corporations) have similarly contributed to social and economic conditions of populations and economies. Similarly, gender-based employment strategically removes not only barriers to social mobility and economic advancement of the female population, it may also raise educated female population into higher levels of social representation across public organizations.

Three cases may illustrate how strategically key positions can play a significant social, economic, and political role in public personnel administration in the United States. First is the long-standing struggle of the blacks and Hispanics who constitute a substantial percentage of the population, have historically and systematically suffered discrimination and exclusion from equal opportunities and promotion to important positions of public employment; affirmative action and new attempts to improve their situations have since the 1970s improved their conditions, but they still mostly lack access to key strategic positions in the federal bureaucracy and public administration. The second group are women who, after suffering a long period of similar discrimination and exclusion, have since the last two decades made significant strides toward inclusion and occupation of important positions in par with dominant white males, and indeed, many are positioned in "strategic" positions in most of the public organizations and institutions of higher education; they have passed the earlier stage of "overrepresentation at the bottom" and taken some commanding heights and are able to challenge and even exclude the dominant whites as well as other minorities, especially people of foreign origins.

The third group of people overcoming earlier struggles and potential discrimination or exclusion consists of unspoken and unspeakable people of minority religions, namely Jews, Hindus, Muslims, and others. Of these three subgroups, Jews seemed to have faired a lot better by blending in the mainstream and through extensive political and economic lobbying and organizational power. They have made a remarkable stride in positioning themselves in key "strategic positions" in almost all organizations of governance—legislative, executive, and judicial branches—at all levels of government as well as in nongovernmental, nonprofit, and community organizations, including institutions of higher education and policy think tanks. Once in a key position, they open opportunities for their own potential newcomers and provide powerful legal and network protections toward faith-based representation through seamless neutral competence and expertise in the competition process. Hindus and some other religious groups have also made somewhat fair in public employment and academic institutions, but it is the latter subgroup, the Muslims who have suffered most in the predominant religious-cultural environment of "Judaia-Christianity," a self-declared alliance of the conservative religious Right that claims self-righteousness and superiority over all other religions.

In the post-9/11 social and political environment, there has also been a de facto "crusade war" (using George W. Bush's own term) declared against Muslims in public organizations, institutions of higher education, and other organizations across the country. They are now subjected to exclusion and discriminatory practices almost everywhere, and by the white males, women, and "chosen" or preferred people who are in key strategic positions of organizations. In this era of self-declared global clash of civilizations—of the West against East (Huntington, 1993), Muslims often find themselves discriminated against, excluded, and subjected to arbitrary treatments, with doors of opportunities shot at their face. This is done more often rather silently and painfully, with rationality. Coming from a Middle Eastern or Islamic origin means an almost automatic subjection to exclusion and differential treatments.

These examples do not even include the Native Americans who once owned this land but have for over a century been subjected to the caging confinement of "reservations" and virtual extinction. Thus, strategic social representation is a prediction for substantive policy and program representations in government and other organizations of society. Strategic public personnel administration is therefore key to bridging such a huge gap that exists in a country whose political elites claim slogans of democracy and representation but have a long way to go, first to correct the past injustices and undemocratic practices at home and abroad, and then to practice what they preach worldwide. Strategic public personnel administration is a central mechanism through which such unfair and unequal treatments can be corrected in action.

Social representation is strategically significant though not enough in changing the outcomes of public service and administration. However, it does contribute to a change of character of public personnel administration by opening the doors to knowledge and talent development, new managerial capacity, and culture of

administration sensitive to equality and fairness. The higher the levels of organizational employment, the higher the strategic contributions to the values of
public personnel administration, public management, and organizational behavior. It also contributes to the normative feature of power relationship that defines
organizational leadership and behavior.

Managerial and Organizational Issues

Organizational and managerial dimensions are the two fundamental and most
important areas that cover numerous issues of strategic human resource or personnel management in government and nonprofit organizations. Organizational
issues define the locus and focus of key positions and people in strategic locations, identify and place priorities in organizational structure and process, and
emphasize the importance of culture cultivated through leadership and organizational behavior. The managerial issues develop and evolve functions and behavior that act as glues in the multiple web systems of organizational structure,
behavior, and performance. They make things possible, and activate or reacti-
vate the organizational performance engine through strategic personnel administration processes and functions, from planning and recruitment to training and
development to compensation and retirement programs or lack of. In essence, organizational and managerial dimensions form the constitution of public personnel
administration.

Many issues form this category, and they include structural flexibility or rigidity, location of personnel system in the overall organizational system, staff or line
emphasis of personnel functions, coordination and synchronization of external
and internal market domains for recruitment and selection processes, politics or
merit issues, specialization or generality in knowledge requirement, centralization or decentralization, command and control system, supervision and authority
relations, report and accountability matters, cutbacks or growth decision issues,
growth and development, and many more. It is these and many other issues that
make organizational and managerial dimensions central to strategic public personnel administration.

Human Capital: Knowledge and Skills

We live in an age of human capital development, that is the age of knowledge,
skills, and attitudes, all of which constantly define and redefine the structural,
process, and cultural/behavioral requirements for an effective and productive personnel management in government. Knowledge means ideas and technologies,
and technologies require new skills and training for their acquisition and development. Knowledge then becomes power, but power can become concentrated
not necessarily by those possessing the knowledge and skills, but in the hands of
those who control the means and organization of knowledge and skills. They are
the elites, the power elites who by the virtue of ownership, control, and ability

to make decisions affecting large number of organizations and peoples in society are able to command and control the management of public and private organizations. With the increasing mergers of organizations, shrinking public sector organizations, privatization, and outsourcing public service functions, more concentration of power is taking in the hands of few elites who tend to dominate large number of organizations and determine the future of governance and administration.

Human capital development and management then becomes key to progress, decline, growth, performance and productivity in public and private organizations. New human capital requires new knowledge management skills, skills that are needed badly to envision, plan, and develop ideas for organizational innovation and productivity. Knowledge management demands investment in human capital building, development, and management, especially in the age of globalization characterized by rapid change and culture shocks. The new culture demands new attitudes that make or break performance and productivity standards. Human capital and knowledge management are needed in all areas of technical, intellectual, service, and operational areas, and at all levels of government from local to global. Complex environments require complex organizations, knowledge base, and management.

Legal and Constitutional Issues

Legal and constitutional dimensions create and define issues that are borne out of the labor management relations, individual rights and responsibilities, laws and regulations that govern employee relations, an organizational interaction with its environment. The constitutional concerns of discrimination, liberty, freedom of speech and expression, privacy, due process, fairness, equal rights and treatment, discrimination, and many other related issues that affect the working environment and functions of public personnel management.

Strategically, these and other related legal and constitutional issues require special knowledge development and competence by application, an essential basis of legal competence not only for current but also future performance in public personnel administration. They demand capacity building in today and tomorrow's public personnel management in the categories of specialist and generalist functions of personnel, managerial and operational, and technical and service areas.

Merit and Professionalism

Merit and meritocracy are the core values of any effective strategic personnel administration. Merit systems ensure the identification, recruitment, selection, and development of right human capital, with knowledge, talent, and skills that are needed to perform specialized and general functions of an organization. These attributes form the basis of professionalization of personnel administration and

organizations within which it operates. Professionalization of personnel administration promotes professionalism with standards of excellence, ethical norms and
values, and performance quality in public and private organizations.

The issues of merit and professionalism define the central values of efficiency
and effectiveness of a public personnel administration system. They have at the
same time become the center of academic and political debates in governance
and administration worldwide. Merit values can clash with the values of representation and fairness in a broader context of society, where different groups and
classes of citizens with disparate educational and knowledge bases seek representation in the government bureaucracy and market organizations for employment
and opportunity for social and economic mobility but lack necessary skills and
qualifications to compete with well-to-do and better educated workforce. Merit
and professionalism may also conflict with political values of partisan and ideological demands for control and command, change, and particularistic group
interests. Thus, merit and professionalism cover a wide range of issues with
far-reaching consequences for governance and public administration. They form
strategic issues of public personnel administration, primarily concerned with values of efficiency, effectiveness, and broad-based "public interests." They also promote representations and democratic values through adherence to excellence in
quality performance, professional standards, and ethical and accountability criteria.

Politics and Patronage

A central issue of all civil service systems is the extent to which politics and patronage play a role. Politics reflects not only the policy preferences of the time, but
also the personal and partisan and a host of institutional, organizational, managerial, ideological and other forms of politics. However, the most important issue
of politics in civil service is patronage as opposed to merit and professionalism
noted above.

All civil service systems carry with them a degree of patronage, or running
a bureaucracy with personal and partisan criteria, from recruitment to development to promotion and retirement. This issue of patronage has been the subject of
numerous studies, books, and debates in governance and public administration.
Should meritocracy and professionalism guide the organization and management
of governance, or patronage and politics be the criteria? Patronage was pervasive
as the dominant model of administration during the 19th-century American federal government. It produced the spoils system with massive corruption, which
in turn led to the reform movement and the enactment of the U.S. Civil Service
Reform Act of 1883. The Act aimed at abolishing corruption and replacing the patronage system with a merit system for efficiency and professional effectiveness.

After several decades of progress in professionalism and meritocracy in the
civil service, the federal bureaucracy became the subject of a renewed wave of
patronage during the Reagan administration in the 1980s, a decade of massive

practice of patronage at all levels, too often rationalized for policy and partisan purposes. Patronage has taken a new twist in George W. Bush's presidency by appointment of individuals with questionable qualifications for the jobs or agencies they are expected to lead. An example of this problem has been the disastrous and scandalous case of handling of the Hurricane Katrina disaster in New Orleans that led to massive policy and administrative failures on the part of the Federal Emergency Management Agency (FEMA) under Michael Brown, a close friend of Bush by virtue of financial campaign contributions. As this book is being prepared for production, a whole series of federal government failures, specifically of the Department of Homeland Security (DHS) under Chertoff, is being investigated through Congressional Hearings. The issue has gone beyond an agency failure and has touched the largest bureaucracy of the world in America, DHS.

A political scientist, Charles Jones (1984), once noted, "the causes of policy failures are, at root, political" (p. 1). Yes, when politics, not professional qualifications, guide a professional agency like FEMA in the face of disasters, the result often is disaster itself, produced by mismanagement and leadership crisis, especially at the federal level where all the institutional and logistic capacities were available but not utilized due to political failure.

Ethical and Accountability Issues

Almost anything done, or not done, in government has ethical and accountability implications. Ethical issues arise when conflict of interests, bribery and embezzlement, and nepotism and favoritism, among others, are practiced and tolerated without impunity. Accountability is a safeguard against corruption, but its violation or unaccountability in decision making, policy initiation, and implementation occur when policymakers and administrators are not held accountable for their actions or inactions that cause harm or destroy public trust.

After almost 2 years of the invasion of Iraq, the CBS *60 Minutes* (Sunday, February 12, 2006) program reported that over $8 billion of U.S. federal money given to friendly corporate contractors was totally gone and unaccounted for. Ethical and accountability issues, therefore, are central to good and sound governance and administration; they transcend civil service and all governmental processes. Ethics, accountability, and transparency along with responsibility constitute central principles of good and sound governance and administration; they often are in short supply in practice, including in self-declared democracies—or rather plutocracies—like the United States, where secrecy and unaccountability are easily rationalized under security pretexts.

Labor/Union-Management Issues

Labor-management relations have been the subject of contention between employees and workers on the one hand, and employers or managers on the other hand, ever since the ancient times. With each side seeking to maximize its own interests, the process often leads to confrontation, disputes, and at times even violence. With the rapid changes through sweeping privatization and outsourcing strategies to the degree of attempts to dismantle a century-long tradition of labor gains through struggles, and now with the full swing process of corporate globalization, the labor/unions are being pushed to the corner again and forced to losing many if not most gains they had acquired for over a century.

We will expect a return back to the practices of the medieval age, indeed worse than that age. Unlike the medieval feudal or slavery ages, where the masters and slave owners had the obligation of providing the basic subsistence of food, shelter, and security to their servers and slaves, the modern globalizing social order of corporate capitalism does not see any such obligation, moral or otherwise. Under the new order, everyone is expected to fend for himself or herself in the jungle of the market system. Yet, despite this new "market absolutism," the labor cannot be reduced to a totally "disposable commodity" for the sake of profit. New skills and knowledge are needed in the knowledge society, and knowledge management needs trained labor/employees to run the business of government and private organizations. Thus, the issue of labor will persist with contention.

Technological and Other Issues

Technological issues pose a serious challenge to public personnel administration, as innovations and advancement constantly require new knowledge and skills, as well as financial capacity to acquire them. Technological issues present both positive and negative challenges to personnel systems, freeing labor forces from hard work, while causing at the same time potential for work-related incidence of injuries and illness as well as displacements through downsizing and loss of job security.

Aside from the select issues outlined above, every stage or step taken in the process of personnel administration, in both government and business enterprises, raises many other critical issues. These include human resources planning, recruitment, selection, training and development, placement and evaluation, rewards, benefits and pay, disciplinary action, and more. And at each of these stages, all issues outlined above immediately appear and play a major role, such as patronage or merit, ethics and accountability, social and economic consideration, fairness and equal rights, etc.

These crosscutting issues transcend the entire public personnel system, and strategically define or redefine its process and outcome. Yet recruitment, development, and performance of qualified employees in the age of knowledge management is crucial, a subject of numerous studies and debates.

Globalization and Global Issues

Globalization and global issues have been redefining almost everything the worlds of government and administration have experienced so far. The mega changes and consequences these changes of globalization—a process through which world-wide integration is taking place economically, politically, and socially—are producing is beyond the clear imagination of any manager or politician. The consequences are serious, and the need for a strategic public personnel administration with a new capacity to look into the horizon and produce competent personnel and managers that can strategically guide the ships of progress and development in the high tides of change that affect government and nonprofit organizations in the age of rapid globalization has never been so great. Thus, globalization raises numerous issues and concerns for effective management of strategic public personnel administration. Indeed, globalization sets the broadest possible context in which the new, strategic, public personnel administration must operate.

PLAN OF THE BOOK

This book is organized into four parts and twenty-four chapters. Each part carries several chapters under a common theme, and they all contain freshly presented material with the most up-to-date information and data on strategic public personnel administration. While some chapters focus on the personnel system in the United States, the overall tone of the book has universal application in mind regardless of cultural boundaries. The aim is to present instructional material that serves graduate and undergraduate classrooms, teachers, students, researchers, policymakers, public personnel practitioners, analysts, and consultants worldwide.

Part I covers seven chapters on historical, conceptual, and meanings of strategic public personnel administration. Specifically, Chapter 2 by a leading scholar of the U.S. civil service history, Paul Van Riper, sets a historical background of public personnel administration in the United States. Chapter 3 provides a new perspective on strategic personnel administration in government and nonprofit organizations; this is done by another public personnel scholar, Donald Klingner with an associate Gamal Sabet. In Chapter 4, Steven Ott and Lisa Dicke present accountability challenges that face public sector personnel mangers in an era of downsizing, devolution, diffusion, and disempowerment.

Chapter 5 is a thorough analysis of making the transition to strategic human resource management; this is done by yet another expert scholar, Steven Hays. In Chapter 6, Marc Holzer, Hedy Isaacs, and Seok-Hwan Lee offer an interesting discussion of the context and strategies for productive human resource management in the 21st century. In Chapter 7, another leading scholar of public personnel management and organizational behavior, Frederick Thayer, challenges us all by arguing that "government does strategic planning while pretending it does not." He is right on target and his challenge needs to be taken seriously, as often students, scholars, and practitioners are given the impression that strategic "planning" is a socialist idea and not practiced in corporate America. Obviously, such an impression is a false idea and must be cleared. Finally, in Chapter 8, Ali Farazmand presents an in-depth analysis of innovations in strategic human resource management for building capacity to meet the challenges of the globalization age.

Part II deals with bureaucracy, civil service, and politics, with five chapters covering several key issues that define the character of public personnel systems in all times. In Chapter 9, Robert Maranto argues for politics and patronage in public personnel management in the United States, leaving little doubt about its drawbacks. Chapter 10 is presented by Sally Selden, who makes an argument for ending civil service paralysis through a discussion of the emerging practices and trends in state personnel management systems. This is followed by a "modest proposal" in Chapter 11 by William Murray and Gary Wamsley, regarding political appointees to solve the current crisis of the U.S. civil service and personnel management. Finally, in Chapter 12, Ali Farazmand presents a strategic analysis of civil service reforms in the United States in an historical perspective, from past to the present, with future directions and implications for education and training. This is a political economy analysis, with implications for winners and losers, management and labor, and theory and practice.

Part III covers a number of topics and dimensions of organizational behavior and strategic public personnel management in a broad-based perspective. Five chapters present burnout, job mobility, high performance work teams, performance appraisal, and ethical concern of conflict of interests of off-campus consulting activities of public administration and affairs faculty. Specifically, Chapter 13 by Robert Golembiewski and Thomas Myers offers an interesting discussion of how phase model of burnout as leverage in meeting "future forces" that challenge human resource development and management across cultures.

In Chapter 14, Lois Recascino Wise and Barbara Lamb offer an analysis of "job mobility assignments" as mechanisms for human resource capacity development. Chapter 15 by Michael Klausner presents an important discussion of high performance teams and their role in strategic public personnel administration. Chapter 16 by Behrooz Kalantari is also an interesting discussion regarding the linkage between performance appraisal and organizational strategic planning in public personnel administration. Finally, in Chapter 17, James Bowman and Carole Jurkiewicz challenge all academic scholars and teachers with their powerful discussion of how conflict of interests and ethical dilemma can develop when on-campus faculty of public administration go town as off-campus consultants to corporate business organizations and government agencies.

Part IV covers six chapters dealing with a wide range of important issues and trends central to public personnel administration. Chapter 18 by Jack DeSario and James Slack presents a powerful argument regarding new challenges facing public personnel administration, namely the issues of equal opportunity, affirmative action, and the Constitution. Discrimination and violation of individual rights are key issues of concern in workplaces all over the United States and around the world. In Chapter 19, Lloyd Nigro and William Waugh, Jr. present a significant perspective on workplace violence and human resource management in the

United States. Security and individual safety is at issue here, and the authors offer a very good discussion of how to prevent and manage workplace violence.

Chapter 20 focuses on gender. Here, Mary E. Guy and Jennifer Killingsworth offer a persuasive argument for gender-based equality and equity in workplace organizations, and against the disparate impacts of traditional human resource management practices in the United States. In Chapter 21, Carole Jurkiewicz argues for application of new technologies to functional purposes of strategic public personnel management. Chapter 22 deals with public sector labor relations and unions. Here David Carnevale offers a very important and lengthy analysis of strategic public sector relations with different approaches of confrontation and cooperation across high performance workplace organizations. Finally, Chapter 23 by Ali Frazmand offers a lengthy analysis of the current worldwide trends of Total Quality Management (TQM) and globalization, with a focus on the changing role of government, challenges, and opportunities that they can present to public personnel managers, government executives, and ordinary personnel. The chapter also offers what governments should and should not do in the age of globalization.

REFERENCES

CBS. (2006). *60 Minutes*, Sunday, February 12.

Cook, J. M. (1983). *The Persian Empire*. New York: Schocken Books.

————. (2001). Learning from Ancient Persia: Administration of the Persian Achaemenid World-State Empire. In Ali Farazmand (Ed.), *Handbook of Comparative and Development Public Administration*, 2nd ed., pp. 33–60 (expanded and updated). New York: Marcel Dekker.

Frye, R. (1975). *The Golden Age of Persia*. New York: Harper & Row.

Ghirshman, R. (1954). *Iran: From the Earliest Times to the Islamic Conquest*. New York: Penguin Books.

Huntington, S. (1993, Summer). Clash of Civilizations. *Foreign Affairs*: 22–49.

Jones, C. (1984). *An Introduction to the Study of Public Policy*. New York: Harcourt Brace & Company.

2

U.S. Public Personnel Administration in Historical Perspective

PAUL P. VAN RIPER

Enduring governments have always had organized civil service systems. This is the basic thesis of Max Weber's famous essay on the importance for governmental survival of a bureaucratic structure, recruited for expertise, and functioning within rules and regulations based on law.

That is, the governmental administrative systems of the great empires of the past—Mesopotamian, Chinese, Indian, Persian, Roman, Byzantine, and Turkish—had much in common. For the Western world this experience was lost during the feudal fragmentation of the Middle Ages. The creation of modern administrative systems and their permanent civil service staffs came with the development of the sovereign nation state in Western Europe during the 16th and 17th centuries. As Leonard D. White concluded in his 1930 study, *The Civil Service in the Modern State*, "Richelieu in France, Henry VIII and Elizabeth in England, and the Great Elector (Frederick William of Brandenburg, later Prussia) are among the chief architects who reconstructed the concept of the state, of office, of civil life and of permanent officials out of the debris of the feudal system."

This evolution came in three stages. Under the monarchs there had arisen by 1750 an embryonic administrative system plus the beginnings of a permanent corps of officials to manage it. Then, as the royal systems were converted into constitutional institutions responsible to parliaments and politicians, the civil offices became "the patronage" and pawns in partisan, often corrupt, political power games. In a third and modern stage, political reform brought with it the concept of a civil service merit employment system embodying the three ideas of tenure, partisan neutrality, and open competition.

Such developments came to full fruition earliest in England, followed by France and Germany, the nations whose experience would set the example for much of the rest of the world. Most of the older nations have gone through such a cycle, as are many of the new nations now.

Following experimentation in India by the British East India Company, the merit system became a reality in Britain itself through the creation in 1855 of an impartial board called the Civil Service Commission, to supervise open examinations on a limited scale. Then an 1870 Order in Council gave the Commission full jurisdiction over examinations for most entry positions. With tenure in office and political neutrality already established, this completed the British pattern, which soon became a model for the United States.

The U.S. civil service system, in turn, has derived from a complicated set of foreign and indigenous influences. Formed by an amalgam of constitutional interpretation. partisan political practice, mid-19th-century British civil service reform, and a cultural predisposition for an open mobile society, the modern U.S. system of public personnel administration—and it is very much a system— has ended up unique in the world of governance. There have been a few influences from U.S. private enterprise and the military, but these have been distinctly secondary.

One last introductory note: this historical review deals largely with personnel administration at the federal level. This is justified because federal, state, and local governmental personnel systems in the United States have almost all derived from the same source, the civil service reform movement of the late 19th century. The principal lasting product of this movement was the federal Pendleton Act of 1883. This became a model for subsequent personnel reform efforts at all governmental levels.

TERMINOLOGY

The French word "personnel" came into English usage in the 19th century as a noun roughly synonymous with "employees." However the term "personnel management" is a 20th-century invention not widely used in either public or private circles until after World War I.

During the 19th and into the early 20th century, the phrase "civil service reform" denoted the emergence of a personnel management function within U.S. civil governments. Within U.S. industry, an embryonic personnel function was first known in the late nineteenth century as "welfare work." By the first decade of the 20th century this had been transformed into "employment management." As late as 1916 an entire issue of The Annals (Vol. 65) was devoted to industrial employment management, with no reference whatever in the text to the term "personnel." The military G-1 (personnel) staff function was a product of World War I

(Hayes, 1978; Nelson, 1946). Before then personnel functions in the uniformed military were viewed merely as normal aspects of command management.

In the United States and perhaps the world, apparently the first use of the word "personnel" to characterize any separate and distinctive managerial function is found in the annual report of the U.S. Civil Service Commission for 1909 where a heading refers to the "Personnel of the Commission" and a brief report from the Postmaster General is titled "Personnel and Salaries." In the Commission's 1910 report there is reprinted a document prepared by the Secretary of Commerce and Labor, titled simply "Personnel," and the managerial concept of personnel was here to stay. From there the term gradually permeated private industry and the military during and after World War I.

A half century later there was still another terminological shift. Within private industry by the 1970s the phrase "human resources management" began to replace personnel management as the preferred term. Thus far, however, the new term has been slow to be accepted within civil government or the military.[1]

CONSTITUTIONAL INFLUENCES

The most pervasive constitutional influence affecting U.S. public administration at all levels, and especially public personnel management, is that of the separation of powers. The general, overall consequence is that all U.S. public administration is controlled by at least two bosses—one executive, the other legislative—and sometimes a third, the courts. It is this lack of unity of command that is the pivotal factor differentiating public from private administration in the United States, including personnel. In private enterprise the personnel director is responsible solely to the Chief Executive Officer. In U.S. governments the personnel officer is responsible not only to a chief executive, but also must enforce many legislative regulations on a boss (e.g., Hatch, wage and hour, loyalty and security, etc., and acts), must advise employees on appeals procedures (often against a boss's actions) and, if in doubt, is expected to respond in terms of the public interest.

There are many consequences of the separation of powers, but two need discussion here not only because of their special relationship to the personnel function but also because of the great political as well as administrative importance frequently associated with their changing interpretation and development through two centuries.

The Constitution vests the bulk of the appointment power in the President, though for inferior officers, Congress may authorize appointments by department heads or the courts. However, only Congress can create or abolish offices, provide the essential perquisites of pay and allowances, and establish hours and conditions of work.

Potentially more limiting on the President's power of appointment is the Senate's authority to advise and consent on nominations, a practice unknown elsewhere in the world except in Latin America where constitutions have been patterned after that of the United States (Harris, 1953, vii). Deriving from the 18th-century efforts of popularly elected colonial legislatures to control the patronage of royal governors, the system was carried into the Constitution of 1789 (Savelle, 1942, 354–355). By mid-20th century more than 26,000 civil and nearly 100,000 military offices were involved. With the removal of postmasters from confirmation by the Postal Reform Act of 1970, the civil group has been reduced to under 2,000 (Senate Print, 1992, 102–509). Fortunately for the President, the Senate has rarely turned down nominees, but the requirement of consultation plus an executive need for legislative support has at times resulted in considerable partisan patronage. This was especially true during the Great Depression of the 1930s when there was 10 to 20 percent unemployment and great pressure on legislators to find jobs for constituents.

The most uncertain legal question about appointments was faced in the mid-19th century on the issue of the constitutionality of civil service reform itself. The matter came to a head when in 1871 Congress passed a one-paragraph rider to a sundry appropriation bill authorizing President Grant to appoint a board to operate a selection system and advise him of qualified candidates for appointment. Grant in fact appointed what has become known as the First Civil Service Commission, which functioned between 1871 and 1875, when Congress refused more appropriations.

However, this first commission did not feel it could proceed until it received an opinion from Attorney General A.T. Akerman as to the constitutionality of its being inserted in the appointment process between the appointing officer and the actual appointment, with, in effect, the power to veto consideration of large numbers of persons. Viewing the matter as "a question of degree," Akerman wrote that "though the appointing power alone can designate an individual for an office, either Congress, by direct legislation, or the President, by authority derived from Congress, can prescribe qualifications, and require that the designation shall be made out of a class of persons ascertained by proper tests to have those qualifications," as long as the appointing power "would still have a reasonable scope for its own judgment and will" (1871, 516, 525). In effect, Akerman's opinion still governs. A byproduct has been that the well—known "rule of three" derives more from constitutional necessity to give an appointing officer "reasonable scope" for choice than from any notions of good administration. The Constitution of 1789 was even more obscure on the power to fire—the removal power—in that the document is silent about removals except by impeachment. This prompted the first debate in the first congress of 1789. The question was whether the President should have an unrestricted power of removal or whether the removal power should parallel that of appointment and be subject to senatorial confirmation. Finally, a bill creating the first federal agency, a Department of Foreign Affairs (now State), and granting the president an unrestricted power of removal as incidental to the general executive power, was passed, but only by Vice President John Adams breaking a tie vote in the Senate. However, the matter was not permanently settled until the post–Civil War Radical Republicans sought to reverse the so-called "decision of 1789" through the enactment of the Tenure of Office Act of 1867, which required senatorial confirmation of many removals. The failure of the Radicals by the narrow margin of one vote to impeach President Andrew Johnson for flouting the act left the President's removal power not only intact but greatly strengthened.

Indeed, the question then became: Was there no possible limitation on the executive removal power? Late 19th-century civil service reform and the Pendleton Act of 1883 did not depend on any limitation of the removal power. If the "front door" to appointment was closed by requiring prospective appointees to pass an examination, then the "back door" of removal could be left open and unguarded. During the course of the debate on the Pendleton Act, Senator George F. Hoar, a Massachusetts Republican, noted that the measure "does not assert any disputed legislative control over the tenure of office. The great debate as to the President's power of removal ... which began in the first Congress, ... does not in the least become important (in) ... this bill ... It does not even ... deal directly with the question of removals, but it takes away every possible temptation to improper removals" (*Congressional Record*, 1882, 274).

But the continued punitive use of the removal power for both partisan and antiunion purposes brought the civil service reformers to push in the 1890s for better tenure protection. President McKinley responded in 1897 with an executive order requiring "just cause" for removal from that part of the civil service covered by Pendleton Act appointment procedures and known as the "classified service," with reasons to be given in writing and the right of the employee to make a written reply. But no hearing was required and there was no penalty attached. Even this mild protection evaporated under Theodore Roosevelt, only to return under President Taft who found himself in conflict with both Congress and the labor unions for not only continuing Roosevelt's famous "gag orders," preventing civil servants from testifying before Congress except through department heads, but also for allowing use of the removal power, notably in the Post Office, to help break the growing strength of postal unions.

Finally, a combination of congressional retaliation and national labor union agitation led by the American Federation of Labor on behalf of the postal unions, in a context of the growing power of Progressive political strength, resulted in the passage of the Lloyd–LaFollette Act of 1912. This embedded in law the mild McKinley removal process; ended the Gag Orders by allowing civil servants, either individually or collectively, to petition Congress and congressmen directly; and authorized postal employees to join unions and to affiliate these unions with the national labor movement. Interpreted to authorize unionization throughout the federal service, this portion of the act provided a base for federal civil service labor policies for the next half century.

The Lloyd–LaFollette provision for federal labor unions proved effective, but that governing removals did not. Under a developing doctrine of public employment as a privilege and not a right, the courts consistently refused to intervene in removal cases and pass on their merits. Labor historian Sterling Spero has concluded that by the 1920s "the guarantees of the Lloyd LaFollette Act thus become mere moral remonstrances, unenforceable if the employing authorities choose to circumvent them" (1948, 43).

This conclusion was underscored by Chief Justice Taft in 1926 in *Myers v. United States*, which involved a postmaster appointed by the President with the consent of the Senate, who was summarily removed before the completion of his term of office. Upholding the removal, ex-President Taft implied an almost unrestricted power of removal as a prerogative of the President's general executive power.

Nevertheless, Lloyd—LaFollette authorized the Civil Service Commission to request a record on removal cases and it could report on the adequacy of the procedures involved. It created a Board of Appeals and Review in 1930, but it was not until the Veterans Preference Act of 1944 that there were any enforceable provisions supporting tenure for any civil servants, and then only for veterans. Within another 5 years veterans were able to obtain amendments to the act of 1944 giving the Civil Service Commission real enforcement powers and authorizing the award of back pay. Theoretically, such limitations might have been contested, but only Presidents might have effectively done so, and post–World War II presidents have seldom opposed the veterans lobby. Finally, in 1962 President John F. Kennedy applied the veterans' preference procedure fully to nonveterans and established an appellate system within agencies by executive order, supported in turn by several pieces of legislation (Case, 1986). There was, of course, no question about the President's authority to limit his own power. However, the climate of political and judicial opinion had changed greatly since the 1920s. There were great advances in labor legislation beginning in the 1930s, which produced unemployment insurance and the social security system, both eventually applied to civil servants. The rights-privilege distinction concerning office-holding was disappearing in the courts by the 1960s, and a liberal Supreme Court was breathing new life into the freedom of speech clause in the Bill of Rights. There were notable consequences for public personnel administration, among them a resolution of the historic controversy over the removal power.

This came in the Civil Service Reform Act of 1978. While it did not change the basic nature of the federal personnel system, it removed all doubt about Congress' authority over removals. The largely permissive Pendleton Act and its executive orders were superceded by mandatory law, and much of the authority wrested from Congress by the first President Johnson was quietly handed back by President Jimmy Carter when he signed this reform statute a century later. That is, there was no longer any argument over the power of Congress to protect the tenure of civil servants who were veterans or who had been hired through merit system procedures.

But it remained for the final blow to the executive power of removal—this time at all levels of government—to come in the form of a most unexpected Supreme Court decision in 1976, *Elrod v. Burns*. As an infringement on the First Amendment's guarantee of freedom of speech, removals for partisan political reasons were declared unconstitutional even when applied to offices, which had been considered legitimate patronage since they were created. That is, traditional political patronage, unquestionably legal for two centuries, was suddenly outlawed everywhere with the single exception that the decision did not apply to policymaking posts. Chief Justice Burger's dissent expressed outraged disbelief and no one thought the court really meant it until it was reaffirmed several times. The Court then even expanded its antipatronage position to forbid any personnel action based on partisan political considerations. Indeed, the change was so unexpected and complete that the patronage driven government in the state of Illinois soon found itself almost without any personnel system at all (Katz, 1991).

PRE-PENDLETON EMPLOYMENT SYSTEMS

All through the 19th century employment was a normal and ordinary part of general management, primarily involving record keeping. Until the 1920s this function fell under the purview of the then all-powerful Chief Clerks of the departments and agencies, sometimes assisted by "appointment clerks." The duties of the Appointment Clerk of the Department of Agriculture in 1897 have been summarized as follows: assisted by two more clerks, it was his duty

> ... to prepare for the signature of the Secretary the documents effecting all appointments, promotions, reductions, transfers, furloughs, and resignations for the entire Department; to maintain a biographical record of each employee; to conduct the business of the Department with the Civil Service Commission; and to advise the Secretary on the application of the civil service law, rules and regulations; to keep records of all transactions of his office, and to brief and file all documents relating to the work thereof. (Stockberger and Smith, 1947, 83–84)

Except for the reference to the Civil Service Commission, this job description would have covered the typical personnel record keeping work of Chief Clerks' offices for the previous century. However, employment attitudes varied considerably during these years.

The relatively stable civil employment in the U.S. federal government between 1789 and 1829 is well known. The patronage exploitation of the royal colonial governors was still a vivid memory. There was no formal merit system after 1789 but employees of character and competence were generally sought as Presidents endeavored to set the new nation on a firm foundation. The system was even pointed to in England as an example of what might be done to reform the civil service system of George III, known as "The Old Corruption" (Finer, 1952, 329).

Nevertheless, the system began to deteriorate soon after 1800. Believing in a fair division of the offices between the major parties and observing that vacancies "by death are few, by resignation, none," President Thomas Jefferson concluded, "Can any other mode than that of removal be proposed?" (Padover, 1943, 518). He as much as President Andrew Jackson can be associated with the early stages of the notorious spoils system which was in full sway by the late 1830s. Again, this story is well known.

Even before the Civil War there was great concern about the growing corruption associated with wholesale patronage. But the best reform measure that the Jacksonian Democrats' Whig opponents—including Clay, Calhoun, and Webster—came up with was a proposal to reverse the decision of 1789 and subject removals to the approval of the Senate. This became known as the Whig theory of civil service reform. It was never attempted except in a mild form when the Confederacy included the following in its Constitution of 1861:

> Art. II, Sec. 2, Cl. 3. The principal officer in each of the executive departments, and all persons connected with the diplomatic service may be removed from office at the pleasure of the President. All other civil officers of the executive departments may be removed at any time by the President, or other appointing power, when their services are unnecessary, or for dishonesty, incapacity, inefficiency, misconduct, or neglect of duty and when so removed, the removal shall be reported to the Senate, together with the reasons therefore.

This went in the direction of the Lloyd—LaFollette Act of 1912, but there has been no study of the effectiveness of the Confederate provision (Van Riper and Scheiber, 1959, 458).

PENDLETON ORIGINS

Serious efforts to reform the U.S. federal civil service had to await not only settlement of the removal controversy but also the invention of a more effective reform measure than legislative confirmation of removals. Both requirements were met not long after the Civil War. The failure of the Andrew Johnson impeachment made it impossible to activate the Whig solution. Meanwhile, in both the United States and abroad the concept of qualification through examination was slowly gaining acceptance.

The use of examinations in the U.S. public service first developed in the military. The Gilmer Committee of the House of Representatives reported in 1842 on "the advantage of preliminary examinations ... cadets, midshipmen, and applicants for appointments as surgeons in the Army and Navy have for years been subject to this test. The Committee has no doubt that the application of the same principles in the original appointment of clerks would be attended with beneficial results" (Titlow, 1979, 138). Under the auspices of Senator Robert M. T. Hunter of Virginia, later Confederate Secretary of State, a law of 1853 required passage of a modest qualifying test known as a "pass-examination" for clerical appointments and promotions. The examinations were to be given by departmental boards. Intermittently enforced at departmental discretion, the statute, enacted 2 years before a similar British requirement, remained in effect until superceded by the Pendleton Act of 1883 (Van Riper, 1958, 52–55).

This 1853 law suggested another approach to civil service reform: that testing could be used in conjunction with the patronage, to weed out incompetents but not otherwise interfere with appointments. But the Civil War intervened and the patronage itself came under full-scale attack. The 1850s experience also made it clear that lasting reform could not be left in the hands of department heads alone. There needed to be a central focus for policy and control.

By the late 1860s the British version of civil service reform was well under way and had begun to be known in the United States. Reform measures introduced by Sen. Charles Sumner of Massachusetts in 1864 and Representative Thomas A. Jenckes of Rhode Island in 1865 and 1867 were based on the British concepts of competitive entrance examinations administered by an independent Civil Service Commission, followed by partisan neutrality in office. There was considerable support for these ideas and they provided a base for later developments. Meanwhile, they were overshadowed by the bitter conflict over the Johnson impeachment.

There were, of course, other foreign models to consider—French, Prussian, Persian and Chinese, for example—and there were reports to Congress about all of these. But the primacy of the British example in the minds of U.S. reformers is clear. Sumner, Jenckes, and George William Curtis, the developing leader of the reform movement as a pressure group, all were in voluminous correspondence with their counterparts in Great Britain, especially Thomas Macaulay, generally recognized as the inventor of the British type of civil service reform, and Sir Charles Trevelyan, leader of the British reform group. Moreover, there was the English cultural connection and the major elements of the British reform system met U.S. needs.

Feeding on patronage scandals, the reform movement gained momentum. After Republican reverses in the congressional elections of 1870, even President Grant came out for reform in his second inaugural. However, patronage strength and the failure of the reformers to focus on a single proposal led to defeat of the more encompassing bills. Nevertheless, a one-paragraph rider approved by Grant was tacked on to a sundry appropriation bill approved on March 3, 1871 permitting, as noted above, the creation of a civil service agency by executive order, known today as the First Civil Service Commission.

This permissive statute, avoiding any controversy over the appointing power, authorized the President to set up rules for entering the civil service and for ascertaining the fitness of candidates. To the surprise of nearly everyone, Grant took the law seriously. He appointed a commission of seven members and designated George William Curtis, the leading reformer, as chairman. New rules based on British experience were developed for competitive examinations, which were given on a limited basis in Washington and New York. Congress provided modest funds and the first presidential staff agency was in being. Many of the precedents for modern public personnel procedures derive primarily from the 1871 law and only secondarily from the Pendleton Act 12 years later. As Lionel Murphy, author of the principal study of the Grant Commission, reminds us:

> Much of the terminology and many of the concepts employed in the proceedings, reports, and other records of the [Grant] commission still prevail. Among these are: "Civil Service Commission rules," "application," "test," "grade," "eligible," "ineligible," "register," "military preference," "position," "vacancy," "apportionment," "probation," "promotion," "classification," "superannuation," "political assessment," "pernicious political activity," "boards of examiners," "ratings of 70 per cent," "three highest eligibles," "policy deciding officials," "certificate," and many others. (1942, 322)

Dorman B. Eaton, a wealthy New York attorney in whose living room the National Civil Service Reform League was founded, succeeded Curtis as chairman of the Commission, The new system did not please many politicians, however, and Congress withdrew appropriations by 1874. Grant did not abolish the Commission but revoked its rules in 1875 and operations were suspended. Nevertheless, the First Commission demonstrated that civil service reform on the British model could work.

The origin of the Pendleton Act of 1883 in the wake of the Grant scandals, the disputed election of 1876, the assassination of President Garfield by a disappointed office-seeker, and the rise of civil service reform to a major national issue is well known. Less understood is the unique role played by Dorman B. Eaton. After he had been chairman of the Grant Commission, he played a main part in the transference of British experience to the United States. In 1877 President Hayes asked Eaton to make a special study of the British reform since 1850 and report back to Hayes. Eaton spent the summer and early fall of 1877 in England. On return, he gave his findings to Hayes and then concentrated on writing a book, which was published by Harpers in 1880 under the title of *Civil Service in Great Britain*, with considerable sales of both hard cover and paperback editions.

In 1880 the distinguished Democrat and former vice-presidential candidate, Senator George H. Pendleton of Ohio, introduced a new reform measure based on previous bills. It was getting nowhere when Eaton went to Pendleton and proposed that a bill drafted by a New York Civil Service Reform Association committee, chaired by Eaton, be substituted for the senator's bill. Pendleton agreed and Eaton defended the bill in detail before a Senate committee. Great Democratic gains in the congressional elections of 1882 stimulated new interest among Republicans in civil service reform, which could promise some protection to Republican officeholders in case of a Democratic presidential victory in 1884, which in fact came about. Pendleton's bill was quickly brought forward. There was extensive debate in the Senate but none in the House. Both houses passed the bill by large majorities and President Chester A. Arthur signed it into law on January 16, 1883.

Arthur then appointed Eaton to head the second Civil Service Commission. Though a Republican, Eaton was reappointed by Cleveland and held his office for nearly 3 years. New rules based on the work of the Grant Commission and recent developments in Britain were established and the new employment system was soon firmly in being. Eaton's role throughout the creation of the Pendleton Act may have been unique in U.S. political history. Certainly few persons have been in a position to pretest a major administrative device, as he did while chairing the Grant Commission after Curtis, then to direct the design of a new bill placing that device into effect, and, finally, to supervise the execution of that bill as a statute. At last the merit system, a term probably coined by Eaton in the 1870s, was in place in the United States.

THE PENDLETON SYSTEM

The Pendleton bill, as originally drafted by Eaton and his associates, would have installed the British civil service system almost intact in the United States. That is, as presented the bill proposed entrance into a partisanly neutral civil service, only at a young age and only at the bottom, through competitive examinations administered by a central agency termed a Civil Service Commission. The result would have been the kind of closed career system found in the British civil service, most uniformed military services here and abroad, and the U.S. Foreign Service.

However, the U.S. Senate, in adjusting the proposal to U.S. predispositions, made one addition to and one deletion from the bill, that, together, changed the entire thrust of the system. The Senate feared testing that might be too theoretical and ordered the tests to be "practical in character" and closely related to the work to be done. Liking even less the idea of entrance only "at the lowest grade," the Senate deleted the phrase, the necessary motion being made by Senator Pendleton himself (Van Riper, 1958, 100–101). These two changes were enough to turn the British closed career system into the open, program-oriented system the United States still has today—characterized by entrance at any age, lateral entry, and occupational specialization. The Senate debates offer no evidence that its members had any particular concept or theory in mind other than a general predisposition toward practicality and social and occupational mobility. The conversion of the British system into the Pendleton system came really by accident, with the result that the U.S. merit system was then and is now unique in the world.

The Pendleton concepts remain at the center of the employment systems of the federal government and most state and local jurisdictions. It should be noted, however, that the idea of employment through competitive examinations—or any kind of test—did not come from private enterprise, here or elsewhere, It was not until the 1920s that the Pendleton employment system was picked up by a substantial number of firms, in a movement from government to business, not the reverse.

PERSONNEL ADMINISTRATION

Not until after World War I was there a mix of activities worthy of the designation of "personnel administration." It took the years between the two world wars for that mix to coalesce into a unified staff function. Only a few aspects of that intricate development can be considered here in a rough chronological sequence.

The first call for the transformation of the Civil Service Commission into a central "bureau of personnel" came in 1913 from President Taft's Commission on Economy and Efficiency (Van Riper, 1958, 222). Change did come soon in increments, but with new functions not always assigned to the Civil Service Commission. In 1912 Congress gave the coordination of efficiency ratings to a new Division of Efficiency within the Civil Service Commission, but 4 years later turned the division into a separate Bureau of Efficiency. Civil pensions came in 1920, their administration divided between the Civil Service Commission and Interior's Bureau of Pensions, later the Veterans Administration. Workmen's compensation, generally applied to the federal service by 1920, was placed in the Department of Labor. Position classification, invented in Chicago around 1910, was applied to the federal government in 1923. However, a Congress reluctant to give the executive branch more control over positions and salaries gave administration of the system to a peculiar separate agency called the Personnel Classification Board, composed of one representative each from the Bureau of the Budget, the Bureau of Efficiency and the Civil Service Commission. In a few departments, however, there was consolidation. The first to create a moderately full personnel system as a staff entity was the Department of Agriculture in 1925, followed by the Treasury and Interior.

It remained for President Hoover, aided by economy pressures from the Great Depression, to bring about the demise of competing agencies and to consolidate all major federal personnel functions within the Civil Service Commission by 1934. President Franklin D. Roosevelt completed the system in 1938 when he ordered all federal agencies to create personnel departments. The other side of the coin was dealt with when the Hatch Acts of 1939 and 1940 were passed. These closed many patronage loopholes and forbade partisan political activity by federal merit system employees and by state and local employees paid from federal funds.

By 1940 close to 75 percent of the federal civil service was under the merit system; seventeen states had relatively complete merit systems; and all states had at least some merit employees as a result of federal grant-in-aid requirements. That is, just prior to World War II, workers in these jurisdictions, plus many of those in over 850 cities and a few counties and special districts, came under varieties of the Pendleton system of public personnel administration (Civil Service Assembly, 1940, 8). Judged by today's standards, however, there still were notable functional gaps in personnel. There were yet, for example, few provisions for employee health, safety, or training in U.S. governments.

The United States entered World War II with close to 1.3 million federal civil servants plus 3 million state and local. The latter figure was stable during the conflict but the federal service increased to 3.8 million at the height of the war, with most of the increase designated as temporary employment for the duration. The federal service declined to 2 million by 1948, rose to nearly 3 million during the Korean and Vietnam conflicts, then leveled off at 2.8 to 3 million where it has remained for the longest period of no growth—actually a decline in proportion to population—in its history. During the same years state and local employment, encouraged both by new functions and large grants of federal aid, grew from 4 to more than 12 million employees. That is, contrary to many popular suppositions, most of the post–World War II bureaucracy in U.S. governments—expressed in numbers of civil employees—has not been in the nation's capital but largely spread out close to home in the state and local governmental systems.

From the close of World War II in 1945, to the end of the 1970s, economic prosperity brought with it the longest period of labor shortages, especially among professional, scientific, and technical personnel, in our history. The Cold War, ensuing prosperity, and great organizational growth, public and private, brought with them considerable expansion in personnel functions.

For the first time loyalty and security became peacetime concerns, with the U.S. Civil Service Commission becoming the largest investigating agency in the country. There were new developments in ethics, nondiscrimination via a special Equal Employment Opportunity Commission, executive development through a new Federal Executive Center and several satellite units, and in the expansion of formal labor relations at all governmental levels. By the middle 1960s labor shortages produced "positive recruiting" by most public agencies, as well as for the first time a view of personnel as a cybernetic system, commencing with labor analysis and forecasts, on to training and development, utilization, and replacement. From the financial side the principal innovation came in vastly expanded fringe benefits, increasingly offered as cafeteria plans and soon totaling in costs a third or more of base pay. Much more personnel authority was finally delegated to the new federal personnel entities within agencies, coordinated at the federal level through a combined agency—Civil Service Commission inspection system.

Nevertheless, continued prosperity, greater and greater requirements for skilled personnel and, as noted earlier, the gradual closing of the backdoor to public employment were causing management and political executives to become restive over the rigidities still remaining in governmental personnel procedures. Shortly after the passage of the federal Civil Service Reform Act of 1978, Alan K. Campbell, former chairman of the Civil Service Commission and the first director of the new Office of Personnel Management, explained (Campbell, 1979, 3):

> Over the years, the continuous addition of laws and regulations applied protection to salary increases, promotions and retention in the public service, producing a

system in which most personnel decisions were based on automatic considerations.... Positions were filled by selecting one of the top three on a list of eligibles.
Promotions were based primarily on time in grade. Salary increases were determined
by cost-of-living or, again, time in rank. In short, it had become a system I often like
to describe as one largely untouched by human thought.

The Reform Act attempted to loosen federal personnel bonds by several novel
measures. Through the act plus executive orders, the Civil Service Commission
itself was divided into an Office of Personnel Management, headed by a director
appointed by and reporting to the President, and a genuinely independent Merit
System Protection Board, to hear employee appeals and to keep an eye on the
federal personnel system. Both were guided by a new set of positive merit system
principles combined with a list of prohibited personnel practices. A third agency,
the independent Federal Labor Relations Authority, was created to supervise the
first general federal labor relations statute (Title VII of the Reform Act) to mandate
collective bargaining with civil servants. At the top of the system a Senior Executive Service (SES) was created from the old GS 16 through 18 "supergrades,"
removing some job protections and making it possible for SES members to be
moved around as needed, and to be motivated by new concepts of merit pay and
bonuses, about which more shortly. There was a new provision to protect whistle-
blowers, some lessening of the evidentiary requirements for removals for inefficiency, and abolition of veterans' preference for field grade and higher officers. A
closing section of the act offered another unique proviso permitting experiments
in personnel procedures involving up to 5,000 employees. These federal personnel measures echoed throughout many state and local jurisdictions and produced
more experimentation. The Reform Act gave a kind of electric jolt to the entire
public personnel system nationwide.

Among the responses, the only theme that has seemed to hit a popular chord
among both workers and bosses has been that aimed at the creation of a more
family friendly workplace. This is a development common to both public and private work systems. An interesting mixture of ingredients includes cafeteria plans
of fringe benefits; flexitime work schedules; liberal provisions in a Family and
Medical Leave Act, taking effect in 1993; a return to the preindustrial concept
of the home work station, made increasingly possible by the new information
technology; plus increasing provision for the use of part-time workers, especially
women, as a major means of bringing highly qualified talent to the workforce in
a time of labor shortage.

Most of the remaining civil service reform efforts of the last half century can
be divided into two categories, one involving pay and the other fair employment
and diversity.

Pay reforms began in 1970 when Congress startled the world of public administration by authorizing unlimited collective bargaining in the U.S. Postal Service,
a newly created government corporation. This led almost immediately to a novel
group incentive pay system. The Reform Act of 1978 went further. If there no

longer was much managerial discretion in the hiring or firing of civil servants, the act provided managers with new authority over pay. Most pay raises were subjected to performance criteria, and in the manner of business—for the first time among U.S. governments—$10,000 to $20,000 annual bonuses were authorized for top executive performance. Under the Reform Act's experimental proviso there soon were successful experiments in both pay banding and gain sharing. Other experiments were made elsewhere. A number of state and local governments are, for example, sharing portions of demonstrated savings or budget surpluses as rewards to the employees involved.

A system for adjusting federal white-collar pay to that of the private sector has existed since the Federal Pay Comparability Act of 1970. This has produced annual increments, but the Federal Pay Reform Act of 1990 finally authorized a system for the annual adjusting of federal white-collar pay to the prevailing rate in job localities, which has been used to determine blue-collar wages since the Civil War. Approaching pay from another perspective, there have recently been serious efforts to simplify job classification systems, whose tight work descriptions have long impeded employee movement of all kinds. Recent federal initiatives have experimented with very broad occupational guides designed to be inclusive across a number of occupational groups, and to provide greater delegation to managers and agencies.

However, despite such loosening up of rigid pay and classification schemes, the rise of the federal debt and state and local taxpayer revolts have tended to hold a tight lid on public pay costs, which average 70 percent of budgets in most state and local jurisdictions. Managers seeking to obtain scientific and professional talent in a period of low unemployment and high demand from private industry are still having great trouble finding qualified applicants. That is, many of the rigidities in public personnel procedures derive from current citizen and legislative reluctance to match the true going rate for scarce talent. There is much flexibility in pay systems, but the money still isn't there to take full advantage of them.

The other set of developments goes back to World War II in origin and derives from an array of statutes and procedures which now tend to be lumped together under the equal employment opportunity (EEO) and affirmative action labels. These involve a mass of detailed controls over employment and employee utilization processes as they concern minorities, women, and veterans. Most of these requirements are well known and cannot be discussed in detail here. Perhaps the most rigid in their requirements are the essentially male-oriented veteran preference statutes, which Congress is even now considering tightening up rather than loosening. Given the origins of the U.S. population, diversity is a must, but equal employment opportunity procedures are a maze, with navigation through it fraught with the threat of lawsuits, which the recent tendency of federal courts to expand the tort liability of public managers has made ever more dangerous. The voting public, elements of which stand to both gain and lose from various forms of affirmative action, remains ambiguous in its attitudes, abolishing affirmative action in California but recently renewing it in, for example, the city of Houston, Texas, and the U.S. Congress.

The controversies involved in both public pay and affirmative action are joined in the issue of comparable worth. Comparable worth argues that many pay differences between men and women are the result of discrimination. Opponents argue that they are the result of impartial supply and demand. The federal courts have thus far, in effect, been on the side of the latter. However, more than a thousand public jurisdictions, including twenty states, have required by law that some or all public jobs be paid according to their worth to a jurisdiction rather than to the marketplace (Pynes, 1997, 179).

IN THE NEW MILLENNIUM

By the late 1990s the underlying trends of personnel management in government were flowing in opposite directions. Pointing one way is the reinvention of government movement, stressing downsizing, elimination, or the contracting out of governmental functions, including much of personnel. The Office of Personnel Management has contracted out its massive investigative function to a corporation formed by its former employees, who are bidding successfully for investigative work wherever it may be found, public or private. There is no reason why much recruitment and employment, as well as training, cannot be done as well or better by private organizations subject to competition. Governmental collective bargaining has frequently been handled by consultants.

Return pay and fringe benefit procedures to departmental chief clerks; and give classification, promotions, and dismissal back to management from whence they came, to join performance ratings and discipline, which are already there. End the inflexibilities in public personnel management by ending 20th-century public personnel management. In the new dispensation, who needs it? Or, as a subhead in Nicholas Henry's 1995 public administration text puts it (282): "Does human resource management have a future?"

In response professional personnelists—or human resources managers if one prefers—are stressing a "strategic" concept of personnel management. Unfortunately, conventional personnelists have been thought of as controllers and enforcers, which to some extent they must be if merit is to be preserved in the face of strong partisan pressures. Strategic personnel management stresses control less and assistance to management more, in the belief that personnel considerations are basic to realistic planning in all organizations, public or private. In other words, bring to management a modernized and flexible systems approach to personnel with an emphasis on the personnel department as an indispensable aid to and agent of management.

To this end the International Public Management Association for Human Resources, the premier association of public personnelists and public personnel agencies, is in the process of preparing a training guide for a Human Resources Competency Model, based on 1996 research by the National Academy of Public

Administration. The initial elements of this new training program, the first such guidance ever provided for public personnel management, were presented at the IPMA International Training Conference held in Minneapolis in September 1997. The format thus far is strategic and managerial as compared to technical and procedural, and might well become the basis for the accreditation of both public personnelists and public personnel programs in the future.

CURRENT OPPORTUNITIES

Public personnel management is very much at an exciting crossroads today. In a battle cry for more flexibility in personnel systems, some have adopted as their motto "let's go back to the spoils system." But this is the way to madness. At no time in our history has merit been more required for the management of the affairs of the world. But what can be done, and quickly? There are many examples of the new strategic approach.

At the federal level, the OPM has eliminated the 10,000-page *Federal Personnel Manual*, providing agencies with much more choice in almost all activities. It has delegated recruiting and examining to the departments and agencies, simplified the present classification system, and permitted agencies to create their own performance rating and reward systems. And it has speeded up almost everything.

If someone in a jurisdiction really cares, it is possible to make at least two more major improvements today without new legislation. One can provide a vastly improved information system about both available jobs and, for managers, about alternative procedures. In addition, there are all kinds of ways to speed up the examining and appointment process. This is especially needed in times like these, of great labor shortages. Walk-in examining and rostering were common in both world wars and should be more so now. With some legislative help—as recently in Missouri, New Jersey, Wisconsin, New York, California, and an array of local governments—any jurisdiction can open up classification, start toward pay banding, undertake experiments, simplify appeals through alternative dispute resolution, simplify the use of temporaries and provisionals, tie pay into performance through group incentives, establish flexible senior civil services, develop interest-based bargaining with unions, expand and better use probationary periods, and, especially, pay attention to managerial and citizen complaints and do something about them. In a time of extraordinary prosperity, there may even be some loosening of purse strings.

In many jurisdictions major problems lie in veterans preference, especially as it affects reductions in force (diversity is being RIFFED many places these days); the rule of three and similar restrictions; classification and pay systems rigidly embedded in statutes; the infrequency of examinations when shorthanded; requirements for promotion exams; and inadequate training of both managers and personnel people in modern personnel system functions and procedures.

That is, a lot of legislation needs to be revised, and there are special problems with employee unions, veterans groups, and the professional associations who prefer rigid classification guidelines. But, again, Missouri, New Jersey, Wisconsin, and many smaller entities have demonstrated that a new wave of civil service reform is possible in the strategic direction. Thus far the spotlight has been on the public personnel function. Now, in conclusion, let us turn the discussion around for a moment. When it comes to two things, there is no evidence managers really want to manage. They will not handle individual performance ratings well: group incentives are much more effective and much more easily managed. Second, there is no evidence that managers really want to take back the personnel functions they once had fifty to a hundred years ago. They don't want to take the time to search for people and to worry about the myriads of details that staff people must handle. Finally, in these times of downsizing and RIFS, reemphasis on "at will" employment, and replacing of older and experienced workers with underpaid part-timers, managers have to show they are a lot more caring about their human resources or their human resources aren't going to care about them.

NOTE

1. Part of the governmental reluctance stems from the fact that any change in official terminology would require a good deal of new legislation. Moreover, the term is unfortunate for its connotations suggesting the treatment of people as a commodity and for the term's possible confusion with welfare.

REFERENCES

Campbell, Alan K. (1979). *The Politics and Substance of Civil Service Reform*. Louisville, KY: University of Louisville.

Case, H. Manley. (1986). Federal Employee Job Rights. *Howard Law Journal*, 29: 283–306.

Civil Service Assembly. (1940). *Civil Service Agencies in the United States*. Chicago, IL: The Assembly.

Congressional Record. (1882). 47th Cong., 2nd sess., XIV, part 1. Washington, DC: Government Printing Office.

Finer, S. E. (1952.) Patronage and the Public Service. *Public Administration*, 30: 329.

Harris, Joseph P. (1953). *The Advice and Consent of the Senate*. Berkeley, CA: University of California Press.

Hayes, James H. (1978). *The Evolution of Military Officer Personnel Management Policies*. Santa Monica, CA: Rand Corporation.

Henry, Nicholas. (1995). *Public Administration and Public Affairs*, 6th ed. Englewood Cliffs, NJ: Prentice-Hall.

Katz, Jeffrey L. (1991). The Slow Death of Political Patronage. *Governing*, April: 58–629.

Murphy, Lionel V. (1942, January, July, and October). The First Federal Civil Service Commission. *Public Personnel Review*, 3.

Nelson, Otto. (1946). *National Security and the General Staff*. Washington, DC: Infantry Journal Press.

Padover, Saul K. (1943). *The Complete Jefferson*. New York: Tudor Publishing Co.

Pynes, Joan E. (1997). *Human Resources Management for Public and Nonprofit Organizations.* San Francisco, CA: Jossey-Bass.

Savelle, Max. (1942). *A History of Colonial America.* New York: Henry Holt.

Spero, Sterling. (1948). *Government as Employer.* New York: Remsen Press.

Stockberger, Warner W., and Virginia B. Smith. (1947). *Personnel Administration Development in the United States Department of Agriculture.* Washington, DC: Dept. of Agriculture.

Titlow, Richard E. (1979). *Americans Import Merit.* Washington, DC: University Press of America.

U.S. Attorney General. (1871). *Opinions Attorney General,* 13.

U.S. Senate. (1992). *Policy and Supporting Positions.* Committee on Governmental Affairs, 102nd Congress, 2nd session, Senate Print, 102–509. Washington, DC: Government Printing Office.

Van Riper, Paul P. (1958). *History of the United States Civil Service.* Evanston, IL: Row, Peterson.

Van Riper, Paul P., and Harry N. Scheiber. (1959). The Confederate Civil Service. *Journal of Southern History,* 25: 450–467.

———— 3 ————

Toward a New Perspective in Strategic Human Resource Management in the Public Sector

DONALD E. KLINGNER AND GAMAL SABET

ENVIRONMENTAL CONDITIONS THAT AFFECT CONTEMPORARY PUBLIC PERSONNEL MANAGEMENT

Changes in the Organizational Environment

The environment of contemporary organizations is characterized by increased uncertainty, specialization of labor, and rapidity of change (Heclo 1977). The competencies needed to solve contemporary organizational problems therefore need to be more specialized. The rapidity of changes is in part due to technological innovations in a dynamic international economy. The more competitive the market, the more responsive private businesses expect government to be. And for them, responsiveness means rapid, flexible action by public agencies and employees. Those public personnel systems that can adapt to these demands will be those that have the best chance of surviving in the future (Osborne and Gaebler 1992).

Changing Demographic Tendencies

Labor force diversification is a concept that describes the constantly expanding range of employee characteristics (Judy and D'Amico 1997). It includes differences among applicants and employees with respect to race, gender, ethnicity, national origin, language, religion, age, education, and competencies related (and unrelated) to job performance. Almost all employees, married or single, constantly balance family and work obligations. Achieving this balance is difficult for employees, and causes problems for managers and personnel directors.

Emergent Market Values That Conflict with Civil Service

In the United States, the development of public personnel administration has proceeded according to a model that demonstrates the underlying conflict between four traditional values and three emergent antigovernment values. The four traditional values (political responsiveness, efficiency, employee rights, and social equity) represent an implicit approval of collective action to achieve common goals. The three new values (individual responsibility, limited and decentralized government, and community responsibility for social services) can be traced back to declining confidence in government. Proponents of these new values say that if government cannot resolve certain social problems, let the market, let individuals, or let community-based organizations do so instead. Cutbacks in public employment, privatization, service contracting, and employment of temporary and part-time workers outside of civil service are all results of this shift in values away from collective action through government (Klingner and Nalbandian 2003).

Today, it can be said that in the United States public personnel management represents equilibrium between these competing values. Each personnel system represents a particular value for assigning scarce public jobs in a complex and unstable environment. And it can be expected that this conflict demonstrates the mixing of technical decisions (for example, how to do a certain personnel function) with political decisions (for example, which value to favor or which system to utilize).

THE CONSEQUENCES OF THESE ENVIRONMENTAL CHANGES ON THE FIELD OF PUBLIC PERSONNEL MANAGEMENT

Change from the Administration of Positions to the Administration of Work and Employees

In the past, legislators and chief executives tried to ensure bureaucratic compliance, efficiency and responsiveness through budgetary controls and position management (limiting the number and type of personnel that an agency could employ). Frequently, imposing median grade level restrictions as well reinforced these position and budgetary controls.

Due to a variety of political and economic pressures, the focus of public personnel management has shifted from the management of positions, which had occurred in traditional civil service systems, to the accomplishment of agency objectives through the administration of work. Through personnel departments, personnel managers have tried to achieve the efficient allocation of job tasks and the equitable distribution of rewards. Public managers have objectives to achieve but limited resources within which to achieve them. The rhythm of change influences the extent to which the knowledge, skills, and abilities of today will be appropriate to the future. Recruitment based on a typical, traditional job description can ensure appropriate competencies for today, but limit the organization's ability to respond to future challenges.

Employees have a third objective—employee management. For them, the willingness to do the work and their ability to learn and perform well is more important than their actual ability. They want their abilities and competencies to be fully used in a way that contributes to organizational productivity and to their personal career development. They want to be managed as individuals through a continual process of supervision, feedback, and reward. The majority of supervisors share this perspective. They want to be able to assign tasks to employees in a flexible, intelligent fashion that recognizes changes in work demands and differences in employees' competencies, even among employees with the same job title. They want to be able to use and reward employees based on their contributions to the work group. At heart, they view job descriptions and classification systems as "administrative trivia," required to justify budget requests and to keep personnel managers happy, but not directly related to agency mission or day-to-day supervision.

Precise Differentiation between "Permanent" and "Contingent" Workers

Personnel management requires choosing the personnel policies and techniques related to management of human resources within the organization. Taken as a whole, these procedures and value preferences send messages to employees, administrators, and interested groups outside the organization concerning the value the agency places on human resources. Therefore, public personnel directors have had to adopt reasonable policies (at least from the agency's perspective) to assign responsibilities and control costs.

First, employers continue to select and employ key administrative, professional, scientific, and technical employees through a civil service system. Relatively high pay, benefits, and job security go with these positions because they are considered essential for long-term employee retention and productivity. This includes employee assistance programs that ensure employee productivity and well-being, funded through employer-sponsored health plans.

Second, employers have tried to adapt themselves to changing job duties, limit costs, and to avoid legal responsibility by utilizing secondary labor markets (such as contract or contingent employment) for many positions that previously would have been filled through civil service. While use of the secondary labor market is recognized as a common contemporary labor force technique, the exact number and proportion of contingent workers is under debate among economists and personnel managers. Their calculations vary between 2 and 16 percent of the labor force. The higher figure is more likely correct because it includes not only contingent workers, but also independent contractors and other self-employed workers (Caudron 1996).

The Disadvantages of a Traditional Civil Service System

Civil service systems are based on a set of fundamental assumptions about the nature of work. The following ideas have been considered essential in the historical development of civil service systems from out of the era of patronage. They have provided a reasonable guide to the design and implementation of public personnel systems for many years. They are:

Work can be divided into individual segments of work and responsibility called "jobs."

Jobs are characterized by stability over time because government work is achieved through bureaucracies designed to provide stability and routine.

The competencies required of workers can be evaluated in relation to specific jobs, and personnel management functions can be based around positions rather than the employees who occupy them.

Job analysis and the relationship of each position to others provide a rational system for pay, recruitment, selection, and performance evaluation.

Today, as a result of the previously mentioned changes in the nature of work, some experts argue strongly that these traditional assumptions are no longer relevant for elected and appointed officials, managers, or employees in the contemporary era of environmental turbulence and instability. For these critics, traditional civil service-based assumptions function more like an obstacle and less like a useful tool for managing human resources. The flexibility demanded by specialization, the rapidity of change, and the need to balance work and family responsibilities have led to the obsolescence of the assumptions of stable and routine jobs, and of impersonal position management that characterize traditional civil service. A fundamental notion in civil service is the maintenance of rationality and equity through legal and quasilegal restrictions on administrative discretion. But an environment that demands flexibility, responsiveness, and efficiency in disciplinary action and grievances has led many personnel managers and managers to question the effectiveness of a system designed to reduce managerial discretion and favoritism (Cohen and Eimicke 1994).

This complexity and specialization require that persons work together in teams. Frequently, changing conditions require that problems be solved through the formation of task forces and other temporary organizations. The notion of working in teams is quite different from the traditional assumption that work can be divided into individual units of tasks and responsibilities called jobs. Rather than being concerned with individual administrative or professional positions, contemporary public employees are required to focus on directing work teams. In teams where interpersonal dynamics prevent the achievement of group objectives, the most important element is the ability of employees to work together, rather than their skills or abilities as individual employees. The "civic behavior" of employees and personal qualities such as courtesy, ability to solve problems together, sensitivity, and the ability to persuade and to communicate verbally across cultures and languages, become key components to effectiveness. Yet these are difficult to measure and evaluate through the use of traditional job descriptions. In this sense, employees' tasks and responsibilities as team members are more important than a job description of what the employee does as an individual.

The Growth of Alternative Organizations and Mechanisms

The emergence of antigovernment values (individual responsibility, limited and decentralized government, and community responsibility for social services) has created new and different personnel systems. Their primary objective is to limit government power and reduce the number of public employees. In fact, two methods are used to achieve this objective. First, services previously through government agencies utilizing appropriated funds have to be delivered through private enterprise. These alternative mechanisms include service contracting, privatization, franchise agreements, vouchers, volunteers, and regulatory and tax incentives (Savas 1990).

Second, for those public policy objectives that continue to be achieved through public employment, employing an increasing percentage of temporary, contract, and part-time employees enhances the flexibility of employment relationships. The emergent market-based values have replaced the traditional practice of accomplishing public employment objectives through civil service employees paid out of appropriated funds. And as long as these values continue to gain strength, this trend can be expected to continue.

The Consequences of These Challenges for Leadership and Employee Performance

The clash between these new environmental conditions and the assumptions underlying traditional civil service systems creates large conflicts and problems, both political and administrative. The traditional employment contract between public employees and the public has been affected by changing economic conditions in two important respects. Most obviously, working for the government is less stable and secure. In the past, public employees would implicitly exchange lower pay for the higher benefits and job security of the public sector. Also, the emergent antigovernmental values lead them to increasingly question the value of working in the public service. In the past civil service was considered desirable because it offered the opportunity to serve the public. But after years of continued negative publicity concerning the inefficiency or ineffectiveness of public administration, it is not surprising that public employees have come to think of themselves as part of the problem rather than part of the solution. The old idea that the objective of public administration is the public's welfare rather than private profit has come under fire. And many public employees find it difficult to accept this situation when their own jobs are at stake or when they feel under attack by the public or elected officials (Peters and Savoie 1994).

The resurgence of market values and the continued advance of privatization and service contracting have caused most public employees, at least at some point, to doubt their career choice. Are there any important differences between the values, job objectives, and competencies required of personnel managers in the public and private sectors? Are there any principles and values of civil service systems that fundamentally cannot be privatized? If the majority of the functions previously performed by public administrators are privatized or contracted out, what impact does this have on providing public service or on the values underlying public employment?

The Need to Unify Political and Administrative Perspectives

In this environment, conflicts have both political and administrative dimensions, and trying to resolve them requires cooperation. Sometimes it seems like elected and appointed officials, and civil service employees, operate in two different worlds. The world of elected and appointed officials tends to be larger than the world of administrators, and public administrators and employees approach their jobs in a very different manner. One way to understand the differences between politics and administration is to view political and administrative logic as alternative perspectives on reality, or two different frames of reference for action. In Table 3.1 we can see the differences in general terms (Nalbandian 1994).

For a politician, the primary value is responsiveness to the will of the people. This means sometimes acting to promote efficiency, social equity or individual rights; sometimes representing the interests of a few; and sometimes doing what is good for the majority over the long run. The elected official's focus is primarily outside of the organization and into the community or environment of political interests that rally for and against specific policies and solutions to problems. Even when elected officials "meddle" internally, it can be justified in terms of an external role like "oversight," or helping citizens find their way through an administrative agency's labyrinthine procedures.

To some extent politics differentiates itself from administration in that part of it can only be understood as a game, with its own rules and strategy and tactics. We even refer to the game of politics. Partially, it is a game because the boundaries are so broad and vague. Elected officials must manage their own careers. They cannot count merely on hard work and conscientiousness to keep them in office, and they operate in a world of values where compromise and negotiation are valued more than right answers. They come to their office with no special expertise and often without much relevant experience. They are chosen because they represent something their constituents believe will serve them well.

Because the world of politics is a world of conflicting values, communication is often through symbols that reveal those values. Politicians love to tell stories and, in return, constituents tell them stories—stories about the (in)efficiency of government, about fairness, about the special needs they want represented. The currency is power. The bottom line for an elected official is the ability to influence

TABLE 3.1.

	Politics		Administration
VALUES	Political Responsiveness		Efficiency and Effectiveness
FOCUS	The environment		The organization
ACTIVITY	The game of politics		Problem Solving
PLAYERS	Representatives	Top-level managers and political administrators	Experts
TYPICAL CONVERSATION	"What do you hear?"		"What do you know?"
MEANS OF COMMUNICATION	Interests and symbols		Information, money, concrete results
MEDIUM OF EXCHANGE	Power		Knowledge
THE DYNAMIC	Conflict, compromise and short-term solutions		Harmony, cooperation, and continuity

other elected officials and build community consensus in order to get things done, and there is no formula for success.

Hierarchy removes so much uncertainty from the lives of administrative officials that it is difficult for them to imagine the uncertainty that elected officials work with. It is hard for the outsider to identify how power is acquired and who is powerful, again because in most legislative bodies there is no hierarchy. In addition, in some governing bodies there is no specialization. The elected official's time perspective is shorter than an administrator's because for most elected officials, elected office is not intended to be a career. Even when it is, managing that career requires making short-term, noticeable achievements in an environment of conflicting values.

The administrative world is very different, especially at the level of the personnel specialist, the planner, the engineer, the water plant operator, the scientist at the Environmental Protection Agency, the systems analyst at the Department of Defense, the agronomist at the Department of Agriculture, the budget analyst, and so on. To these people, administration is not a game; it is about the rational, analytical application of knowledge to solve problems. While the problems may have an external origin, the focus is internal; the work is largely internal. The water plant operator may never interact with a citizen unless it's on a tour of the water treatment plant; the same is true for the budget analyst and the personnel specialist. Their professional/technical knowledge and the hierarchy they work in bound their world. They are experts whose knowledge has been acquired over years of education and experience. They were selected for their work on the basis of their knowledge, skills, and abilities, and not because they appealed in some abstract way to a group of voters.

"What do you know?" invites a very different response than "What do you hear?" It suggests a factual exchange where those with the most knowledge are the most valued. Problem solving requires cooperation, and fairness in the implementation of public policy relies on continuity. The administrative specialist thinks in terms of a career, and knowing that he or she is going to be around for the long haul, the vicissitudes of electoral politics are likely to be shunned rather than respected.

These perspectives differ, but successful governance, including the survival of administrative agencies, requires a blend or at least some understanding of the other perspective. It is too much to expect the politician to understand the world of the budget analyst; nor can the wastewater treatment plan operator be expected to know what it is like to see the world from the council chambers. Those who speak both languages, understand both technical and political rationality occupy the middle ground. This is one of the crucial roles of the chief administrative officer and other senior administrative officials and political executives or their senior staff. In effect, they are called upon to interpret—to translate the world of administration into value questions and to transform value issues into problems subject to administrative expertise.

HOW THESE CHANGES AFFECT THE ROLE OF THE PUBLIC PERSONNEL ADMINISTRATOR

In the end, like at other points in time during the past century, we can only speculate on the emergent role of the public personnel manager as the field continues to evolve. But if the past is any indication, it is likely to include four key roles: technician, professional, human resource management specialist, and mediator (Klingner and Nalbandian 1981).

Technician

Entry-level public personnel managers are usually technical specialists or generalists. In a large personnel department, technicians are expected to know how to perform specialized functions within civil service systems.

Staffing specialists administer examinations, establish lists of eligible applicants, and refer eligible applicants to line managers for interviews and selection. This job requires knowledge of personnel law and recruitment and selection procedures, and experience in employment interviewing and affirmative action.

Job analysts or position classifiers analyze jobs to determine the appropriate competencies and minimum qualifications, respond to managers' requests for reclassification (to determine if duties, competencies, and minimum qualifications have changed over time), and recommend the appropriate salary for a position (based on job worth factors or market conditions). This job requires task analysis, knowledge of job classification and evaluation procedures, and survey research.

Testing specialists developing valid and reliable selection criteria for positions, and defend the reliability and validity of current tests. This job requires knowledge of testing, measurement, and test validation procedures.

Pay and benefits specialists administer the payroll system, enroll new employees in benefit programs, advise employees of changes in benefit programs, and ensure compliance with federal pay and benefit laws. This job requires knowledge of pay and benefit systems; employment contracts; pensions; federal laws with respect to wages, hours, and benefits; and health, life, and disability insurance.

Affirmative action compliance officers are responsible for compliance with equal employment opportunity and affirmative action laws and regulations (U.S. Equal Employment Opportunity Commission), the Americans with Disabilities Act (ADA), gender equity with respect to pay and benefits (U.S. Department of Labor), and the Age Discrimination in Employment Act. They are the persons most concerned with recruitment, selection, and promotion activities within civil service and affirmative action systems. This job requires knowledge of state and federal AA/EEO laws and compliance agencies, and of related personnel functions (primarily staffing, pay, and benefits).

Training and development specialists determine training needs, develop and conduct training programs, and evaluate their effectiveness. Trainers must have training or experience as adult educators.

Employee assistance program directors coordinating employee assistance programs offered by the organization or by contract providers, as a response to personal employee problems that become workplace issues: alcohol and drug abuse, financial counseling, domestic and workplace violence, life-threatening diseases, legal assistance, and psychological counseling. They should know federal laws protecting the rights of employees with physical or mental disabilities (such as the Americans with Disabilities Act and the Family and Medical Leave Act); be able to conduct informal counseling with supervisors and employees; and be able to advise employees of the health and insurance benefit programs offered by the employer.

Risk managers are responsible for developing or enforcing personnel policies designed to limit the organization's exposure to legal or financial liability due to violations of employee rights, unsafe or unhealthy working conditions, or poor management practice. In particular, personnel managers who function as risk managers are responsible for reducing employer liability for workers' compensation, disability retirement, and negligent hiring, retention, or referral claims. This function may also be shared with the organization's attorney and budget officer. Risk managers must know personnel law, Occupational Safety and Health (OSHA), workers' compensation systems and procedures, and the Family Medical Leave Act.

Contract specialists' responsibilities vary depending upon the personnel system. Under collective bargaining systems, they are responsible for developing

background information to support management's positions during contract negotiations or for administering collective bargaining by ensuring that labor and
management comply with negotiated agreements. Under alternative systems, they
are responsible for developing and negotiating fee for service contracts with outside vendors, or individual employment contracts with employees or independent
contractors. Contract specialists have experience with business law, policy analysis, contract negotiation, or contract compliance.

The Professional

The issue of whether public personnel managers are professionals has been debated for years. In many practical ways, the issue seems to boil down to the extent
to which personnel managers can engage in the conflicts among public personnel systems and values, and yet keep from being captured by any one of them.
Conceptually, the issue seems to focus on the extent to which there is an iden-
tifiable body of competencies that define the occupation of the human resource
manager, an accepted process of education and training for acquiring these competencies, and a standard of ethics that guides their application. For academics
who develop theory in the field, the issue of professionalism seems to focus on
the extent to which there is an underlying body of theory that forms the basis for
developing and implementing alternative approaches to the personnel functions;
setting these approaches theoretically within the governmental context; and then
describing the extent to which role strain or role conflict among the conflicting
expectations of alternative personnel systems are an aberration or "come with the
territory."

   If the previous discussion of competing values and systems has demonstrated
anything, it is that public personnel managers will continue to be responsible for
making the difficult decisions required to implement not only competing pro-
government values but also their opposing antigovernment values. More than
ever, good job performance will require that they recognize the inherent conflicts
in their role, and yet continue to make sound professional decisions in a climate
of political and economic uncertainty (Riccucci 2005).

Human Resource Management Specialist

Pay and benefits constitute about two-thirds of the operating costs of the typical organization. Human resource management specialists are—or should be—
experts consulted by other managers who wish to improve their ability to manage
people. So in addition to professional and technical capabilities, personnel directors are responsible for experimentation, technology transfer, and education
within the organization. Each of these roles merits discussion. Experimentation
means the testing of personnel policies or procedures to determine their impact
on a desired value (such as the effect of a new benefit, or a new performance evaluation method, on employee productivity or turnover). But personnel directors

rarely initiate personnel management innovations. Usually, these are developed in one setting and transferred to others where variables and objectives are similar. From this perspective, innovations such as privatization or use of independent contractors are administrative innovations that have been introduced initially in one government as experiments, and then adapted and adopted in other settings as a technology transfer process. Lastly, human resource management specialists function as educators for employees and other managers concerning public personnel systems—the laws, policies, and procedures used to manage employees in an organization. This educational function is performed formally, through training and development, and informally, through organizational interactions, as they perform the four personnel functions.

Mediator among Conflicting Values and Systems

Initially, civil service reformers sought to establish the credibility of personnel management by emphasizing its political neutrality and focusing on administrative efficiency. This emphasis served to establish public personnel management as a technical field with a body of techniques used to perform human resource management functions, and it separated public personnel administration from politics. Ironically, however, this emphasis on political neutrality and insistence on discovering the "one best way" to manage human resources had an opposite effect on the field as well. It isolated public personnel managers from the value conflicts that characterized the world of other professionals (such as law and medicine) and minimized the ethical dilemmas that constantly confronted them—dilemmas that grew out of the political context in which all public employees operate. This created the illusion among public officials (and among personnel directors and specialists themselves) that the field was value-free. It focused personnel management on administrative techniques instead of broad human resource policy questions. This devalued the status of the profession and downgraded the importance accorded the study of personnel systems and values.

Traditional public personnel managers are usually impatient or complacent with ethical choices. In their view of public personnel administration, ethical dilemmas are easily resolved because this system is based entirely upon the civil service system as a moral ideal, with the political patronage system as its archenemy and moral opposite (or at best something to be continually wary of). The competing claims of alternative systems (politics, collective bargaining, and affirmative action) are considered challenges to the morally superior civil service system. Public personnel managers operating under these beliefs function either as "true believers" or as pragmatists. They are inclined to consider *ethics* unnecessary, because it is easier to think of administrative actions as purely technical and rational and infused with moral superiority, or impractical because competing claims require pragmatic compromise.

Today, the extent to which the three emergent antigovernment values will diminish the impact of the traditional four is uncertain. But if the past is any indication, it is likely that the inherent weaknesses of the new values will be self-limiting and that there will be a swing back toward the pro-government alternatives. Therefore, it is reasonable to predict that public personnel managers will continue to play their traditional role as mediators among conflicting values, albeit on a smaller scale because of the diminished role of government in society.

The Changing and Complex Role of the Public Personnel Administrator

Contemporary public personnel managers need various types of competencies in order to perform their roles well. Public personnel managers need to place continued emphasis on productivity and efficiency. They have to be competent—and keep themselves competent—in personnel law, procedures, and quantitative and qualitative analytical techniques. They have to be viewed as human beings by employees, have a positive attitude toward organizational administrators and objectives, and maintain close working relationships with other personnel professionals inside and outside the organization. Even though no administrator can be an expert in every aspect of the field, the complete personnel department cannot avoid having someone on staff who is competent in all of them.

Traditional public personnel management requires that personnel directors know the laws and regulations that control practices within a particular system, as well as the techniques used to perform personnel functions within that system. For example, traditional civil service-oriented personnel management requires knowledge of civil service rules and regulations (such as competitive examination procedures, or how to select from a list of eligible applicants), as well as how to develop and administer examinations, write job descriptions, administer pay and benefit programs, and process personnel actions.

Contemporary public personnel management requires these skills and more. It requires knowledge of public personnel management techniques, an understanding of historical developments in the field, and the ability to resolve ethical dilemmas among competing values under conditions of change and uncertainty. Personnel rules and procedures are not value-neutral; rather, they are the implicit or explicit implementation of a particular public personnel system (or compromises among several such systems). This means that each selection or promotion decision must be viewed not merely as a technical exercise, but as a case that reflects and exemplifies this historical conflict over alternative values, power, and public personnel systems.

Public personnel directors must be sensitive to the need for administrative systems to be responsive to legitimate political values and public participation in governance, especially in local government. These kinds of changes inevitably challenge the shield that the rhetoric of merit has provided the traditional manager. Now there is no escaping the political pressure personnel managers must face. They work under consent decrees and with unions that traditionally have set barriers to hiring women and minorities. At the same time, they are expected to respond to their political leaders while maintaining the integrity of the civil service system they oversee. Yet they have no guidance from within the traditional civil service system for how to integrate these increasingly insistent and conflicting demands.

Modern public personnel managers tend to view their world as a conflict and change-oriented environment, rather than as a stable one. First, theirs is a world in which trends such as privatization and contracting out have blurred distinctions between public and private. Second, their world is controlled by a myriad of complex and conflicting laws involving affirmative action, labor relations, personal/professional liability, employee privacy, due process, and pay equity. Third, their world is characterized by constant technological innovations in areas such as data security, teleconferencing, computerized databases and report generation, and applications of interactive video to training and orientation. Fourth, their world is characterized by changes in workforce composition (demographics). For example, robotics and automation have led to the creation and absorption of many middle management and clerical positions; the workforce is aging, and the number of women and minorities is increasing—by 1980, over half the workforce employed outside the home in the United States was female. And the number of blacks and Hispanics is increasing as well (they will constitute 50 percent of the births in the United States by 2076) (Judy and D'Amico 1997). Fifth, this leads to changes in organization such as real-time problem solving, decentralization, and networking.

These changes in the context of public administration have led public personnel managers to adopt a changing definition of the field. In general, there is increased awareness of the impact of environmental factors—among them technology, economics, politics, and social conditions. There is also continued awareness of the importance of human resources to organizational productivity. Within the field of human resource management, this means increased responsibilities in the general area of environmental mediation and adaptation, including interpretation and compliance with government regulations, predicting the effects of changes in technology and workforce composition on jobs, and developing programs and systems to help line managers increase productivity. Examples are job humanization, flexible work schedules and benefits, training and education, and performance-oriented evaluation systems.

Toward an Evolutionary Developmental Model of the Role

The competencies required of public personnel managers have changed historically over time as a result of changing conditions and expectations. Today it can be said that public personnel management in the United States represents a dynamic equilibrium between the previously mentioned conflicting and interacting values and systems. Each value represents a particular system for assigning scarce public jobs to applicants within a complex and changing environment. This conflict demonstrates the intermingling of technical decisions (for example, how to perform a certain personnel function) with political decisions (for example, which

TABLE 3.2. The Role of the Public Personnel Manager in the United States

Stage	Dominant Value	Dominant System	Public Personnel Manager's Role
Patrician (1789–1828)	Responsiveness	"Government by Elites"	None
Patronage (1829–1882)	Responsiveness	Patronage	Recruitment and political clearance
Professionalism (1883–1932)	Efficiency + Individual Rights	Civil Service	Watchdog against the spoils system
Performance (1933–1964)	Responsiveness + Efficiency + Individual Rights	Patronage + Civil Service	Adherence to legislative mandates + watchdog against the spoils system
People (1965–1979)	Responsiveness + Efficiency + Individual Rights + Social Equity	Patronage + Civil Service + Collective Bargaining + Affirmative Action	consultation + balance among competing values and objectives
Privatization (1980–now)	Individual Accountability + Limited and Decentralized Government + Community Responsibility	Alternative Organizations and Mechanisms + Flexible Employment Relationships	Adherence to legislative limits + contract compliance
Partnership (2002–now)	Responsiveness + Efficiency + Individual Accountability + Limited Government + Community Responsibility	Patronage + Civil Service + Collective Bargaining + Affirmative Action + Alternative mechanisms + Flexible Employment Relationships	Compliance + Policy Implementation + Consultation + Contract Compliance + Strategic thinking about HRM + Tension Management + Boundary Spanning

value should be favored or which system utilized in performing that function). The steps in the evolution of the role in the United States, the values, the systems, and role expectations at each stage of development, are shown in Table 3.2.

Up to this point our analysis has focused on the development of public personnel management in the United States. But we also have to think about the relationship between public personal management and democratization from an international perspective, due to the fall of international communism and the resurgence of democratic institutions in parts of Eastern Europe, Latin America, and Africa. This development process varies from region to region, so we will therefore use several Central American republics as an illustrative example.

Despite this consensus on the importance of public personnel management to the development of democratic government and society, there has been little comparative research on the development of public personnel management in Central America or of its relationship to democratization there. Comparative administration texts do discuss civil service reform, though they do not focus specifically on this topic or region. Consequently, critical questions remain unanswered:

> How does the development of public personnel management in Central America compare with its development in other Latin American countries or in other developing countries?
>
> How does the process by which public personnel management has developed in the United States compare with the developmental process in other developed countries?
>
> To what extent are findings about the relationship between democratization and public personnel management in Central America generalizable to the study of democratization in other developing countries?

Comparative analysis allows us to establish some key points about the development of public personnel management, and about its relationship to the democratization process in Central America.

First, each country evidences background characteristics that are similar to and yet different than the others. Among the similarities are a common language, history as parts of the Spanish colonial empire, and structure of government. Yet each also differs from the others in historical, social, political, and economic characteristics. And understanding these similarities and differences is the key to understanding their laws, government structure, and personnel processes.

Second, the history of each country shows that complex and interactive pressures toward democratization and modernization influence the development of each country. For example, there are internal pressures to allow greater political freedom (characterized by the development of political institutions), economic development (characterized by external investment and the creation of adequate private sector employment), and improved socioeconomic well-being of the population (as measured by levels of income, health, and education); and external pressures for enhanced governmental performance and stability, the growth of a stable and adequate economy, and the protection of human rights. While the conceptual and operational relationships between democratization and other variables are debated, an examination of national characteristics demonstrates that a close relationship exists between the effectiveness of a government and the effectiveness of its public personnel system.

Third, public personnel systems within these three Central American republics have developed through a relatively uniform process similar to, yet not identical with, the evolution of the field in the United States. In the beginning there is

TABLE 3.3.   The Role of the Public Personnel Manager in Developing Countries

Stage	Dominant Value	Dominant System	Public Personnel Manager's Role
I – Elites	Responsiveness	Patronage	Recruitment and political clearance
II – Patronage	Responsiveness + Efficiency + Individual Rights	Patronage + Civil Service + Collective Bargaining	Recruitment and Political clearance + "Watchdog" over agency managers and elected officials to ensure merit system compliance
III – Merit	Responsiveness + Efficiency + Individual Rights	Patronage + Civil Service + Collective Bargaining	Recruitment and political clearance + Adherence to legislative mandates + Watchdog against the Spoils system + Contract compliance
IV – Mature Mixed	Responsiveness + Efficiency + Limited government	Patronage + Civil Service + Collective bargaining + Privatization	Compliance + Policy implementation + Consultation + Contract Compliance + Strategic thinking about HRM

a patronage system, then a transition toward merit marked by three milestones (passage of a civil service law; creation of a civil service agency with adequate location, staffing and funding; and implementation of effective personnel procedures). This proposed model is shown in Table 3.3 (Klingner 1996).

In Central America, dominance by elites during the initial stage of independence is followed by patronage-based personnel systems as political leaders seek to maximize political responsiveness. As pressures for efficiency (modernization) and employee rights (democratization) increase, the third stage is a transition to merit systems marked by three milestones: passage of a civil service law, creation of an effective civil service agency, and elaboration of effective policies and procedures. Fourth, if and when this occurs, policymakers must strive to maintain an appropriate balance among the desirable but contradictory objectives that characterize public personnel management in developed countries: (1) Establish an optimum level of public employment, (2) protect public employees' rights yet achieve administrative efficiency, (3) achieve both uniformity and flexibility of personnel policies and procedures, and (4) balance conflicting values and personnel systems.

Although the transition from patronage to merit is due to a number of external pressures, it is also spurred by internal consensus (among a coalition of administrators, academicians, political leaders, and other "change agents") on the general disadvantages of patronage systems: Excessive political appointments are tied to government corruption; (2) the wholesale employee turnover that accompanies elections promotes inefficiency and wastes human resources; and (3) the resultant instability, corruption, and poor government performance discourage international investors and engender cynicism or apathy among the people. The advantages of a merit system are also widely accepted by this reform coalition: it allows (1) governments to predict personnel expenses and control them within a prescribed budget; (2) agencies to manage their own human resources most effectively; and (3) public employees in professional and technical positions to develop as individuals and as a national resource.

While the general developmental process in these three Central American republics appears similar to that found historically in the United States, there are three major differences. First, because in Central America unions are a potent political force against patronage, they emerge prior to (rather than after) the transition from patronage to civil service. Second, because public employment rights for minorities and women are not yet a critical public policy issue in Central America (except in relatively developed countries such as Costa Rica), social equity as a value does not yet have significant impact on personnel systems. So stage three in Central American republics is at present a dynamic equilibrium among three (rather than four) traditional values and their respective public personnel systems. Third, while there exist considerable pressures toward privatization as part of the overall economic policy of international lending organizations to reduce public expenditures and external debt, there is also widespread realization in Central America that the development of a strong civil service is essential to democratization and development. Thus, pressures toward privatization and business models are not as strong there as in the United States. So again, stage four in Central American republics is at present a dynamic equilibrium among three values and their respective public personnel systems.

Although there has been little research into the process by which administrative innovations are developed or transferred from one country to another, this developmental uniformity appears to be based on three factors: (1) Conditions in developing countries, including pressures for modernization and democratization, may parallel (though lag behind) those in the United States; (2) personnel innovations tend to be exotic (introduced into developing countries by consultants from developed countries) rather than indigenous ("home grown"); and (3) international lenders often mandate administrative reform as a condition of continued credit.

HOW DO PUBLIC PERSONNEL MANAGERS GET INTO THE FIELD?

Previous discussion indicated that public personnel management is a set of functions (planning, acquisition, development, and sanction) performed by personnel specialists, managers, and elected and appointed officials. Personnel specialists, in particular, function as technicians, professionals, human resource management experts, and mediators. They perform these multiple roles in a central personnel office or in a public agency. Usually, at least in entry-level positions, they specialize in some aspect of the field, such as staffing, test development, job analysis and evaluation, affirmative action compliance, contract negotiation or administration, training and development, or pay and benefits. In smaller jurisdictions or agencies, the personnel function may be part of another job, and this provides basic exposure and experience.

While the personnel specialist's work involves primarily civil service systems and the employees working in them, it includes other systems as well—collective bargaining, affirmative action, political appointments, alternative mechanisms for providing public services (such as outsourcing), and flexible employment relationships (such as exempt positions, temporary, and part-time employment).

While all students of public personnel management need to know something about the job of the personnel manager as part of learning about the field, some students have a more specific interest—they want a job. Thus, their interest in what public personnel managers do is followed by two other questions: As a student, what courses should I be taking to qualify myself for a job as a public personnel manager? As a first-time job applicant, how do I get a job?

While public personnel management is a profession, it is also a profession of generalists in that people become public personnel managers through a variety of career paths. Most have some formal academic training, undergraduate and/or graduate, in public management or business administration. This may include course work in personnel management from a private-sector perspective, or in public personnel management from the perspective of civil service and collective bargaining systems. There are specialized graduate curricula in personnel management taught by a number of programs; information on public administration programs can be obtained from the *National Association for Schools of Public Affairs and Administration (NASPAA)*; information on business administration programs can be obtained through the *American Association for Schools and Colleges of Business (AACSB)*.

In addition to required courses in human resource management, many graduate programs also include a specialization area in human resource management. While the content of programs differs among institutions, common topics in a specialization are included, either as separate courses or as elements in a curriculum.

Administrative law: impact of rules and regulations on public administration, including personnel management.

Collective bargaining: Impact of unions on public personnel management, legal and political antecedents, and contract negotiation and administration procedures.

Test development: Development and validation of devices for selection, promotion, and placement (sometimes taught by psychology).

Pay and benefits: Job analysis, classification, and evaluation; setting wages and salaries through job evaluation and/or market surveys; statutorily required employee benefits (workers' compensation, Social Security), and optional ones (health insurance, pensions, etc.).

Training and employee development: Design, implementation, and evaluation of orientation, training, and career development programs.

Affirmative action compliance: Work force diversity, equal employment opportunity, affirmative action, and employment equity without respect to gender, race, national origin, age, religion, or disability.

Organizational development and change: Assessing organizational performance, and changing structure and culture to make it more effective.

Role of women and minorities: Changing organizational culture to make it more equitable for women and minorities.

Personnel policies and procedures: "Topics" courses specializing current policy issues (such as workforce diversification, workplace violence, alcohol and drug abuse, and life-threatening diseases).

Productivity improvement: How to make organizations more efficient and effective through the application of policy-analytic techniques.

Comparative or development administration: Offered through public administration, business administration, economics, or international relations programs.

Alternatives to civil service: Use of alternative organizations or mechanisms for providing public services, or of flexible employment relationships for public employees.

University training (a BPA, a Master's degree, or even a graduate professional certificate program in public personnel management) will give personnel specialists added knowledge that can enhance their performance as specialist, professional, mediator, or human resource management expert, thereby enhancing their career options. And because public personnel functions also involve others besides personnel specialists (such as managers, supervisors, and appointed officials), many human resource management courses have more general usefulness for anyone considering a career in public policy or management.

Those without significant personnel management experience may have a harder time breaking into the field. Worldwide changes in labor markets, plus the changing political conditions under which public administrators work today, mean that there is more competition for professional jobs in many fields, including public personnel management. Often, recent college graduates without significant public personnel management experience are competing against experienced professionals who are on the job market because they have been laid off (or, if you prefer current terminology, "out-placed" or "reengineered" out of their jobs). Under pressure to "do more with less," employers will seek to hire employees who will not incur start-up costs. They may prefer to hire the experienced professional over the recent graduate.

How do you "get your foot in the door" under these conditions? The first suggestion is to take courses as part of your university education that provide you with knowledge and abilities needed by public personnel managers, particularly the entry-level positions discussed above. Take enough courses (usually semester credit hours) and the right courses so that you can apply for a major, a minor, or a certificate in human resource management or personnel management. Second, include an internship as part of your university curriculum. Make sure it is with an organization that is looking for employees—one that uses internship programs as a recruitment mechanism rather than just a source of temporary, free labor. Your best gauge of this is by asking your university's internship placement coordinator, your professors, or current employees who started work there as interns. While a formal internship option may not be feasible for the mid career student, expressing interest and aptitude on the job may help with a lateral transfer into personnel work. With some creative thinking and job design it may be possible to share some time in the personnel office or to gain experience by seeking out personnel-related tasks in your own office. Third, tailor your résumé so it highlights the education, experience, skills, and knowledge needed for a job in personnel management. Identify related courses in management, computer sciences, statistics, psychology, law, or other fields. Fourth, practice applying for jobs and taking interviews so you know how to respond to questions interviewers ask. Why do you want this job? What work experience have you had that shows your aptitude or ability for personnel work? If you lack related experience, what skills and abilities do you have that would make it easy to learn? Why are you the best candidate for the position? Good luck!

TAKING CHARGE OF YOUR OWN CAREER DEVELOPMENT AS A PUBLIC PERSONNEL MANAGER

Any preprofessional training begins to become obsolete the moment the course is over. Clearly, it is incumbent upon personnel professionals to take charge of their own self-development through continued self-study and career development. Some suggested sources public personnel managers could use as individuals to enhance their own skills and abilities are professional associations, research libraries, and the Internet (Klingner and Nalbandian 2003).

Professional Associations

Professional associations offer the opportunity to network with other professionals locally, to attend national and regional conferences, and to receive free member services such as newsletters or professional journals. All of these offer continued education and career advancement options for working professionals. Universities, professional associations, and private professional development institutes provide training courses and seminars for public personnel practitioners. Check the continuing studies or university outreach programs of local universities, or the calendars of local chapters of professional associations.

Research Libraries

Research libraries are indispensable for students or practitioners seeking to keep their knowledge of law and practice up to date. People tend to think of libraries as places where books are kept, but in reality, the past 10 years have witnessed their transformation into sources of information, much of it stored or transmitted electronically rather than on paper. A generation ago, students researched papers by checking books out of the library, or by photocopying journal articles. They took the materials home, wrote a draft of the paper, and typed the final copy. Books are a good source of historical data, but they are rarely useful for researching current topics because the long lead-time between writing and publication (usually a minimum of 2 years). Books are cataloged by subject area, usually according to the Library of Congress cataloging system.

Research is totally different today. It's possible to research excellent papers without using books at all, by utilizing alternative information sources: reference books, loose-leaf services, indexes, professional journals, and government documents. Loose-leaf services are serial publications issued on a regular basis to provide researchers, lawyers, and practitioners with current information on specified areas of personnel practice and procedure. Indexes are bound books or CD-ROM disks that provide bibliographic sources on human resource management topics from a range of professional journals and other periodicals. Data are arranged so that references may be located by author, publication, key word, etc. They are published monthly, quarterly, or annually.

Many professional associations publish professional journals to keep members informed about current law, practice, innovations, and issues in the field. These are sent to members, or are available through research libraries. Generally, periodicals in the human resource management area are found in the HF5549.5 area (Library of Congress cataloging system). The federal government, and many state and local governments, routinely send publications to so-called repository libraries throughout the country. These government documents are sometimes hard to locate because they are not indexed by Library of Congress codes (as are books and professional journals). But reference librarians can help you if you can't locate what you need through the indexes of public documents. Or you may contact these agencies directly to request specific documents—most are free or low-cost.

It's also possible to research a popular current topic through newspapers and magazines. While the quality of newsmagazines and newspapers is uneven, some periodicals (such as the *New York Times* and *Wall Street Journal*) are noted for their thoughtful, well-researched coverage. Frequently, this is the only source you can use for current topics, as the lead-time to publication in professional journals is often over a year. Some periodicals (including the two mentioned above) have their own indexes. If your library subscribes to a comprehensive index of periodicals (such as LEXIS/NEXIS), you will be able to search the whole universe for material on a specific topic. Some popular magazines are also indexed in the indexes mentioned previously.

Doing Research through the Information Superhighway

While it is of course possible to do research by visiting the library and browsing through these information sources there, all this information—and a lot more—is available on the information superhighway (Internet). This is the global information network that connects the researcher with a wealth of electronic information. All you need is an office or home computer, a phone line with a modem, and communications software (which may even be provided free by your university or your employer. Using these tools, it's possible to use four major applications of the Internet: e-mail, listservs, browsers, and Web sites (home pages).

E-mail (short for electronic mail) is fundamental to Internet connections, since it provides the computer address from which and to which electronic messages are sent. Electronic messages are sent from one computer to another through each computer's modem, using phone lines as the transmission method across distances. E-mail has several critical advantages over conventional communication by memo, fax, or voice communication by telephone. First, it is paperless, meaning less waste and less transmission time. Second, messages are received and stored automatically for the recipient, who can "pick up the mail" and read it from any software-compatible computer using the individual's e-mail address and a confidential access code. This avoids playing "phone tag," because the complete message or question is stored, waiting to be accessed by the recipient. It also avoids long-distance phone charges since information is transferred instantaneously from computer to computer. Messages can be sent to lists of recipients simultaneously, creating the opportunity for a true communications net among people with common interests.

Listservs are tools that organize and expand the usefulness of e-mail by providing an easy way for persons with common interests to share information. Once people join a listserv, they are automatically sent every message sent on the Internet to every other member of that listserv; and a message they send to that listserv is automatically referred to all other members as well.

The positive implications of the Internet are enormous and obvious. It enables students and scholars to communicate easily and directly around the world. The problems are equally obvious: organization and quality control. With all this data floating around in cyberspace, how do users know where to look for it, and how do they evaluate the correctness or quality of the data out there? Gophers are automated retrieval services used to locate materials on a particular subject, using branching logic trees and key word addresses in a fashion similar to CD-ROM indexes used by reference libraries. Many government agencies, the Library of Congress, and universities engaged in public management research maintain gophers to help scholars find their way around the Web. Individuals, organizations, or agencies may create their own home page, a Web site identified with their particular e-mail address and used to transmit information to users through Internet browsers.

CONCLUSION

Public personnel management has been affected by environmental change as organizations and jobs become less stable, demographic tendencies become more diverse, and emergent market values compete with traditional pro-governmental values and systems. These changes have several critical consequences: (1) change from the administration of positions to the administration of work and employees, (2) precise differentiation between "permanent" and "contingent" workers, (3) growing realization of the limitations of traditional civil service systems, (4) the growth of alternative organizations and mechanisms for providing public services, (5) a continued need to define the values that underlie public service, and (6) the need to unify political and administrative perspectives to make government work effectively.

Public personnel managers may be viewed as technicians, professionals, mediators, and human resource management specialists. Traditional personnel managers (those who operate within a consensus on one system and its underlying values) tend to define themselves, and to be defined by others, as technical specialists working within a staff agency. Contemporary personnel managers (those who operate as human resource management experts or as mediators among competing systems and values) tend to define themselves, and to be defined by others, as professionals whose role involves a blend of technical skills and ethical decision making.

Tomorrow's organization with increased specialization, downsizing, teamwork, and pay for performance all add challenges and anxiety to the work of elected and appointed executives, managers, supervisors, and employees. Organizing work in this type of environment of change highlights the importance of an organization and its members who are capable of dealing with the resultant ambiguity and who are willing and able to learn from their organizational experiences and make personal and organizational changes based on that learning.

REFERENCES

Caudron, Sharon. (1996). Contingent Work Force Spurs HR Planning. *Personnel Journal [Online]*, 48 paragraphs. Available at http://www.hrhq.com/members/archive/2627.html.

Cohen, Steven, and William Eimicke. (1994, Spring). The Overregulated Civil Service. *Review of Public Personnel Administration*: 11–27.

Condrey, Steven. (Ed.) (2004). *The Handbook of Public Human Resource Management*, 2nd ed. San Francisco, CA: Jossey-Bass.

Heclo, Hugh. (1977). *A Government of Strangers*. Washington, DC: The Brookings Institution.

Judy, Richard, and Carol D'Amico. (1997). *Workforce 2020*. Indianapolis, IN: Hudson Institute.

Klingner, Donald, and John Nalbandian. (2003). *Public Personnel Management: Contexts and Strategies*, 5th ed. Englewood Cliffs, NJ: Prentice Hall/Simon & Schuster.

Nalbandian, John. (1994). Reflections of a "Pracademic" on the Logic of Politics and Administration. *Public Administration Review*, 54: 531–536.

Osborne, David, and Ted Gaebler. (1992). *Reinventing Government*. Reading, MA: Addison-Wesley.

Peters, B. Guy and Donald J. Savoie. (1994, September/October). Civil Service Reform: Misdiagnosing the Patient. *Public Administration Review*: 418–425.

Riccucci, Norma. (2005). *Public Personnel Management: Current Concerns, Future Challenges.* New York: Longmans.

Savas, E.S. (1990). A Taxonomy of Privatization Strategies. *Policy Studies Journal*, 18(2): 343–355.

4

Accountability Challenges Facing Public Sector HRM in an Era of Downsizing, Devolution, Diffusion, and Empowerment

J. STEVEN OTT AND LISA A. DICKE

Political ideology and an ideology of empowerment have collectively created an all-but-indisputable truth: *The best decisions are made by people and organizations that are closest to those who will be most directly affected.* It doesn't matter if the question is whether a decision should be made in Washington, DC, or in state houses; in a state house or in city halls; in city halls or in community councils; in corporate headquarters or in geographically dispersed profit centers; in government agency offices or in boardrooms of contracted nongovernmental service providers; or by higher-level public managers or employees who interact with recipients of services. The question has been answered before it is asked: "One size does not fit all. Make decisions as close as possible to the people who will be most directly affected." The strategies for acting on this all-but-indisputable truth in the epoch of the 21st century are self-evident: downsize, decentralize, devolve, diffuse, empower, and contract-out.

This all-but-indisputable truth and its enactment strategies have been fueled by the widely shared public perception that government is incompetent and cannot be trusted to do anything right (Lenkowsky and Perry, 2000; Ott and Shafritz, 1994, 1995). Beliefs that support this truth include: Bureaucracies are not able to provide sufficient incentives to induce government employees to work efficiently and effectively; government managers are rewarded for maximizing the size of agency budgets and staffs; and inhabitants of government bureaucracies become overzealous in exercising regulatory policies that irreparably damage businesses, families, and lives. Strategies to implement this truth represent attempts to circumvent what are widely believed to be the irreparable causes of government incompetence—the rule-bound inflexibility of large traditional government bureaucracies that deliver monopolistic services. Proponents of downsizing, devolution, and diffusion thus envision a release of creative and administrative talents within government agencies and in contracted private organizations that deliver services for government, when centralized rule-based authority structures are removed or, at least, are dispersed (Durst and Newell, 1999; Page, 2005; Peters, 1996).

This all-but-indisputable truth and its implementation strategies also have implications for public human resource management (HRM), managers and departments and for public employees in general (Swiss, 2005). As public organizations are downsized, employee morale often plummets as fears and insecurities infect the organizational culture. Attempts to empower employees and to redesign or enrich jobs are seen as nothing more than manipulative schemes to get employees to "do more with less." The seemingly endless attacks on the ability of government organizations and employees tend to cause talented young people to avoid or leave government jobs thus creating self-fulfilling prophesies (Kearney and Hays, 1998).

Concerns about the loss of accountability and equitable treatment when government agencies are downsized, devolved, diffused, and lower level employees are empowered have been resourcefully dismissed via a second all-but-indisputable truth: *Information technology and performance measurement are able to uphold the core values of accountability and equity.* The combined effects of these two all-but-indisputable truths have substantive implications for the processes, structures, and cultures of public sector organizations and their HRM departments. The most significant challenges these truths have created for HRM are by-products of weakened government accountability and the erosion of core public values, particularly equity (Ott, Boonyarak, and Dicke, 2001). Meeting these challenges will require new roles and skills for public HRM departments as well as considerable effort and creativity. These truths, ideologies, and strategies, and their implications for public HRM are the foci of this article.

Specifically, we argue that downsizing, devolution, diffusion, and empowerment are pervasive and persuasive ideologies, and pressures on government to implement these ideologies will not lessen in the foreseeable future. Downsizing, devolution, diffusion, and empowering provide many performance advantages, but they eliminate the historic notion of accountability flowing up through hierarchies to public officials who are accountable to the public. It has been widely assumed that recent advancements in information technology and performance measurement provide adequate replacements for up-the-hierarchy accountability, but these technologies are not yet at a level of development that they can ensure some important dimensions of accountability in several areas of government services Nicholson-Crotty, Theobald, and Nicholson-Crotty, 2006; Page, 2005; Swiss, 2005). Alternate approaches to accountability are needed, and public HRM managers and departments can play leading roles, but the long-standing

HRM "paradigm" will need to change radically before they will be able to do so effectively.

THE POLITICAL IDEOLOGY OF DOWNSIZING, DEVOLUTION, AND DIFFUSION/OUTSOURCING

House Speaker Newt Gingrich was arguably the most eloquent spokesperson for this political ideology in the 1990s. The Republican Party's "Contract with America" became the symbol for the devolution and diffusion movement. The potency of the ideology has shown little decline. In the infancy of his presidency, George W. Bush signed Executive Orders 13198 and 13199 establishing Executive Department Centers of Faith-Based and Community Initiatives and a White House Office of Faith-Based and Community Initiatives. These orders once again visibly institutionalized the ideology at the national level, and the implications for public sector HRM could not be dismissed lightly. We expect to continue to hear the tenets of the ideology voiced as all-but-indisputable truths by politicians, the news media, and some scholars alike, such as:

Downsize: Government is too big. David Osborne, for example, did not believe that the National Performance Review (NPR) could succeed if it were "sold" as simply an effort to improve the performance of government. Osborne "pleaded with Gore to put the 252,000 personnel reduction goal in the [NPR] report. Had we not convinced him, I don't think the report would have been credible in Washington" (in Light, 1998, 26). Smith and Lipsky (1993) argue that "reducing the size of government" is at least as persuasive as "reducing costs" as another all-but-unarguable justification for contracting services out to the private sector.

Devolve: Better decisions are made close to home. Decentralize. Let go of decisions and resources. In 1996, for example, Congress was persuaded by the governors to turn the administration of Medicaid over to the states. The governors argued that if states were freed from the Health Care Financing Administration's (HCFA's) endless red tape, they would make better decisions that would benefit people in their states, and with the savings from increased efficiency, states could provide the same or higher levels of services with less funding. As has been widely reported, the governors' claims far exceeded what the states were able to achieve.

The devolution movement has not been limited to "returning" power to the states, however. At the same time that the states have been wrestling with Washington over the control of programs and funding, cities, counties, and special districts also have been pleading for increased freedom from state house controls and statewide "mandates."

Diffuse: Government should not engage in (and should withdraw from) the provision of any services that organizations in the private sector can and will provide. Leading proponents of contracting-out, such as E. S. Savas (1982), have argued that the public is served best when interested public agencies and private firms are allowed to compete for public business. Positive results, including higher productivity, lower production costs, and increased customer satisfaction, reportedly have resulted from public-private competition in the U.S. government, states, and cities (Barzelay, 1992;

Chi, 1994; GAO, 1992, 1997a, 1997b; Osborne and Gaebler, 1992; Osborne and Plastrik, 1997; Prager and Desai, 1996). The strength of the political ideology of diffusion, however, has given credibility to the argument that the public sector enjoys an unfair advantage in competition with the private sector, and thus public agencies should not be permitted to compete with private firms for government contracts. For example, despite demonstrated financial and performance benefits to the government that were derived from public-private competitions for Air Force and Navy aircraft maintenance work between 1991 and 1994, the Department of Defense's program of public-private competition was abruptly terminated. In justifying the decision, John Duesche, Deputy Secretary of Defense summarily announced:

With regard to competition between the public depots and the private sector, the Task Force and other related studies and audits have concluded that: Databases and financial management systems in the Department of the Military Services are not capable of supporting the determination of actual cost of specific workloads. Although vigorous attempts have been made to execute fair public/private cost competitions...a level playing field is not achievable in the near term. Based on these findings public/private competition will be discontinued at present. (May 4, 1994, 1)

Studies have concluded, however, that when there are few qualified vendors in the private sector—as is the case with large aerospace firms—the government rarely saves money by contracting-out (Page, 2005). "The simple transfer of a service from public monopoly to a private one is unlikely to yield improvements in either quality or cost savings" (Miranda, 1995, 197).

The strength of diffusion as political ideology in the decades of the 1990s and 2000s has been most evident, however, in the systems for the delivery of state, county, and municipal human services. Virtually *no* human services are provided directly by government employees anywhere. Nonprofit organizations, and in some fields for-profit firms, are *the* deliverers of government-funded human services (Smith and Lipsky, 1993). Where no nonprofit organization exists to deliver human services to clientele groups, state and local departments of human services have helped employees establish new nonprofits expressly for the purpose of contracting-out services to them. In a few states, even some "case management" responsibilities—the system for ensuring accountability for human services—have been contracted-out. In most human services systems, case managers decide which clients should receive which services from which provider(s), and for assuring the quantity, quality, and appropriateness of services they receive.

Downsizing, devolution, and diffusion are accepted tenets of the political ideology of the past two decades. Decrease the size of government, push decisions down closer to home, and push services out into private organizations. Government, governance, taxpayers, the private sector, and the economy all will benefit. Quality of life will improve for individuals, communities, and the nation.

THE IDEOLOGY OF EMPOWERMENT

The ideology of empowerment shares many tenets and themes with the 1990s political ideology, and the implications for HRM are similar. Empowerment ideology, however, has its own foci, targets, and jargon which can be sorted into two primary streams: (1) empower employees to make decisions, and (2) empower recipients of services and other members of the general public to influence government decisions. Empowerment, like devolution, reflects disenchantment with traditional government bureaucracy and inflexible, rules-based, hierarchies.

> The operative assumption appears to be that the best or even the only way to obtain better results from public sector organizations is to adopt some sort of a market-based mechanism to replace the traditional bureaucracy. (Peters, 1996, 21)

Empowerment as an ideology also contains several highly optimistic themes. It is optimistic about the nature of humans if they are provided with "proper and adequate" incentives, and it is optimistic about the knowledge and abilities of lower-level employees if they can be freed from rigid bureaucratic rules and policies. And, empowerment is optimistic about positive results that can be achieved when people who receive government services are empowered, particularly when services are coproduced (Handler, 1996) and when "watchful eye" public interest groups are diligent (Light, 1998, 2000). Employee empowerment has been the more influential of these two streams, and thus the balance of this discussion about empowerment is limited to it.

Empowerment is about higher management "letting go," turning decisions, responsibility, resources, and accountability over to the employees and/or teams of employees lower in the organization who perform the day-to-day tasks. The two overarching arguments for empowerment are: (1) empowerment permits employees to grow and develop as humans; (2) empowered employees who have been adequately developed produce positive benefits to the organization and for its clients, particularly responsiveness to individual client needs and wants. Properly selected, trained, informed, supported, and motivated teams of workers can and will organize, coordinate, control, correct, and otherwise supervise themselves (Bowen and Lawler, 1992; Orsburn and Moran, 2000; Orsburn, Moran, Musselwhite and Zenger, 1990). Multiple layers of supervisors and middle-managers were needed in earlier eras to perform these coordinative and supportive functions, but in the new political ideology they are not needed, do not add value, and impede the progress of empowered employees (Bolman and Deal, 2003). Middle managers only add needless costs and organizational rigidities. "In the latest round of budget cuts, mid-level managers are considered the easiest and more defenseless target" (Walters, 2005, 28). These two overarching arguments for empowerment are mutually self-supporting—as they have been through the past 30 to 40 years of organizational behavior and human resource theories of organization (Ott, Parkes, and Simpson, 2003).

The empowerment ideology argues for reducing or removing hierarchical layers of top-down controls, opting instead to expand employee decision-making or decision-influencing (Deming 1986, 1993; Kettl 1995). It rests on the popular assumption (Clinton and Gore, 1995; Osborne and Gaebler, 1992) that "workers and clients closest to the actual production of goods and services in the public sector have the greatest insight and information about the programs" (Peters, 1996, 48). It also rests on the belief that customer (or client) satisfaction should be the "bottom line" for government agencies. Client satisfaction is the best measure of service quality, and thus client satisfaction should drive decisions, not rules, policies, control systems, or top-down decisions.

The ideology of empowerment has been highly visible in several popular management movements of the 1980s and 1990s, including: *Quality* or *TQM* (Bhote, 1994; Deming, 1986, 1993; GAO, 1991, 1992; Joiner, 1994; Juran, 1992); *National Productivity Review* or *NPR* (Clinton and Gore, 1995; Gore, 1993; Kettl, 1995); *self-directing work teams* (Bowen and Lawler, 1992; Orsburn and Moran, Weisbord, 1991), including the Air Force's highly-studied TQM/self-directed work team pilot project, "Project Pacer Share" (Dutcher et al., 1992; Gilbert, 1992; Gilbert and Nelson, 1991; RAND, 1990). All of these empowerment-based management movements have sought to increase organizational productivity, flexibility, responsiveness, and customer service (or client service) by reshaping organizational cultures. If the organizational culture is changed, work teams can and will coordinate their tasks and discipline their own members. Policies, procedures, and layers of hierarchy can be eliminated. Employees and work teams can have autonomy and discretion.

Information Technology

Government's ability to downsize, diffuse, devolve, empower employees, and contract-out is dependent on rapidly accessible, current, accurate information about performance and, preferably, also about outcomes (Stevens et al., 1995). Empowered employees and contracted organizations need information to manage, coordinate, and redirect activities, schedules, and resources. Higher levels of government managers need information upon which to base decisions about resource allocations and reallocations, and to maintain accountability and control over operations and resources. In traditional bureaucracies, these coordination and accountability/control functions have been performed by supervisors and lower- and middle-level managers.

"Informated" employees (Zuboff, 1988) now can perform these functions. Information technology can enable organizations to advance beyond "automating" to "informating." The import of Zuboff's distinction between automating and informating is reflected in a plant manager's question: "Are we all going to be working for a smart machine, or will we have smart people around the machine?" (1988, 285). Informating is the essence of information technology in the first decade of the 21st century. With it, employees can escape from rigid organizational rules and policies—to empowerment. Information technology thus is also about persons and offices high in bureaucracies letting go—exercising less authority and control. It is about qualitative changes in power and authority in government agencies.

> A technology that informates can have a corrosive effect on the hierarchical organization of work . . . Both groups [management and employees] work together to forge the terms of a new covenant, one that recasts the sources and purposes of managerial authority. (Zuboff, 1988, 285)

Readily available, low cost, highly sophisticated, networked information processing technology permits both employees and managers to access data. Teams of employees can know as quickly as management about backlogged work, the availability of resources, the status of projects or work in progress, work schedules of functionally related teams, and feedback from clients. Information technology is eliminating (or at least greatly reducing) the need for supervisors and lower-to-middle-level managers who used to perform the coordination and accountability/control functions.

Performance Measurement

Although students and practitioners of public management had begun to take notice of performance measurement in the 1980s (Epstein, 1984; Morley, 1986), it became one of the most popular topics in the literature of public management during the 1990s and remains so today (Ammons, 1994; Behn, 1995; Berman and West, 2004; Bouckaert, 1993, 1995; Cohen, 1993; Deller, Nelson, and Walzer, 1992; Eccles, 1991; Gilbert, 1992; Hedley, 1998; Holzer and Callahan, 1998; Kamensky, 1993; Kaplan and Norton, 1992, 1996; Lisoski, 2003; Nichols and Nichols, 1993–1994; Nyhan and Marlowe, 1995; Peters, 1996; Prager and Desai, 1996; RAND, 1990; Sorber, 1993; U.S. Department of Justice, 1995). It had to. Performance measurement became a "hot topic" because *it had to work*. "The absolute worst measure is none at all" (Lisoski, 2003, 16). Devolution within and among government agencies, empowerment, and diffusion through contracting-out and other varieties of "enterprise government" (Halachmi and Nichols, 1997) could not be managed without valid, reliable, timely, and nontrivial measurements of performance (Ott, Boonyarak, and Dicke, 2001). Government accountability cannot exist without it (Altshuler, 1997; Rosen, 1998). Measurements must be available to and accessible by higher-level managers, empowered work teams, and contracting agencies.

Thus both technologies—performance measurement and information technology—must function effectively in order to prevent downsizing, devolution, and diffusion from evolving into government abdication. Unfortunately, the task of measuring nontrivial performance with validity, reliability, and timeliness can be considerably more difficult than it may appear.

There are two primary types of difficulties. First, some services can be extraordinarily difficult to measure such as, for example, quality of life for persons with disabilities and mental illness; and changes in beliefs, attitudes, and behaviors that are "co-produced" by the service provider and the recipient of services (Clary, 1998). Consider, for example, the difficulties involved in trying to measure the sexual activity level of unmarried high school students, the prevalence of certain types of high-tech white-collar crimes, or the frequency with which crimes are committed against prostitutes, drug dealers, or pedophiles. Measurement is less difficult when the important elements of the processes, outputs, and/or outcomes can be quantified and/or observed objectively. Thus, for example, the thickness of concrete, the number of pregnant women who attend prenatal classes, the number of contact hours between service providers and patients with Alzheimer's disease, and the number of people removed from a state's welfare roles during a defined period of time, are all measurable without particular difficulty.

The second and often more complex difficulty, however, is that all too often what can be measured is not what is important. Does anyone truly care how thick concrete is if freeways are hopelessly congested, how many pregnant mothers attend classes if they do not change their unhealthy lifestyles, or if the people who are removed from the welfare roles have nowhere to live except on the streets? Often it is not particularly difficult to measure the quantity of inputs, activities, and outputs. It is often quite difficult to measure the quality of activities, outputs, and either the quantity or quality of outcomes. It is yet more difficult and expensive to measure (establish) relationships between activities and outcomes—cause-effect relationships—as is often the situation with coproduced services when activities only *influence* outcomes (Suchman, 1967). When changes in behavior or lifestyle are the desired outcome, such as for example with programs to improve the outcome of pregnancies or for people with chemical dependencies, timeliness of measurements often can pose serious problems. Outcomes can take years or even decades to establish—except through indirect and/or proxy measures, which introduce other difficulties.

We have asserted that downsizing, devolution, diffusion, and empowerment are dependent on performance measurement and information technologies. If so, we are asking more of performance measurement than it is able to deliver yet in many government services areas. Despite its rapid development in the last 15 to 20 years, it cannot yet provide nontrivial information for decisions that is consistently valid, reliable, and timely across many of the government functions that are being downsized, devolved, and diffused.

Downsizing, devolution, diffusion, and empowerment are ideologies, however, and they will continue to draw popular support. The inadequacy of an enabling technology will not diminish the ardor of their proponents.

ACCOUNTABILITY AND CONTROL IN AN ERA OF DOWNSIZING, DEVOLUTION, DIFFUSION, AND EMPOWERMENT

Empowered government employees and personnel in organizations that contract with government agencies need information to manage, coordinate, and redirect activities, schedules, and resources. Higher-level government managers need information upon which to base decisions about resource allocations and reallocations, and to maintain accountability and control. How can accountability be ensured and maintained if one of its key enabling technologies is not yet able? This is one of the premiere challenges for public management in the 21st century. It is also one of today's realities for public managers in general and HRM managers specifically. It is the environment in which many local, state, and national government employees and private sector contractors must conduct the business of government while government is being downsized, devolved, diffused, and employees are being empowered. Government's ability to be accountable for resources, service delivery, and the populations it is responsible for serving, is at risk.

"Accountability" is answerability for one's actions or behavior, often "to higher authorities including elected and appointed officials who sit at the apex of institutional chains of command and to directly involved stakeholders, for performance that involves delegation of authority to act" (Kearns, 1996, 11), a definition that ties accountability to the hierarchy through "an organized and legitimate relationship between a superior and a subordinate, and close supervision or a surrogate system of standard operating procedures or clearly stated rules and regulations" (Romzek and Dubnick, 1987, 228). Yet, "accountability is an ill-structured and underdeveloped concept in public and nonprofit administration" (Kim, 2005, 146).

Government accountability is steeped in traditions of responsibility to society and popular sovereignty (Shafritz, 1992). "The term [accountability] suggests the idea of taking 'into account' the consequences of one's actions for the welfare of others" (Donahue, 1989, 10). The notion of government accountability should not be narrowly equated with the legality of actions. Accountability also requires an internalized sense of duty (Harmon, 1995). "Organizational and professional behavior, political concerns, and the morality of administrative actions are equally important in the accountability domain" (Jabbra and Dwivedi, 1988, 5). Accountability thus also has moral, professional, and ethical dimensions (Dicke, 2002; Dicke and Ott, 1999), dimensions that can be extraordinarily difficult to quantify and measure.

On the other hand, most of us believe that external controls also are necessary for ensuring government accountability, such as legally binding obligations. The written contract is the symbol of this belief. Through contracts, "the state is responsible for actions committed in its name, and those who exercise the power of the state are answerable for their actions" (Jabbra and Dwivedi, 1988, 3). In essence, we have been conceptually assuming that when services are provided by nongovernmental organizations, government's accountability crosses the boundary between sectors via written contracts.

If indeed government has responsibilities in the moral, professional, and ethical dimensions of accountability as well as in the legal and fiscal dimensions, government agencies, and their contractors still need to be answerable for the quality of the services that are provided and the outcomes of these services when services are contracted out to private organizations—as well as for the prudent use of public funds. The performance measurement-information system approach to ensuring accountability usually equates accountability with control. When the quantity or quality of services falls below a predetermined level, the performance deficiency is measured, and information is fed back through the information system to decision makers who take appropriate actions—a classical application of the control system model (Donnelly, Gibson, and Ivancevich, 1987).

Control "derives from one basic property: the ability to determine events or outcomes" (Stout, 1980, 6), a property of government services that seldom exists. The ability to control requires knowledge about the links between activities and results—knowledge about cause-effect relationships. With full knowledge, a manager can control events and outcomes. In practice, managers usually can have (close to) full knowledge about quantities of inputs and activities, because these types of variables usually can be measured relatively easily. The same claim cannot be made about our ability to measure the qualitative aspects of many government activities and outcomes. Thus government accountability cannot be achieved using control systems except in the legal/fiscal dimensions of accountability. Control systems cannot achieve accountability in the moral, professional, and ethical dimensions (Ott, Boonyarak, and Dicke, 2001). Thus our claim: Government managers and their contractors cannot achieve accountability in important aspects of government services by relying on the current technologies of information and performance measurement. Only rarely is there full knowledge about relationships between activities and outcomes in the moral, professional, and ethical dimensions of government accountability.

It is also important to remember the ever-present legislative and public demands for agency officials to be "in control" at all times, a reality that has created a pervasive risk-aversive culture among government agencies and officials. Risk-aversion gives priority to the avoidance of errors over strategic opportunism, a preference set that tends to rely on and to favor the use of control systems. Achievement of the moral, professional, and ethical dimensions of government accountability requires a different mind-set. "Real change must issue from those deep levels of our human being where we are in touch with meaning and value" (Zohar, 1997).

PUBLIC HRM AND AN ORGANIZATIONAL CULTURE OF ACCOUNTABILITY

The crux of our argument has been: (1) Downsizing, devolution, diffusion, and empowerment are powerful, pervasive, and persuasive ideologies; (2) pressures for government to continue to downsize, devolve, diffuse, and empower will not lessen in the foreseeable future; (3) historically, accountability in government has been achieved mostly upward through hierarchies, from employees, through layers of supervisors and middle-managers, to elected officials and, at least in theory, out to the public; (4) accountability in government is broader than a narrow legalistic notion of adhering to the terms of a contract, protecting funds, or counting activities; (5) downsizing, devolution, diffusion, and empowerment eliminate government's ability to achieve accountability through hierarchies; (6) it has been widely assumed that advances in two technologies have provided an alternative means for ensuring accountability for government services that are devolved, diffused, and entrusted to empowered employees: information technology and performance measurement; (7) performance measurement is not yet at a level of development that can achieve accountability or control in many important areas of government services. If this chain of arguments has validity, an alternate approach is needed for achieving and maintaining accountability in government. Public HRM managers and departments can play leading roles in helping to change organizational cultures away from the risk-averse control orientations that have pervaded in many agencies at all levels of government.

Recent literature on the improvement of government has given considerable attention to organizational culture (Ott, 1995). For the purposes of managing government in an era of downsizing, devolution, diffusion, and empowerment, organizational culture performs four functions that may be more important than facilitating change. Organizational culture:

- Provides shared patterns of cognitive interpretations or perceptions so that organization members know how they are expected to act and to think.
- Provides shared patterns of affect, an emotional sense of involvement and commitment to organizational values and moral codes—of things worth working for and believing in—so that organizational members know what they are expected to value and how they are expected to feel.
- Serves as an organizational control system, prescribing and prohibiting certain behaviors.
- Affects peoples' expectations about organizational performance and thereby influence the quality and quantity of performance. (Siehl and Martin, 1984, 228–229)

Organizational culture is the "fabric" of the core of an organization's identity. "A culture is not something an organization has; a culture is something an organization is" (Pacanowsky and O'Donnell-Trujillo, 1983, 126). The culture of an organization is where an organization's identity, personality, and its distinctive values develop and reside. It determines the areas in which an organization can place claims on employees' energies, enthusiasms, and loyalties. Battles to establish and maintain accountability for quality are "won or lost on the basis of individual commitment—a [organizational] cultural matter and not one of bureaucratic regulation or management technique" (Sergiovanni and Corbally, 1984, ix). Perhaps then, the moral, professional, and ethical dimensions of accountability—accountability for quality—can be achieved through the shared cognitions, affects, beliefs, values, and expectations that are established through and maintained by carefully nurtured organizational cultures. Perhaps the inadequacies of the enabling technologies do not necessarily need to result in the absence of accountability as government agencies continue to downsize, devolve, diffuse, and empower.

Changing the culture of a government organization, however, is a daunting task that requires multiple conscious efforts, applied consistently, over several years (Trice and Beyer, 1993; Van Wart, 1998). Failed attempts to change the nature of government organizations are rarely caused by management incompetence (Ott and Shafritz, 1995). More often, the "culprit" is the culture of the organization (McNabb and Sepic, 1995; Moran and Volkwein, 1992). The organizational culture, however, also can serve as the primary keys a manager can use to unlock the status quo, to help an organization change from a culture that is firmly rooted in a control orientation to a culture that is based in the moral, professional, and ethical dimensions of accountability. A culture that is based on values and beliefs consistent with a broad notion of accountability can replace technology as the enabler of responsible downsizing, devolution, diffusion, and empowerment.

Unfortunately, many public HRM departments have been ill-suited for leading change initiatives of this magnitude or complexity, both because they have lacked needed skills and resources, and because they have lacked the inclination. Too frequently, the subcultures of HRM departments have stifled and suppressed people with the abilities and attitudes needed to lead organizational change (McNabb and Sepic, 1995).

The good news, however, is that "work is underway to meet the leadership challenges facing many federal agencies" (Ingraham and Getha-Taylor, 2004, 111). Organizations are beginning to think about succession planning and grooming leaders who can continue the organizations' tasks in the 21st century, including effective planning, creative thinking and acting quickly (Ingraham and Getha-Taylor, 2004).

As the profession of public human resource management has steadily grown away from its personnelist history, it has been growing into a more central role in government agencies, a role that often includes leading change initiatives. Public HRM skills are expanding to include methods and techniques for identifying, interpreting, changing, and maintaining aspects of organizational culture that affect productivity and empowerment. HR managers in many units of municipal, state, and national governments are emerging as pivotal actors in efforts to improve organizational effectiveness. They are leading initiatives that affect managers' and employees' productivity, flexibility, and commitment to values that are central to quality concerns (Ott and Baksh, 2005).

There is a possibility that some public organizations may be able to maintain broadly defined accountability through this era of downsizing, devolution, diffusion, and empowerment even if the technologies of information and performance measurement are not yet completely able to support all dimensions of accountability. Hopefully, recent advances in information technology and performance measurement will continue, and soon they will live up to their promise as enablers of accountability. Meanwhile, both of these technologies *and* HRM-led changes in government organizational cultures are needed. It would be naive to place full faith in either without the other.

Public HR managers and departments must work consciously and effectively to develop and nurture organizational cultures that allow line managers to creatively manage the legal, moral, professional, and ethical boundaries within which employees, units, and contracted organizations flexibly manage resources, processes, and outcomes. This requires a profoundly altered conception of public HRM functions and roles. Management of cultural change would need to take priority over the administration of position descriptions, classification systems, and compensation surveys. This will not be easy to accomplish under any circumstances, but it will be particularly difficult within the current context of the downsizing, devolution, diffusion, and empowerment ideologies.

NOTE

An original version of this chapter was published as "Challenges Facing Public Sector Management in an Era of Downsizing, Devolution, Dispersion and Empowerment—and Accountability? Kluwer Academic Publishers, *Public Organization Review*, (1)/2001: 321–339. Reprinted with kind permission of Springer Science and Business Media.

REFERENCES

Altshuler, Alan A. (1997). Bureaucratic Innovation, Democratic Accountability, and Political Incentives. In Alan A. Altshuler, and Robert D. Behn (Eds.), *Innovation in American Government*, pp. 38–67. Washington, DC: Brookings.

Ammons, David N. (Spring, 1994). The Role of Professional Associations in Establishing and Promoting Performance Standards for Local Government. *Public Productivity & Management Review*, 17(3): 281–298.

Barzelay, Michael. (1992). *Breaking Through Bureaucracy: A New Vision for Managing in Government*. Berkeley, CA: University of California Press.

Behn, Robert D. (July/August, 1995). The Big Questions of Public Management. *Public Administration Review*, 55(4): 313–324.

Berman, Evan M., and Jonathan P. West. (2004). Solutions to the Problem of Managerial Mediocrity: Moving up to Excellence. *Public Performance & Management Review*, 27(2): 30–52.

Bhote, K. R. (Spring, 1994). Dr. W. Edwards Deming: A Prophet with Belated Honor in His Own Country. *National Productivity Review*, 13: 153–159.

Bouckaert, Geert. (1995). Improving Performance Measurement. In Arie Halachmi and Geert Bouckaert (Eds.), *The Enduring Challenges in Public Management: Surviving and Excelling in a Changing World*, pp. 379–412. San Francisco, CA: Jossey-Bass.

Bouckaert, Geert. (Fall, 1993). Measurement and Meaningful Management. *Public Productivity & Management Review*, 17(1): 31–43.

Bowen, David E., and Edward E. Lawler, III. (Spring, 1992). The Empowerment of Service Workers: What, Why, How, and When. *Sloan Management Review*, 31–39.

Chi, Keon S. (October, 1994). TQM in State Government: Options for the Future. *State Trends & Forecasts*, 3(2): 2–39.

Clary, Bruce B. (1998). Coproduction. In Jay M. Shafritz (Ed.), *International Encyclopedia of Public Policy and Administration*, pp. 531–536. Boulder, CO: Westview.

Clinton, Bill, and Al Gore. (September 1995). *Putting Customers First '95: Standards for Serving the American People*. Washington, DC: U.S. Government Printing Office.

Cohen, Steven A. (Fall, 1993). Defining and Measuring Effectiveness in Public Management. *Public Productivity & Management Review*, 17(1): 45–57.

Deller, Steven C., Carl H. Nelson, and Norman Walzer. (Spring, 1992). Measuring Managerial Efficiency in Rural Government. *Public Productivity & Management Review*, 15(3): 355–370.

Deming, W. Edwards. (1986). *Out of the Crisis*. Cambridge, MA: MIT Press.

Deming, W. Edwards. (1993). *The New Economics*. Cambridge, MA: MIT Press.

Dicke, Lisa A. (2002). Ensuring Accountability in Human Services Contracting: Can Stewardship Theory Fill the Bill? *American Review of Public Administration*, 32(4): 455–470.

Dicke, Lisa A., and J. Steven Ott. (1999). Public Agency Accountability in Human Services Contracting. *Public Productivity & Management Review*, 22(4): 502–516.

Donahue, John D. (1989). *The Privatization Decision: Public Ends, Private Means*. New York: Basic Books.

Donnelly, James H., Jr., James L. Gibson, and John M. Ivancevich. (1987). *Fundamentals of Management*, 6th ed. Plano, TX: Business Publications.

Duesche, John, Deputy Secretary of Defense. (May 4, 1994). *Memorandum for Secretaries of the Military Departments, Subject: Depot Competition Operations Policy*.

Durst, Samantha L., and Charldean Newell. (March, 1999). Better, Faster, Stronger: Government Reinvention In the 1990s. *American Review of Public Administration*, 61–76.

Dutcher, Joyce S., Carol A. Hayashida, John P. Sheposh, and David K. Dickason. (November, 1992). *Pacer Share: A Federal Productivity and Personnel Management Demonstration Project. Fourth-Year Evaluation Report*. Washington, DC: U.S. Office of Personnel Management, Personnel Systems and Oversight Group, Office of Systems Innovation (OS92-12).

Eccles, Robert G. (January–February, 1991). The Performance Measurement Manifesto. *Harvard Business Review*, 131–137.

Epstein, Paul D. (1984). *Using Performance Measurement in Local Government: A Guide to Improving Decisions, Performance, and Accountability*. New York: Van Nostrand Reinhold.

GAO. (1991). *Management Practices: U.S. Companies Improve Performance Through Quality Efforts*. Washington, DC: United States General Accounting Office (GAO/NSIAD-91-190).

GAO. (1997a). *Privatization and Competition: Comments on S. 314, the Freedom from Government Competition Act*. Washington, DC: United States General Accounting Office (GAO/T-GGD-97-134).

GAO. (1997b). *Privatization: Lessons Learned by State and Local Governments*. Washington, DC: United States General Accounting Office (GAO/GGD-97-48).

GAO. (1992). *Quality Management: Survey of Federal Organizations*. Washington, DC: United States General Accounting Office (GAO/GGD-93-9BR).

Gilbert, G. Ronald. (1992). Quality Improvement in a Federal Defense Organization. *Public Productivity & Management Review*, 14(1): 65–75.

Gilbert, G. Ronald, and Ardel E. Nelson. (1991). *Beyond Participative Management: Toward Total Employee Empowerment for Quality*. New York: Quorum.

Gore, Al. (1993). *The Gore Report on Reinventing Government*. New York: Times Books.

Halachmi, Arie, and Kenneth L. Nichols. (Eds.) (1997). *Enterprise Government: Franchising and Cross-Servicing for Administrative Support*. Burke, VA: Chatelaine.

Handler, Joel F. (1996). *Down from Bureaucracy: The Ambiguity of Privatization and Empowerment*. Princeton, NJ: Princeton University Press.

Harmon, Michael M. (1995). *Responsibility as Paradox*. Thousand Oaks, CA: Sage.

Hedley, Timothy P. (March, 1998). Measuring Public Sector Effectiveness Using Private Sector Methods. *Public Productivity & Management Review*, 21(3): 251–258.

Holzer, Marc, and Kathe Callahan. (1998). *Government at Work: Best Practices and Model Programs*. Thousand Oaks, CA: Sage.

Ingraham, Patricia, and Heather Getha-Taylor. (2004). Leadership in the Public Sector: Models and Assumptions for Leadership Development. *Review of Public Personnel Administration*, 24(2): 95–111.

Jabbra, Joseph G., and O. P. Dwivedi. (Eds.) (1988). *Public Service Accountability*. West Hartford, CT: Kumarian Press.

Joiner, Brian L. (1994). *Fourth Generation Management*. New York: McGraw-Hill.

Juran, Joseph M. (1992). *Juran on Quality by Design*. New York: Free Press.

Kamensky, John M. (Summer, 1993). Program Performance Measures: Designing a System to Manage for Results. *Public Productivity & Management Review*, 16(4): 395–402.

Kaplan, Robert S., and David P. Norton. (January/February, 1996). Using the Balanced Scorecard as a Strategic Management System. *Harvard Business Review*, 75–85.

Kaplan, Robert S., and David P. Norton. (January/February, 1992). The Balanced Scorecard—Measures that Drive Performance. *Harvard Business Review*, 71–79.

Kearney, Richard C., and Steven W. Hays. (Fall, 1998). Reinventing Government, The New Public Management and Civil Service Systems In International Perspective. *Review of Public Personnel Administration*, 39–54.

Kearns, Kevin P. (1996). *Managing for Accountability: Preserving the Public Trust in Public and Nonprofit Organizations*. San Francisco, CA: Jossey-Bass.

Kettl, Donald F. (1995). Building Lasting Reform: Enduring Questions, Missing Answers. In, Donald F. Kettl and John J. DiIulio, Jr. (Eds.), *Inside the Reinvention Machine: Appraising Governmental Reform*, pp. 9–83. Washington, DC: Brookings.

Kim, Seok-Eun. (2005). Balancing Competing Accountability Requirements: Challenges in Performance Improvement of the Nonprofit Human Services Agency. *Public Performance & Management Review*, 29(2): 145–163.

Lenkowsky, Leslie, and James L. Perry. (July/August, 2000). Reinventing Government: The Case of National Service. *Public Administration Review*, 298–307.

Light, Paul C. (2000). *Making Nonprofits Work: A Report of Nonprofit Management Reform*. Washington, DC: Aspen Institute/Brookings Institution.

Light, Paul C. (1998). *The Tides of Reform: Making Government Work 1945–1995*. New Haven, CT: Yale University Press.

Lisoski, Ed. (2003). If You Can't Measure It You Can't Manage It. *Supervision*, 64(1): 16–19.

McNabb, David E., and F. Thomas Sepic. (Summer, 1995). Culture, Climate, and Total Quality Management: Measuring Readiness for Change. *Public Productivity & Management Review*, 18(4): 369–385.

Miranda, Rowan. (March/April, 1995). Bureaucracy, Organizational Redundancy, and the Privatization of Public Services. *Public Administration Review*, 55(2): 193–200.

Moran, E. Thomas, and J. Fredericks Volkwein. (1992). The Cultural Approach to the Formation of Organizational Climate. *Human Relations*, 45(1): 19–47.

Morley, Elaine. (1986). *A Practitioner's Guide to Public Sector Productivity Improvement*. New York: Van Nostrand Reinhold.

Nichols, Barbara, and Kenneth L. Nichols. (Winter, 1993–1994). What You Measure Is What You Get—Organizational Performance Measures Reward Impact, Not Just Activity. *SPOD News*, 4: 5.

Nicholson-Crotty, Sean, Nick A. Theobald, and Jill Nicholson-Crotty. (2006). Disparate Measures: Public Managers and Performance-Measurement Strategies. *Public Administration Review*, 66(1): 101–113.

Nyhan, Ronald C., and Herbert A. Marlowe, Jr. (Summer, 1995). Performance Measurement In the Public Sector: Challenges and Opportunities. *Public Productivity & Management Review*, 18(4): 333–348.

Orsburn, Jack D., and Linda Moran. (2000). *The New Self-Directed Work Teams: Mastering the Challenge*. New York: McGraw-Hill.

Orsburn, Jack D., Linda Moran, Ed Musselwhite, and John H. Zenger, (with Craig Perrin). (1990). *Self-directed Work Teams: The New American Challenge*. Homewood, IL: Business One Irwin.

Osborne, David, and Ted Gaebler. (1992). *Reinventing Government*. Reading, MA: Addison-Wesley.

Osborne, David, and Peter Plastrik. (1997). *Banishing Bureaucracy: The Five Strategies for Reinventing Government*. Reading, MA: Addison-Wesley.

Ott, J. Steven. (Summer, 1995). TQM, Organizational Culture, and Readiness for Change. *Public Productivity & Management Review*, 18(4): 365–368.

Ott, J. Steven and Abdul M. Baksh. (2005). Understanding Organizational Climate and Culture. In Stephen E. Condrey (Ed.), *The Handbook of Human Resource Management in Government*, 2nd ed., pp. 295–325. San Francisco, CA: Jossey-Bass/John Wiley.

Ott, J. Steven, Pitima Boonyarak, and Lisa A. Dicke. (2001). Public Sector Reform, and Moral and Ethical Accountability: Performance Measurement Technology Cannot Ensure Accountability for Contracted Human Services. *Public Integrity*, 3(3): 277–289.

Ott, J. Steven, Sandra J. Parkes, and Richard B. Simpson. (2003). Individuals in Teams and Groups. In J. Steven Ott, Sandra. J. Parkes, and Richard B. Simpson (Eds.), *Classic Readings in Organizational Behavior*, 3rd ed., pp. 220–231. Belmont, CA: Thomson-Wadsworth.

Ott, J. Steven, and Jay M. Shafritz. (1995). The Perception of Organizational Incompetence. In, Arie Halachmi and Geert Bouckaert (Eds.), *The Enduring Challenges in Public Management*, pp. 27–46. San Francisco, CA: Jossey-Bass.

Ott, J. Steven, and Jay M. Shafritz. (July/August, 1994). Toward a Definition of Organizational Incompetence: A Neglected Variable in Organization Theory. *Public Administration Review*, 54(4): 370–377.

Pacanowsky, Michael E., and Nick O'Donnell-Trujillo.(June, 1983). Organizational Communication as Cultural Performance. *Communication Monographs*, 50: 126–147.

Page, Stephen. (2005). What's New about the New Public Management? Administrative Change in the Human Services. *Public Administration Review*, 65(6): 713–727.

Peters, B. Guy. (1996). *The Future of Governing: Four Emerging Models*. Lawrence, KS: University Press of Kansas.

Prager, Jonas, and Swati Desai. (December, 1996). Privatizing Local Government Operations: Lessons from Federal Contracting Out Methodology. *Public Productivity & Management Review*, 20(2): 185–203.

RAND. (June, 1990). *Pacer Share Demonstration Project: Preliminary Results*. Santa Monica, CA: RAND Corporation.

Romzek, Barbara S., and Melvin J. Dubnick. (May/June, 1987). Accountability in the Public Sector: Lessons from the Challenger Tragedy. *Public Administration Review*, 47(3): 227–238.

Rosen, Bernard. (1998). *Holding Government Bureaucracies Accountable*, 3rd ed. Westport, CT: Praeger.

Savas, E. S. (1982). *Privatizing the Public Sector: How to Shrink Government*. Chatham, NJ: Chatham House.

Sergiovanni, Thomas J., and John E. Corbally. (1984). Preface. In Thomas J. Sergiovanni, and John E. Corbally (Eds.), *Leadership and Organizational Culture*, pp. vii–x. Urbana, IL: University of Illinois Press.

Shafritz, Jay M. (1992). *The HarperCollins Dictionary of American Government and Politics*. New York: HarperCollins.

Siehl, Caren, and Joanne Martin. (1984). The Role of Symbolic Management: How Can Managers Effectively Transmit Organizational Culture? In J. G. Hunt, D. M. Hosking, C. A. Schriesheim, and R. Stewart (Eds.), *Leaders and Managers: International Perspectives on Managerial Behavior and Leadership*, pp. 227–269. New York: Pergamon Press.

Smith, Steven R., and Michael Lipsky. (1993). *Nonprofits for Hire: The Welfare State in the Age of Contracting*. Cambridge, MA: Harvard University Press.

Sorber, Bram. (Fall, 1993). Performance Measurement in the Central Government Departments of the Netherlands. *Public Productivity & Management Review*, 17(1): 59–68.

Stevens, John M., Anthony G. Cahill, E. Sam Overman, and Lee Frost-Kumpf. (1995). The Role of Information Systems in Supporting Total Quality Management and Improved Productivity. In Arie Halachmi and Geert Bouckaert (Eds.), *The Enduring Challenges in Public Management: Surviving and Excelling in a Changing World*, pp. 119–149. San Francisco, CA: Jossey-Bass.

Stout, Russell, Jr. (1980). *Management or Control: The Organizational Challenge*. Bloomington, IN: Indiana University Press.

Suchman, Edward A. (1967). *Evaluative Research: Principles and Practice in Public Service & Social Action Programs*. New York: Russell Sage Foundation.

Swiss, James E. (2005). A Framework for Assessing Incentives in Results-Based Management. *Public Administration Review*, 65(5): 592–602.

Trice, Harrison M., and Janice M. Beyer. (1993). *The Cultures of Work Organizations*. Englewood Cliffs, NJ: Prentice-Hall.

U.S. Department of Justice. (April 1995). *DOJ Manager's Handbook on Developing Useful Performance Indicators* (Version 1.1). Washington, DC: U.S. Department of Justice, Justice Management Division, Management and Planning Staff.

Van Wart, Montgomery. (1998). *Changing Public Sector Values*. New York: Garland.

Walters, Jonathan. (2005). Open Season on Middle Managers. *Governing*, 28–31.

Zohar, Danah. (1997). *Re-wiring the Corporate Brain*. San Francisco, CA: Berrett-Koehler.

Zuboff, Shoshana. (1988). *In the Age of the Smart Machine*. New York: Basic Books/HarperCollins.

5

Making the Transition to Strategic Human Resource Management: Precursors, Strategies, and Techniques

STEVEN W. HAYS

A t this point in the field's evolution, almost no one disagrees with the notion that Human Resource Management (HRM) needs to develop a strategic perspective. The contemporary literature is replete with references to the transformation that has putatively taken place in the roles, functions, and operating philosophies of personnel offices in government and industry (Ulrich, 1998a, 1998b). HRM's traditional emphasis upon control activities is being supplanted, we are told, by supporting behaviors that are far more responsive to the needs of line managers. The age-old preoccupation with policing the personnel system has supposedly given way to a *service* orientation in which personnelists become strategic partners with other managers in a cooperative effort to elevate organizational performance. Regulatory and enforcement functions are being abandoned as human resource professionals strive to enhance their relevancy. As such, today's HRM practitioners are being heralded as the "architects" of organization change (Ulrich, 1998b), and as "facilitators" of management improvements (Whittlesey, 1997).

These reported changes in the fundamental ethos of HRM are prompted by necessity. Public Administration (PA) in general is under assault from a widely discussed cascade of environmental challenges, including fiscal pressures, recruitment dilemmas, a hypercritical public, massive shifts in labor demographics, and an unflattering history of administrative shortcomings (Newland, 1984; Hays, 1996, 2001). Because the personnel function has often been a major part of the *problem* rather than the *solution* to PA's managerial malaise (Volcker, 1989), public personnelists now carry a disproportionate share of the responsibility for modernizing and upgrading their professional performance. The success or failure of much of the celebrated *reinvention* agenda depends upon a much more proactive and effective brand of personnel management within state, local, and federal agencies. Thus, for better or worse, HRM occupies a central role in the struggle to reform public management.

Although there is a near-unanimous consensus that HRM can and must be transformed into line managers' strategic partner, the contemporary literature is somewhat lacking in specifics as to *how* this miracle can be accomplished. Everyone seems to agree on the revised roles and functions that HRM must internalize (Hays, 2001), but few guideposts on the path to reform are provided. What new strategies and operating techniques are required to advance the ambitious objectives of HRM reformers, and what political and/or organizational accommodations will be necessary before these changes can be engineered? The purpose of this chapter is to begin to fill in some of the details. After delineating a number the initial conditions that must be present before strategic HRM can become a reality; an overview of potential alterations in various personnel techniques and practices is provided.

Before launching into this (somewhat self-indulgent) essay, a few important *caveats* need to be mentioned. First, the reader will quickly recognize that the suggested reforms may be impractical and/or politically inappropriate in some settings. Knowing what *ought* to be done does not always translate into action, especially when one is dealing with such sensitive issues as government jobs and career systems. Despite lots of good reasons to change administrative practice, the forces of inertia and/or political reality are powerful. Moreover, there may well be very legitimate reasons *not* to alter a particular personnel system, depending upon the social, economic, and partisan composition of the host jurisdiction. Prescription is always a risky enterprise, and we should never make the assumption that any particular model or ideal is universally applicable or advisable. A related caution stems from the inherent limitations of forecasting. Much of this essay is devoted to predictions (guesses?) as to the types of HRM techniques that will emerge as the 21st century unfolds. Although most of the suggestions are based on supporting literature and/or a small amount of empirical evidence, the limitations of forecasting are self-evident. As the economists say, "Those who make their livings by the crystal ball will often dine on broken glass." Despite being based on best-guess estimates, projections from trends that are already apparent, and academic consensus (in many cases), each prediction must be evaluated with an appropriate amount of skepticism.

PRECURSORS TO REFORM: POLITICAL AND ORGANIZATIONAL REQUIREMENTS

At the risk of stating the obvious, it is a truism that personnel reform does not occur in a vacuum. Making the transition from the merit system's policeman to a strategic player in the internal operation of public agencies requires the cooperation of many actors outside of the typical HRM office. Unfortunately, however, this reality is often overlooked by writers in the field. The personnel profession is often lambasted for being unresponsive and intransigent, yet fundamental changes in most government personnel systems cannot occur without legislative authorization. A quick review of the reform landscape confirms that almost all significant upgrades in state and local HRM systems have been preceded by statutory (and, in some cases, executive) initiatives. In order to dismantle the most oppressive vestiges of old-style personnel practice, legislation is needed to free the hands of both personnelists and line managers.

The current trends toward responsiveness and accountability (which are watchwords of strategic HRM) are built upon the elimination of the excess bureaucracy that surrounds most merit systems. This typically requires a proactive effort on the part of political leaders to reduce merit system protections, to decentralize HRM decision-making to the agency level, and to revise compensation and classification systems that impede managerial flexibility. The most dramatic examples have occurred in such states as Florida (Bowman et al., 2003), Georgia (Nigro and Kellough, 2000), and South Carolina, where the merit systems were essentially abolished. While this move may appear on the surface to be warranted, it has already proven to be a risky enterprise that can threaten the professionalism and neutrality of the civil service (see Bowman et al., 2003; Kellough and Selden, 2003). This problem notwithstanding, further legislative intervention is often needed to encourage refinements in the HRM system, including an adequate employee recognition system (which requires *money*), expedited forms of grievance handling, and simplified recruitment and selection protocols. Because merit systems have been built on a heavy foundation of statutes and executive orders, it takes more than good ideas and intentions to make significant alterations in personnel practice. In short, almost any basic revision of a government personnel system is contingent upon the existence of enabling legislation. To expect personnelists to orchestrate significant improvements in the absence of such measures is unrealistic.

Given the necessity for political approval, it is possible to hypothesize about the likelihood of HRM reform in different jurisdictions. For example, one might reasonably expect change to occur most readily in states and localities where a single party is dominant. In split-party settings, in contrast, reform is likely to come much slower. Where the legislature is divided, or where the executive and legislative branches are controlled by different parties, political intrigue and mistrust will probably discourage aggressive decentralization of HRM authority. A related hypothesis is that local governments headed by professional managers (i.e., the city manager form) are prime candidates for modernization, while highly partisan settings (the strong mayor form, perhaps) are not expected to be fertile reform ground. Similar conclusions can be drawn about the effects of unions. To the extent that unions are present and powerful, basic changes in personnel system operations will probably be restricted. Other exogenous variables that might influence a jurisdiction's tendency to embrace strategic HRM include the form of administration (high levels of gubernatorial power and the existence of an executive cabinet should be positively correlated with strategic HRM), the personnel system's composition (civil service commissions are inversely correlated with reform, while executive personnel systems are likely to encourage innovation), and the overall political culture of the region (moralistic areas would be expected to be more reform-oriented than are traditionalistic jurisdictions). A recent surge in the number of activist governors who are "on a mission" to overhaul their states' personnel systems is one indication not only of the types of reforms that can be implemented, but also the serious *risks* associated with ideologically motivated transformations of public institutions.

Although all of these relationships are logical, there is little reliable empirical data to validate or refute the underlying hypotheses. The essential point, however, is that HRM reform ultimately depends upon effective (and hopefully *enlightened*) *political* leadership. Acting alone, personnelists can only introduce change at the margins of the field. Their capacity to engineer meaningful transformations from within is severely restricted by the legalistic and statutory construction that characterizes any highly articulated merit system.

The second major precursor to the acceptance of a strategic role for HRM is the need to alter the perceptions of a skeptical labor force. HRM's poor internal image has been a major theme of the professional literature for over 30 years (Holt, 1994; Stewart, 1996). The personnel function is widely viewed, even today, as a narrowly focused and ineffectual anachronism. Sometimes referred to as "the organizational equivalent of Siberia," the personnel office was (is?) a mysterious and unfriendly place staffed by unresponsive specialists who delighted in enforcing irrelevant bureaucratic requirements. For line managers who have spent the bulk of their careers harboring such negative perceptions, the internalization of an expansive "strategic" role will require more than a propaganda campaign. Stated simply, HRM practitioners must *convince* the management community that they deserve a "place at the table." After decades of wandering aimlessly in the administrative wilderness, personnelists bear the burden of proof in demonstrating to other managers that they have something of value to offer the organization.

Recommended solutions to HRM's image problem abound. The theme that permeates every set of recommendations is that personnel practitioners need to redefine who and what goals they are supposed to serve. Instead of emphasizing rule enforcement, they must view line managers and other employees as their primary clients. Control activities would thereby be supplanted by supporting behaviors, and the personnel office would become much more attentive to the impact of its activities on the bottom line. In other words, practitioners must learn to act strategically, to link their activities with the broader goals of the organization, and to assess each procedure on the basis of its contribution to the agency mission. Concerns such as organizational productivity, programmatic outcomes, lowered staffing ratios, and elevating employee morale would take precedence over traditional staffing priorities (as exemplified by rule compliance, merit system operation, and grievance processing). Terms that have been used to describe this revised organizational role include "facilitator" (Whittlesey, 1997), "partner" (Santry, 1996), and "service provider" (Roussel, 1995).

Obviously, a role transformation of the scope described above doesn't "just happen." An incredible number of hurdles block the path to change. Professional inertia, a slow learning curve, statutory and procedural impediments, and an inadequate tool kit of appropriate staffing techniques all constitute potential pitfalls. To this list we must add the probability of managerial reluctance, since HRM's redefined role may well be too much for many managers to easily accept. Therein lies a conundrum: How do personnel practitioners achieve a sufficient level of credibility with fellow managers to be allowed to demonstrate their new competence? Other public administrators must be willing to allow personnelists to participate aggressively in the strategic mission of the agency, yet their instincts will probably encourage resistance because of personnel's past reputation for inflexibility and failure. In a sense, the personnel profession is confronted with a chicken/egg controversy. What comes first, inclusion in the decision-making process (which would be perceived as a risky enterprise by traditionalists), or a clear demonstration that the human resources department is positioned to make important contributions to the agency's mission? Many managers are prone to await the latter, a situation that often precludes the former.

Although this fundamental dilemma will probably take decades of experience (and experimentation) to completely resolve, there are two essential requirements that must be met for HRM to have any hope of receiving broad managerial acceptance. First, the function must be *decentralized* in order to expedite decision making, enhance responsiveness, and improve the likelihood that personnelists can make themselves relevant to other managers. Second, progress must be made in improving the *transparency* of the personnel system. Policies and procedures should be reviewed according to their contributions to the agency's mission. Any requirement that is redundant, inefficient, unduly burdensome, or opaque should be abolished or revised. The ultimate necessity is to streamline the traditional facets of the personnel function so that greater attention can be devoted to activities that enlarge HRM's role in the pursuit of strategic objectives. Some of the specific roles and techniques that might assist in this endeavor are addressed below.

ROLE TRANSITION: EXPANDING HRM'S ORGANIZATIONAL RELEVANCY

An implicit assumption of the preceding discussion is that the human resources function is destined to either expand its organizational mission *or* to lose whatever remaining relevancy it possesses within modern public agencies. Indeed, in the absence of a reconfigured and invigorated HRM department, most staffing activities will probably be targeted for outsourcing, as has occurred in many private corporations (Rubino, 1994).

Prescriptions for reform inevitably emphasize a plethora of new roles for personnel practitioners. According to the conventional wisdom, the development of a strategic perspective—coupled with involvement in the management mainstream—requires that personnelists engage in activities that have heretofore largely been foreign to the profession.

Before we can even begin to list the types of roles that HRM offices will be asked to assume, another critical precursor to successful reform must be addressed. Specifically, the *modus operandi* of practitioners will have to undergo a fundamental transformation. Instead of specializing in narrow technical areas (e.g., recruitment, classification, benefits, and administration), there is widespread agreement that the personnel function must be practiced by *generalists* who have broad organizational outlooks and diverse skills. Obviously, this fact presents a serious and multifaceted challenge. Individuals who have spent decades performing narrow specialties are unlikely candidates to become "strategic partners" with line managers. The transition to an expanded brand of HRM will require *time* (as the old generation of personnelists retires and/or retools), *training* (the next generation of human resource managers will require new competencies that are rarely available today), and *new modes of service delivery* (including new job duties and role expectations).

There is no shortage of prescriptions for how personnel practitioners should behave when functioning "strategically." Because HRM's emerging roles are so thoroughly (even exhaustively) explained elsewhere (Hays, 2001; Hays and Kearney, 2001; Stright, 1993; Tokesky and Kornides, 1994), only a brief summary of their major new responsibilities is provided below. For the most part, the essential components and advantages of each role are both predictable and self-evident.

Buffering Environmental Change

One of the most effective ways for HRM to become an accepted partner in strategic decision-making is to enable the agency to cope with rapid change. This responsibility transcends and permeates all of the other roles that are forecast for HRM.

Because most of the challenges of environmental turbulence involve *people*, the personnel function must logically be a frontline warrior in the agency's struggle to remain viable. Varying facets of this responsibility include (a) the recruitment and retention of a competent labor force; (b) development of a reliable human resource planning system that correctly anticipates and prepares for worker shortages and bulges; (c) creation and maintenance of an adequate system of employee recognition and reward; (d) design of an employee development program that recognizes employee potential and "builds a leadership bench" (Ulrich, 1998b); and (e) involvement in the regular diagnosis and treatment of organizational maladies that could impede mission accomplishment.

A wide array of specific programs and activities might conceivably be involved in this imposing list of obligations. Government training programs, for example, have typically fallen far short of what will be required to "empower" the workforce of the 21st century. According to most experts in the field, the traditional emphasis on skill building is counterproductive in an era characterized by rapid obsolescence. HRM's dilemma here is to help their agencies to become "learning organizations" by inculcating abstract abilities—for example, analytical thinking, goal flexibility—that are pliant and universally applicable (Kemske, 1998). In addition to the obvious need for much more sophisticated systems of employee training and development, HRM will be expected to engineer innovations in performance evaluation (which represents a *notorious* technical deficiency), recruitment (where *flexibility* is becoming increasingly essential), and employee motivation. Taking the pulse of the organization through regular employee attitude surveys, and maintaining the competitiveness of the salary structure by conducting periodic wage surveys, should have already become almost routine in any well-developed public personnel system. Other initiatives that will be demanded of personnelists are *succession planning* technologies (Carey, 1997), *applicant tracking* systems that enhance the agency's ability to monitor and attract qualified personnel (McCausland, 1999), and *environmental scanning* capabilities (Tokesky and Kornides, 1994), just to name a few. Insofar as environmental scanning is concerned, the ultimate objective is for the HRM office to monitor legal, economic, and labor force changes that might affect the agency's workforce. The role requires not only an awareness of external factors that are potentially significant, but also the ability to interpret their impacts and communicate relevant implications to line managers.

Once personnelists are able to adopt this proactive professional posture, the basic composition of the HRM function will be transformed. As has long been advocated, they will (hopefully, anyway) assume the role of internal *consultants* who advise other managers on how to build and protect a healthy workforce. The personnel office could thus become a source of *ideas* rather than the creator of bureaucratic minutiae. Over time, other managers might then begin to expect the HRM office to initiate policy proposals and to aid in their implementation. This encapsulates the "partner of line manager" concept that has been so exhaustively advocated, and implies additional contributions that would logically accrue if the expanded model of HRM were to actually spread throughout public personnel systems.

Building Leadership Capability

Next to helping them to cope with rapid change, perhaps the most critical responsibility that HRM can assume is to assist public agencies with the leadership crisis that pervades government. This involves not only the attraction and retention of desirable employees (which, in the current context, is a massive challenge in itself), but also the cultivation and nurturing of leadership talent once it is recognized. Every component of the personnel system must be involved in this strategic mission, since any weak link in the chain can result in worker disgruntlement, apathy, and/or attrition.

In effect, the HRM office must design and maintain a leadership development *program*—an integrated set of steps and tools that ensures the steady progression and refinement of both executive ability and worker competence. Essential components of such a program would probably include many of the following: an extensive orientation program for new employees (something that is typically lacking in the public sector); a succession planning strategy that projects future leadership requirements and identifies promising candidates for fast-track promotions; a system of peer, subordinate, and group evaluation (the so-called 360-degree evaluation) that emphasizes developmental goals over control and punishment; job rotation and multifunctional assignments to enlarge the managers' vision and job skills; a rank-in-person (as opposed to rank-in-job) career system that enables the organization to assign individuals on the basis of their interests and talents; competency-based training programs to upgrade abstract leadership skills; the proactive use of *mentors* to guide and instruct prospective leaders; and an appropriate reward structure (broadbanding is one promising innovation, as is skill-based pay; most experts are reluctant to endorse "merit pay" due to its checkered history in the public sector).

Once again, the potential benefits to both the HRM office and the agency should be apparent. The symbiotic relationship between the human resource function and all other components of the management infrastructure are especially evident within the leadership development arena. By building an aggressive career ladder for public managers, HRM practitioners can cut many channels into the administrative mainstream.

Technology Transfer

Another prime opportunity for HRM to expand organizational capacity is presented by the pressing demands of the information revolution. Compared to much of the private sector, public agencies are ill equipped to adopt and utilize emerging information technologies (IT). Recruiting and retaining IT personnel are nearly impossible objectives in some settings due to salary disparities between the two sectors. As a result, the HRM function is confronted with a daunting challenge. To the extent that it can assist with the development and retention of IT personnel (and thereby aid the agency in integrating new technologies), additional credibility can be gained with line management.

For the most part, the greatest strides in this regard have occurred in agencies that follow a "grow your own" IT strategy. That is, human resource departments are best served by enlisting members of the current workforce in developmental programs that bind them to the agency for specified periods of time. Interested employees are singled out and provided with subsidized training opportunities, after which they have a contractual obligation to remain in the organization for 2 to 3 years (or else they must reimburse the agency for the costs of their training and related expenses). An essential supplement to this type of program is more generalized training strategies that help other workers harness the technological tools upon which future work will depend. This necessity again accents the importance of training within the expanded OHR office, and suggests that personnel practitioners will be expected to *lead* the agency's efforts to stay ahead of the technology tidal wave (Johnston, 1996).

Upgrading Human Resources Practices and Techniques

The final major shift in HRM focus stems from the profession's need to heal itself. Much of the personnel function's celebrated image problem can be traced to the fact that many of its favored techniques simply don't work. Despite the investment of enormous quantities of resources in the pursuit of effective staffing strategies, the field is replete with failed and counterproductive methods of recruitment, testing, performance evaluation, discipline, grievance handling, *ad nauseam*. To truly emerge into the sunlight, HRM must do a much more thorough job of assessing the utility of its activities, jettisoning those that do not contribute to strategic objectives, and searching for better ways of performing its various functions.

In effect, a primary new role for HRM practitioners is to be more aggressive in the pursuit of *best practices*. Because each public personnel system is a potential laboratory of experimentation, and because innovation within HRM offices has become widespread in recent years, there is usually no need to reinvent the proverbial wheel. All that a personnelist needs to do is to survey the relevant literature and to import any new human resource technique that has shown promise in other jurisdictions. This task is greatly simplified by the existence of Internet Web sites that trumpet successful efforts to improve personnel system operations. The most visible source of such information is made available by the joint efforts of the National Association of State Personnel Executives (NASPE) and the International Personnel Management Association (IPMA). These two organizations sponsor an awards program that recognizes especially notable "best practices" and makes the relevant information available to any interested users in state and local government. Similarly, nonprofits such as the Annie E. Casey Foundation have invested considerable resources in identifying and chronicling HRM Best Practices that are being effectively employed in social service agencies (see Center for the Study of Social Policy, 2001).

Although much work remains to be done in this regard, the amount of progress that has occurred in the past decade is quite stunning. For organizations that are known for inflexibility and inertia, public personnel systems currently demonstrate an astounding proclivity to modernize and embrace change. This phenomenon bodes well for the future, since the ultimate success of strategic HRM depends upon the profession's ability to perform its basic responsibilities effectively.

TRANSITIONAL STEPS

Anyone who is familiar with the way that HRM has traditionally been practiced will undoubtedly recognize the scale of the task ahead. If personnelists are truly destined to become strategic partners with other managers, then merely delineating a number of new role responsibilities will not suffice. Good intentions must be translated into action. As has been noted, some of the most significant prerequisites for success are not within the purview of personnel practitioners. The cooperation of politicians and line managers cannot be taken for granted, and is generally an absolute necessity for systemic changes to occur.

With or without the support of those outside of the HRM profession, however, there are a few obvious steps that might be taken to promote progress toward the goals that have been articulated. Depending upon the legal framework of any particular jurisdiction, worthwhile improvements can be made in HRM operations merely by tinkering with the specifics. And, with the cooperation of a sympathetic agency director, much more ambitious alterations may be within reach of the typical personnel director.

Taking an Aggressive Posture Toward Best Practices

The identification and adoption of relevant best practices is by far the most accessible reform that any HRM office can implement. With few exceptions, some jurisdiction somewhere has experimented with a new strategy for performing virtually any facet of personnel operations. Moreover, a consensus seems to have formed around the utility of many techniques and strategies that are relatively straightforward and readily transportable. There is little disagreement, for instance, about the advantages of wide salary bands over narrow step systems (broadbanding), *any* type of behaviorally based performance evaluation over the trait-based rating scales that still predominate in some areas, and flexible recruitment protocols (e.g., "on the spot" hiring) over rigid formats such as the widely detested "rule of three." Relatedly, experience within the private sector supports the notion that one of the best means of attracting qualified workers is through *referrals* from current employees, that skill-based pay (i.e., paying workers additional compensation as they acquire new abilities) is preferable to most other forms of "merit" compensation, and that well-developed orientation programs reduce turnover and training costs. In the current vernacular, it doesn't take a rocket scientist to figure out that these types of "reforms" are widely applicable and well worth the investment.

In addition to the formal literature on best practices, there is a considerable volume of research focusing on the expected directions that the field will take over the next decade or more (Newland, 1984; Stevens, 1995). Whether or not these prognostications should be given much weight is certainly subject to debate. Yet, since much of the research is derived from surveys of supposed "experts" in the field, it is not unreasonable to assume that their opinions are worthy of some (perhaps slight) consideration. Canvassing decision leaders in a given field, primarily through the use of Delphi techniques, is a routine forecasting tool.

The most comprehensive survey to date (Hays and Kearney, 2001) consists of the opinions of two professional groups involved in public sector HRM, the members of IPMA (who are primarily agency personnel directors) and the membership of the Section on Personnel and Labor Relations (SPALR) of the American Society for Public Administration (an entity that is largely composed of faculty who teach HRM). Their predictions are remarkably consistent both with each other and with the broader literature. They overwhelmingly anticipate a much heavier reliance upon technology within HRM, as exemplified by the increased presence of computer-assisted testing, resume databases, automated customer service, and the delivery of training to differing worker populations. Consistent with much of the reinvention agenda, they also predict the heightened importance of temporary workers, contracting out provisions, 360-degree evaluation, job rotation, and performance management. Likewise, they expect health care and employee development to become the primary job benefits; retirement plans are likely to become far less lucrative with a rapid shift from defined benefit to defined contribution systems. Other predicted trends include the declining use of position classification and rank-in-job career systems, the end of rating scales as a means of performance evaluation, continued emphasis on pay for performance, and the virtual elimination of paper and pencil examinations.

Although each of these trends must be taken as a mere possibility, the overall direction of the anticipated changes ought to sound a warning bell in many personnel departments. Given the state of affairs in some locations, these expected changes are coming far too quickly to HRM professionals who are completely unprepared for the consequences. Also, each reform program represents a potential threat to traditional notions of the civil service. As has become evident in over twenty states, HR reform often takes shape as an assault upon career public servants and the expansion of managerial prerogatives (including the conversion of more and more positions to an at-will status). Hopefully, calls for the strategic involvement of the personnel department will at least motivate some of the effected parties to examine reform options before it is too late, and to take appropriate steps to ensure that "reform" doesn't backfire.

Structural Revisions in HRM

The expansive new vision of HRM that has been described thus far cannot occur without corresponding alterations in the structure of agency personnel departments. A consistent theme among critics of the field is that it is overly specialized, a condition which contributes to introversion, narrowness of focus, and excessive reliance upon bureaucratic procedures (i.e., an emphasis on process over outcomes). To ameliorate this dilemma, the fixation with job specialties must be reduced or eliminated.

As was noted earlier, the concept of a *personnel generalist* is ascendant. Under this configuration, personnelists assume a wide range of responsibilities rather than spending their careers as classifiers, testers, or employee relations specialists (to name just a few of the possibilities). A generalist might be assigned to a subunit of the agency and therein serve as the line manager's advisor for the full array of human resource needs. He or she would probably handle all recruitment chores, conduct exit interviews, survey employees about job satisfaction and related concerns, mediate employee relations disputes, and handle any number of related assignments that affect the human resources function. Alternatively, a central personnel agency might cross-train its employees, and then assign each person to a specific organization. Their roles would then be to serve as liaisons between the HRM office and the agency. As advisors and consultants to line management, they would assist with problem solving in any area involving staffing, evaluation, or labor-management disputes. With luck, they would be welcomed into the agency's decision-making network and thus help to realize the ambitious goals of strategic HRM.

To accommodate this new operational format, one author has proposed that HRM offices will soon resemble "three-legged stools." Those specializations that have not been decentralized to subunits—such as record maintenance, benefits administration, and perhaps some recruitment activities—would be housed in the first leg. Conceived as a "service center," the purpose of the unit would be to process paperwork efficiently and to assist line managers with their technical human resource needs. Training and employee development activities would be vested in the second leg, a structural indication of the heightened importance that such activities ought to enjoy in the near future. The third leg would house the personnel generalists who would function in the "consultant" role that has been described repeatedly above. In effect, the internal structure of the OHR office would directly reflect the revised image that the personnel function hopes to achieve.

HRM Benchmarking

A final step that personnel practitioners can take without undue hardship is to establish performance standards or *benchmarks*. HRM is already the most heavily benchmarked facet of management, thanks in part to the fact that so many aspects of the function can be measured or otherwise evaluated (Brecka, 1995; Holt, 1994; Struebing, 1996).

There are several important reasons why personnelists (especially those in the private sector) are so enamored with performance standards. One immediate benefit is that they enable personnelists to critically evaluate the effectiveness of their procedures. Once the assessment process is set in motion, the odds are that some inefficient practices can be purged. Similarly, benchmarks provide quantifiable proof of the contribution that the human resource function makes to the agency's mission. Targets such as staffing ratios, turnover rates, and absenteeism provide insight into the health and dynamics of the organization. After a baseline measurement has been established, the agency can compare its performance across time, with other public agencies, or under different sets of procedures. Another promising idea is to develop benchmarks relating to the personnel office's success in aligning human resource goals with the organization's strategic plan. If this can be accomplished, personnelists are better able to assert the legitimacy of their claims on the strategic decision-making process. One final benefit is that decentralization of the personnel function is aided when operating units can be held accountable to an agreed-upon standard of performance. This ensures that no agency misinterprets its charge, violates legal requirements, or adopts practices that are contrary to established policy. Thus, for example, a central personnel office might enforce benchmarks covering such contingencies as test validation requirements, the distribution of merit raises, frequency of performance evaluations, and cost/benefit calculations (e.g., the number of personnel managers per worker). Authority is decentralized in this arrangement, but accountability mechanisms remain intact. This result can be used to assuage the concerns of some officials about the potentially negative consequences of HRM decentralization. With quantifiable performance standards in place, those who might seek to exploit government positions for private or partisan gain are at least partially restrained.

SOME CONCLUDING THOUGHTS

In summary, personnelists are in a position to make important strides toward the strategic HRM model, provided that they are willing to internalize a new set of operating strategies and philosophies. Even a single administrator in a small jurisdiction can make a difference, since the raw materials for change are readily accessible. Although few public agencies are likely to completely embrace the strategic perspective, HRM can solidify its organizational status through incremental advances. The process will undoubtedly take time, but seldom has there been such wide consensus concerning the intended direction of reform. Compelling justifications propel HRM toward a different paradigm, and the road to change is unusually well marked.

Perhaps the most serious threat to reform—other than apathy—is the risk that personnelists will overreach. The tasks at hand are so expansive that it would be easy for many professionals to become "caught up in the moment" and exceed their capabilities. Given the fact that most practitioners have not been trained to perform strategically, caution is especially important early in the reform process. This point has been hammered home several times in the private sector literature, where strategic HRM has a much longer and more successful history. Even where high-level support is present and other conditions are favorable, our counterparts in business and industry urge us to "aim for evolution, not revolution" (Stright, 1993, 69). The most successful reforms have occurred in settings where "top-gun HR functions concentrate their intellectual and organizational firepower on a limited number of high-stakes targets" (Down et al., 1997).

For most public agencies, this implies that personnelists should initially focus on targets of opportunity, such as the implementation of best practices that are particularly appealing. Benchmarking, too, can proceed without an enormous investment of time, resources, or prestige. Only after they have had an opportunity to acquire needed skills and credibility with their peers should the finer points of strategic HRM be attempted. If HRM practitioners can prove themselves worthy, then the ultimate potential of the public personnel function might be realized.

REFERENCES

Bowman, James, Marc Gertz, Sally Gertz, and Russell Williams. (2003). Civil Service Reform in Florida State Government: Employee Attitudes One Year Later. *Review of Public Personnel Administration*, 23(4): 286–304.

Brecka, Jon. (1995, April). Human Resources Is Top Benchmarking Process. *Quality Progress*, 17–19.

Carey, Dennis. (1997, Fall). Succeeding at Succeeding Yourself. *Directors and Boards*, 22: 72–73.

Center for the Study of Social Policy. (2001). *HRM Innovations in the Human Services.* Washington, DC: Center for the Study of Social Policy.

Down, James, Walter Mardis, Thomas Connolly, and Sarah Johnson. (1997). A Strategic Model Emerges. *HR Focus*, 74(6): 22–26.

Hays, Steven. (2001). Changing Roles and Duties within Government's Human Resources Profession: Contemporary Models And Challenges. In K. T. Liou (Ed.), *Handbook of Public Management Practice and Reform*, pp. 205–223. New York: Marcel Dekker.

Hays, Steven. (1996, Fall). The "State of the Discipline" in Public Personnel Administration. *Public Administration Quarterly*, 20: 283–304.

Hays, Steven and Richard Kearney. (2001, September–October). Anticipated Changes In Human Resource Management: Views from the Field. *Public Administration Review,* 61 585–597.

Holt, Blake. (1994, June). Benchmarking Comes to Human Resources. *Personnel Management*, 26: 32–41.

Kellough, J. Edward, and Sally C. Selden. (2003). The Reinvention of Public Personnel Administration: An Analysis of the Diffusion of Personnel Management Reforms in the States. *Public Administration Review*, 63(2): 165–176.

Johnston, John. (1996, Winter). Time to Rebuild Human Resources. *The Business Quarterly*, 61: 46–52.

Kemske, Floyd. (1998). HR 2008: A Forecast Based on Our Exclusive Study. *Workforce*, 77(1): 46–58.

McCausland, Richard. (1999, June). HR Consulting Goes Strategic. *Accounting Technology*, 15: 30–35.

Newland, Chester. (1984, Summer). Crucial Issues for Public Personnel Professionals. *Public Personnel Management*, 15–45.

Nigro, Lloyd and J. Edward Kellough. (2000). Civil Service Reform in Georgia: Going to The Edge? *Review of Public Personnel Administration*, 20(4): 41–54.

Roussel, Charles. (1995, April). Promises to Keep: Affecting Organizational Transformation. *HR Focus*, 72: 13–16.

Rubino, Alan. (1994). Repositioning the Human Resource Function at Hoffmann-LaRoch. *Human Resource Planning*, 17(2): 45–50.

Santry, Kerry. (1996). Bridges Says Workers Must Flex and Change with the Needs of the Job Market. *Management Journal* (36): 36–39.

Stevens, L. N. (1995). *Civil Service Reform: Changing Times Demand New Approaches.* Washington, DC: Government Printing Office.

Stewart, Thomas. (1996, June). Taking on the Last Bureaucracy. *Fortune Magazine*.

Stright, Jay. (1993). Strategic Goals Guide HRMS Development. *Personnel Journal*, 72(9): 68–76.

Struebing, Laura. (1996, April). Group's Clients Most Often Use Benchmarking for Human Resource Improvements. *Quality Progress*, 20–22.

Tokesky, George, and Joanne Kornides. (1994). Strategic HRM is vital. *Personnel Journal*, 73(12): 115–118.

Ulrich, Dave. (1998a, January–February). A New Mandate for Human Resources. *Harvard Business Review*, 124–134.

Ulrich, Dave. (1998b, January). The Future Calls For Change. *Workforce*, 87–91.

Whittlesey, Fred. (1997, Spring). The Future of Human Resources Management. *ACA Journal*, 12–15.

6

Productive Human Resource Management for the 21st Century: Context and Strategies

MARC HOLZER, HEDY ISAACS, AND SEOK-HWAN LEE

The context of management in the 21st century is dynamic. Characterized by private competitiveness, demands for existing and new services, budget and other resource constraints, pressure for high performance, community involvement, as well as political pressures, these impulses pose challenges for managers in the public and private spheres.

Managers of contemporary public organizations are confronted with convergent demands from civil society. They are influenced by demands for responsiveness and effective government, for citizens' rights, social equity, greater involvement in governance, and changing workforce attitudes and expectations. The political-administrative interplay juxtaposes the requirement for modern and transparent governance with government provision of more services for society, although it often has fewer real resources. In democratic states, whether they are developed or are in transition, public managers face the challenge of responding through strategic quality management. Managers are forced to respond with innovative rather than traditional orientations to managing their resources. In particular, productive public organizations require innovative approaches to human resource management. Managers require an effective approach to human resource management that helps to create and maintain an environment conducive to a productive workforce.

No aspect of productive public management in public organizations is more important than people—government's most extensive and expensive investments are people. Fifty to eighty-five percent of government budgets are spent on salaries and benefits for employees. Guy (1992a) emphasizes the importance of people in productive public organizations:

> The easiest way to make quick productivity gains is to mechanize a process. The most difficult, but most enduring, way to make productivity gains is to develop each worker's desire and ability to be maximally productive. The reason is simple: It is people who, in the long term, control the productivity of any organization. (307)

As Minzberg (1996) asserts, an organization without human commitment is like a person without a soul: skeleton, flesh, and blood may be able to consume and to exert, but there is no life force. Government desperately needs a life force. Thus, recognizing and responding to emergent human resource management demands is directly connected to improving productivity in public organizations.

Productive organizations are humane and show genuine concern for meeting employees' needs. This characterization of productive organizations is in synch with the view that managing human capital is largely about satisfying human needs and balancing people's needs with those of the organization (Holzer and Callahan, 1998).

Human resource management, according to Isaacs, is the totality of people concerns and the ability of the organization to manage these concerns. When managers deal with these concerns effectively, they are likely to achieve agency mandates as well as satisfy employees' needs: challenging work, job satisfaction, recognition for achievement, pay that allows them to live comfortably, a safe and healthy working environment, and a healthy labor relations climate (among other factors). Agencies need a competent, productive, motivated workforce in a working climate that encourages harmonious relations between managers and employees (Isaacs, 1996).

Human resource management is no longer simply about conforming to personnel processes. It is no longer simply about protecting employees and the integrity of personnel systems from management abuse. Under traditional management models there was an emphasis on adherence to processes. Under performance improvement models there is now an emphasis on achievement of organizational outcomes—of explicit and implicit promises to the public (Cooper, 1998). The purpose of human resource management is to support managers and employees with the goal of better serving the public. Systemically, this requires the traditional HRM elements of:

- hiring appropriate personnel to achieve agency mandates;
- training and developing personnel; and
- rewarding personnel using material as well as psychological rewards—setting up the organizational climate that encourages loyalty and cooperation at the workplace.

In this era of limited resources, decline of public trust, and demands for high level of performance, HRM systems now also require:

- creating and maintaining a quality workforce that is diverse;
- empowering employees;
- enabling employees to manage work and family responsibilities, and holding managers accountable for merit principles and EEO (Naff, 1993);
- identifying different types of employees' motivational bases; and
- identifying factors affecting cooperative culture at the workplaces.

The challenge that productive public organizations face is even greater when we consider their dynamic context. Changing social, technological, legal, political, and physical factors in the external and internal environments are likely to influence how we manage our organizations' most important and complex assets: People.

In this regard, the purpose of this chapter is to provide an overview of the dynamic context of human resource management and important strategies for managing human resources productively for the 21st century.

THE DYNAMIC CONTEXT OF PRODUCTIVE HUMAN RESOURCE MANAGEMENT

Overall, productive human resource management should be understood in the context of an open system in which external and internal environments are interconnected. These environments for human resource management constitute a dynamic, open-world system (Cooper, 1998). Such a system is likely to influence government's ability to attract and retain personnel to perform new, often more complex, tasks in an environment in which government competes with the private sector for human resources and changes in technology result in greater demand for knowledge workers and for information systems that support management decisions. Bohlander and Snell (2007) opine that rapidly changing technologies obviously require a higher quality workforce and adaptive strategies.

Furthermore, the changing demographic profile of society requires a workforce that is diverse. Holzer and Callahan (1998) advocate human resource management that values all employee differences. This view is supported by Bohlander and Snell (2007), who argue that diversity requires a mutually beneficial relationship. Public organizations benefit from diversity by recognizing differences and potential concerns of employees. In this regard, the increasing presence in the work force of women and racial and ethnic groups has given rise to a body of literature focusing on diversity in organizations (Golembiewski, 1995; Rainey, 1997).

Permeable boundaries of public agencies and jurisdictions also pose challenges for human resource management. Cooper (1998) points out that the important problems to be solved do not stop at organizational or jurisdictional boundaries. In many instances government agencies or jurisdictions do not have authority over each other. In all likelihood, problems are solved collaboratively or not at all. In this context a supportive human resource management process requires that public managers acquire problem solving skills, and these skills are likely to be most effective in a collaborative organization ethos. Making things happen is not a top-down affair, but requires human resource management that recognizes competency requirements of agencies and provides needed training and development.

Within organizations, department and unit boundaries are also permeable. This requires that the human resource management department take a team player approach and work with other departments toward attaining organizational objectives.

The changing legal environment also requires human resource management that facilitates management's awareness of relevant laws. In the absence of this awareness, public organizations run the risk of lawsuits and ridicule.

Internal factors, in particular the values held by agency leadership, and the related culture of the organization, are likely to influence human resource management. In particular, agency leadership determines the importance of human resource management to the agency. If the heads of agencies minimize the importance of people to the agency's overall success, so will line managers. In turn, the human resource department will undertake only routine-level human resource management rather than the innovative, productive approaches that require greater efforts.

Leadership's concern for employees who are an agency's internal customers influences the quality of human resource management as well. Employee-centered leadership recognizes the totality of people concerns, demonstrates that employees are valued, and has the vision to create strategic plans for human resource management. Holzer and Callahan (1998), in their account of public agencies that are productive, add credence to the view that the commitment of top management is a necessary first step for disseminating values throughout the organization. These values influence how organizations manage people.

It should be noted, however, that no productivity increment is a product of a single employee's efforts. Even if there is top management support and commitment, we cannot expect productivity improvement in public organizations unless public employees are all committed to improving productivity. Empirical research undertaken by Holzer and Olshfski (1990–1996) confirm that recipients of Exemplary State and Local Awards (EXSL) indeed have committed personnel at all levels along with having support from top agency executives. It turned out that having committed personnel was the most important factor for innovation (Holzer and Olshfski, in Holzer and Callahan, 1998).

The agency culture represents its value system. Individual and organizational performance, and the feelings that people in an organization have about that organization, cannot be understood unless one takes into account the organizational culture (Schein, 1988). The culture that eventually evolves in a particular organization is a complex outcome of external pressures, internal potentials, responses to critical events, and probably, to some unknown degree, chance factors that could not be predicted from the knowledge of either the environment or the members. This organizational culture is one of the important factors affecting employee's motivational bases for productivity improvement (Romzek, 1990). The culture typically indicates how agencies regard their customers, the environment, and their employees (Huber and Schuler, 1993). Culture is often reflected in human resource management processes. Agencies that have a culture of caring for and respecting individuals are likely to provide benefits for a variety of employee needs. In this way, employees learn the culture of the agency through human resource management activities: how the agency selects personnel for hiring and promotion, what criteria it uses to evaluate them, and whom it compensates most highly.

The future hardly turns out to be what we expect. In a dynamic organizational context, where the only constant is change, organizational leadership is required to make change a part of the organizational culture. Such a culture typically reflects the importance that the agency places on people, while not denigrating the importance of materials and machines. This culture typically reflects a leadership that views change as a challenge and an opportunity to improve. According to Mills (1994), the leader in a culture of change creates new ways of doing things, engenders new worlds.

The political-administrative interface may keep the public agency on its toes. Human resource management in public agencies may have political ramifications. Attempts at politicization by elected or other officials will not be received uncritically. Human resource management processes, such as hiring and firing, are no longer backroom activities and must be able to stand scrutiny. Many agencies come into play depending on the issue: Agency interdependence is evident, for example, when policy questions concerning performance appraisal in the federal government are being resolved. Several agencies—the Equal Employment Opportunity Commission, the Office of Personnel Management, the Federal Labor Relations Authority and the Merit Systems Protection Board—have become involved in these policy issues. Productive human resource management in such organizations balances attempts at politicization with principles of merit and equal employment.

Our argument above is that factors in an agency's external and internal environments are likely to influence human resource management. Recognizing these factors and their effects helps to prepare human resource managers to respond to human resource management challenges and to carry out an agency's responsibilities in this regard. In productive organizations, those persons with responsibilities for human resource management recognize these factors as opportunities rather than problems. Such responsibilities are dispersed throughout an organization. Agency heads and their top management team, managers, and human resource managers have a shared responsibility for human resource management. Thus, virtually all agency managers, as Naff (1993) points out, are the human resource management department's customers. With the support of the human resource management department, agency managers maintain the quality workforce; empower, develop, and train employees; and are held accountable for observing justice, fair play, and (above all) merit principles at the workplace. In that dynamic context, human resource managers facilitate change, and guide, advise and facilitate implementation of human resource management plans and processes. In effect, human resource management departments provide supportive processes so that agency managers may deliver better services.

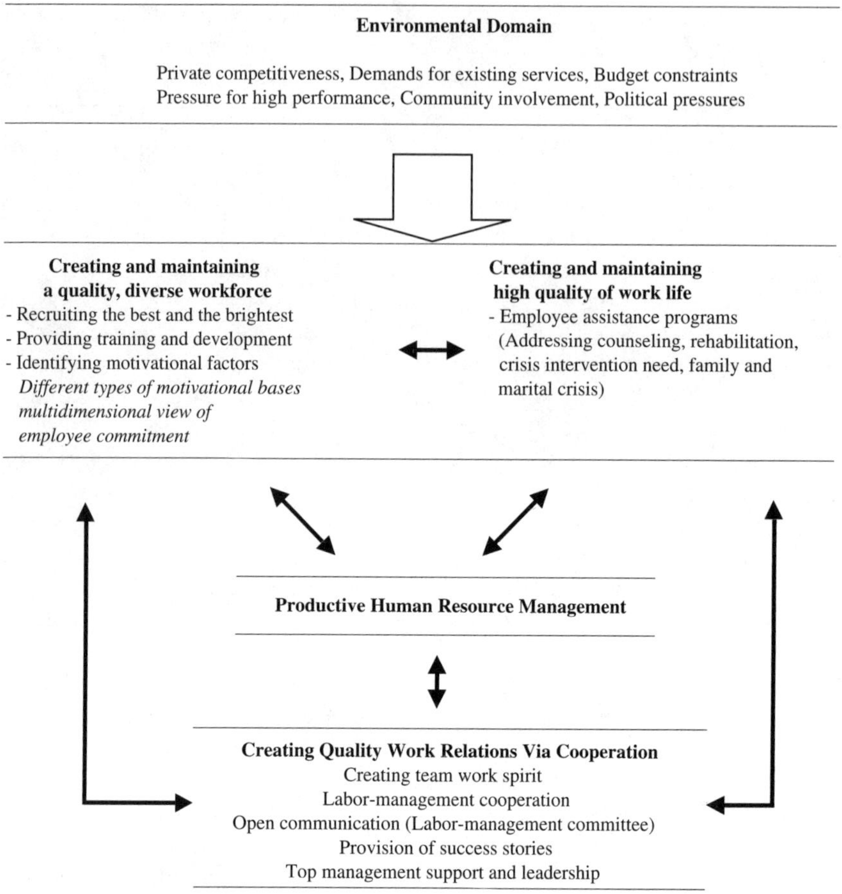

Environmental Domain

Private competitiveness, Demands for existing services, Budget constraints
Pressure for high performance, Community involvement, Political pressures

**Creating and maintaining
a quality, diverse workforce**
- Recruiting the best and the brightest
- Providing training and development
- Identifying motivational factors
  *Different types of motivational bases
  multidimensional view of
  employee commitment*

**Creating and maintaining
high quality of work life**
- Employee assistance programs
  (Addressing counseling, rehabilitation,
  crisis intervention need, family and
  marital crisis)

Productive Human Resource Management

Creating Quality Work Relations Via Cooperation
Creating team work spirit
Labor-management cooperation
Open communication (Labor-management committee)
Provision of success stories
Top management support and leadership

FIGURE 6.1.   Strategies for Productive Human Resource Management in a Dynamic Context

STRATEGIES FOR PRODUCTIVE HUMAN RESOURCE MANAGEMENT

As productive human resource management is a function of a variety of factors, it is necessary to understand it in an open system where internal and external factors are effectively interconnected.

From this perspective, we suggest that a range of strategies be required to effectively manage human resources in productive organizations. These strategies are based on the following three categories:

- creating and maintaining a quality, diverse workforce;
- creating and maintaining a high quality of work life; and
- creating quality work relations via cooperation.

Figure 6.1 shows how a variety of strategies could affect a productive human resource management in a dynamic context.

CREATING AND MAINTAINING A QUALITY, DIVERSE WORKFORCE

Many organizations fail to create and maintain the quality workforce they need to improve agency productivity (Holzer and Callahan, 1998). It is a difficult and time-consuming task. Improving productivity requires developing the capacity and desire of the workforce to function at the highest levels. Their compendium of innovative public sector approaches for managing human resources confirms that this task can be accomplished, an optimistic perspective on the future of human resource management in public organizations.

Creating and maintaining the workforce involves human resource management processes of finding and hiring appropriate people, systematically developing and training them, and then motivating, rewarding, and evaluating the workforce.

Workforce planning, as a strategy for acquiring, utilizing, training and retraining persons, is not simply forecasting the number of persons required now and in the future. It is concerned with the quality of personnel, their development, their optimum utilization, and their retention. Workforce planning has an evaluative role and addresses the future effects of employment as a function of present-day decisions.

Recruiting the Best and the Brightest

Sustained assaults on the public service discourage many of the best and the brightest students from pursuing careers in the private sector (Holzer and Rabin, 1987). Government cannot afford to be complacent about the recruitment and retention of high quality employees. Public service is at risk because it is losing some of its best people to alternative employment (Romzek, 1990, 374). Empirical research conducted by Jurkiewicz et al. (1998) of fifteen motivational factors relevant to public sector employees in America indicates that "high prestige and social status" ranked fifteenth (Jurkiewicz et al., 1998, 235).

In this context, identifying and hiring appropriate people are becoming critical issues and require innovative approaches. Agencies should recruit the "best and the brightest" widely from new graduates, persons who have been downsized, older workers, volunteers, etc. Some public agencies have pioneered hiring innovations that Holzer and Callahan (1998) cite as more efficient, responsive, and user friendly than the traditional civil service hiring procedures. For example, these innovations include the Walk-In Civil Service Testing and Job Opportunity Bulletin System implemented by Wisconsin state government. Furthermore, Holzer (1991) suggests a number of strategies for attracting the best and the brightest into the public sector: For example, in terms of advocacy activities, it is important to keep public service on the public agenda and argue that an effective public service is a prerequisite to productive private sectors. With regard to education for the public service, public service should be perceived as both a necessary investment and an obligation. Thus, it is important to require public service for graduation from all students. A sensible level of compensation, increased managerial discretion, and the control of resources are also important factors for attracting the best and the brightest to the public sector.

Providing Systematic Training and Development

In a productive public agency, training and development are ongoing processes. For the 21st century agencies require a climate where organizational learning is continuous (Mills, 1994). Training starts with orientation on entry and continues throughout an individual's work life to satisfy the needs for new skills, knowledge, and attitudes (KSAs). Development, a long-term program of activities that may include training and education, prepares employees for upward mobility or career progression. Training is vital to improving performance and reduces the likelihood of employee obsolescence in a changing environment. Staff training and development efforts are critical to achieving manpower plans as well as improving competencies of individuals.

The importance of training employees is so often found in the fact that public employees must work in an environment in which politics plays a role. Because of the traditional dichotomy between politics and administration, the legislative environment is commonly foreign to public employees. As a result, public employees do not effectively work in it. Therefore, public employees will be more productive if they understand the legislative environment (Lewis and Raffel, 1996).

Isaacs (1996) asserts that the effectiveness of training and development efforts, and the receptiveness of the trainees to training and development programs, is likely to affect employee productivity. The effectiveness of program design, delivery, and evaluation, and the extent to which employees are allowed to use new skills, also affect agency productivity.

Productive organizations tailor-make their training and development efforts to satisfy both the agency's and the individual's needs. Ideally, these efforts are not based on imagined needs or, as we might say, "a wish list" (Isaacs, 1996). The delivery of training has to be carefully monitored to ensure that stated training objectives are achieved.

Experience has shown that when agencies utilize employees' new skills and knowledge, employees are more likely to be productive. Likewise, productivity is likely to suffer when there is resistance to applying these skills and employees are made to feel impotent and frustrated in their efforts to use the skills (Isaacs, 1996). The benefits to be derived from encouraging employees to use newly acquired skills are manifested by the systematic and innovative approach to training and development taken by the Illinois Department of Employment Security. This approach has proved to be timely, cost effective, and of high quality; a pool of employees are trained to identify training needs and carry out tailor-made training in-house (Holzer and Callahan, 1998).

Motivating Employees

General Factors Affecting Employees' Motivation

Motivating for productivity is not simply a function of better pay and benefits. What Carl Stone's Report on Work Attitude Survey (1983) imputed then, and the Report of the Task Force on Work Attitudes (1983) subsequently emphasized, is still true today: More and more workers are driven by the desire to find some place in society in which their qualities are recognized, where they are regarded as human beings with desires and aspirations, where they see the purpose of their work, and where they are given an opportunity to be consulted on those matters that have an influence on their working lives. Improved worker-management relations, clearer communication, more training to improve skills, and improving the physical work environment may all serve to motivate the workforce in productive organizations. According to Holzer and Callahan (1998), government agencies that have been the recipients of exemplary awards typically use a range of state-of-the-art approaches to motivate people. These agencies recognize that money, though an important motivator, is not the only motivator. Such high-achieving agencies take an integrated approach to human resource management by linking human resource management policies, plans, and processes. Isaacs (2003) points out that motivating and rewarding public employees requires constant attention to employees' needs and expectations from the time that the employees enter the agency until the time that they leave. Humanistic management values, strategies, and ethos that couple employees' needs, expectations and attitudes with employees' aptitudes, abilities and knowledge in a particular job context, may provide scope for improving employees' productivity.

Productive agencies use a well-conceived and managed performance appraisal process as a developmental tool and a motivational option. They recognize that interdependent factors contribute to creating a productive work environment (Guy, 1992a): an organizational culture that relies on team building, maximizing the strengths of employees while compensating for their weaknesses, open communication channels, flexibility in the midst of predictability, and balancing the needs of the organization with the needs of employees.

Agency mandates translate at the operational level into real tasks for teams or individuals. These tasks provide a starting point for the performance appraisal process. Employer and employee may now discuss and agree on allocation of tasks to the employee's team or position. At the point the standard of performance of those tasks is agreed upon, an opportunity is provided for an audit of the skill or training needs of the employee and the appropriate developmental plans are laid (McDonald, 1995).

In productive organizations performance appraisal is also used to develop employees and improve performance. The effectiveness of performance appraisal as a developmental tool rests on facilitating openness between manager and worker. Appraisal is a means of identifying the strengths and weaknesses of employees' performance on an ongoing basis, providing regular feedback to employees about their performance, counseling employees, and finding ways to improve performance. If carried out effectively, performance appraisal is likely to result in employees' becoming aware of whether or not they are satisfying the expectations of the job. When carried out effectively, performance appraisal may also build employees' confidence, boost morale, and improve performance (Isaacs, 1996).

Conflict is inherent in the appraisal process, but there are ways of reducing it. Employees need to know what is expected of them. Managers may do this, by providing job descriptions to reinforce expectations discussed, discussing with employees attainable standards of performance expected of them, having standards that indicate quality, quantity and timeliness of the work to be done, and using standards as yardsticks for measuring performance. According to McDonald (1995), identifying standards is an important precursor to the performance appraisal process as it provides the employee with a framework within which to do self-assessment and also to set the agenda for the formal appraisal session. Goal and standard setting in the performance appraisal process significantly removes the subjectivity and the historical nature of the traditional form of appraising performance as employees are able to assess their own performance as a result of knowing the standards by which they are being appraised.

The value of performance appraisal as a developmental tool is enhanced when appropriate techniques are used and efforts are made to minimize the inherent conflict in the appraisal process. Productive organizations require trained appraisers to assess performance accurately and to take a problem-solving approach to formal appraisal. Managers who appraise performance play a key role in improving employees' performance and developing an organization's human resources (Isaacs, 1996).

Identifying Different Types of Motivational Bases and Employee Commitments

Needless to say, human motivation is a fundamental factor that should be addressed in designing an effective human resource management. The conventional wisdom that public employees are lower on their motivational bases, including organizational commitment, as compared to their counterparts in the private sector, is still controversial among scholars and practitioners. However, Holzer and Olshfski (1990), in their empirical research of EXSL winners, find that the public service ethic seems to be alive and well in the preeminence of "to do the right thing" (requoted from Holzer and Callahan, 1998).

Other scholars argue that there are three types of motivational bases of public services, namely:

- a rational base motive, including participation in the process of policy formulation, commitment to a public program because of personnel identification, and advocacy for a special or private interest;
- a norm-based motive, including a desire to serve the public interest, loyalty to duty and to the government as a whole, and social equity; and

- an affective motive, including commitment to a program from a genuine conviction about its social importance, and patriotism of benevolence.

Based on these three motivational bases, they propose that in public organizations public service motivation be positively related to individual performance. In order for public organizations to be productive, managers should carefully attend to these different types of motivational bases in their organizations (Perry and Wise, 1990).

With regard to employee commitment, its importance is found in its relationship to performance and productivity. Much of the literature on employee commitment finds that commitment to organization is positively associated with job satisfaction (Bateman and Strasser, 1984; Mowday, Porter, and Steers, 1982), motivation (Mowday, Steers, and Porter, 1979), and attendance (Mathieu and Zajac, 1990; Steers and Rhodes, 1978) and negatively related to such outcomes as job performance, absenteeism, and turnover (Angle and Perry, 1981, Balfour and Weschler, 1996; Clegg, 1983).

However, the previous concept of organizational commitment has been criticized by scholars because it may not tell the whole story about important outcome variables such as desire to remain with the organization and willingness to make an extra effort on behalf of the organization (Balfour and Weschler, 1991, 1996). Following O'Reilly and Chatman's (1986) model of three dimensions, Balfour and Wechsler (1996) developed a distinctive definition and measure of organizational commitment: identification commitment (membership), affiliation commitment (belonging), and exchange commitment (extrinsic rewards). What they discovered was that only affiliation commitment was associated with extra-role behavior, while identification commitment was the least important determinant of desire to remain.

Furthermore, it should be noted that employees could be committed to other subjects beyond their organizations. In fact, the conventional view of commitment has exclusively focused on commitment to organization. In contrast to this conventional view, a number of researchers have begun to view employee commitment as having multiple foci and bases (Becker, 1992; Becker, Randall, and Riegel, 1995; Meyer, Allen, and Smith, 1993; Reichers, 1985, 1986). The theory underlying the multiple commitments literature holds that an employee's commitment to the workplace cannot be adequately explained by commitment to the organization alone, because the coalition nature of organizations leads employee commitment to be multidimensional (Reichers, 1985).

Research suggests that employees could also be differentially committed to occupations, top management, supervisors, coworkers, and customers (Becker, 1992; Meyer, Allen, and Smith, 1993; Reichers, 1986). Among other subjects of commitment, commitment to supervisor is an important motivational base for increasing individual performance. As extrinsic rewards controlled by one's supervisor are now seen as a major means for directing and reinforcing managerial and executive behavior (Perry and Wise, 1990), it is possible to expect that those committed to a supervisor are likely to be motivated to improving productivity. Some employees may say that they are working hard not because of their organization, but because of their supervisor. They might want to remain with the organization because they feel emotionally attached to their supervisor rather than to their organization. It is also possible to expect that where a teamwork-based organizational culture prevails, people are likely to be committed to their work group, thereby increasing their willingness for group-based performance. Distinguishing among the foci of employee commitments does help to explain variances in key dependent variables such as extra-role behavior and desire to remain, and turnover. What this argument implies is that public managers now must pay much attention to this multidimensional view of employee commitment and try to identify which types of employee commitment are common among their employees. It should be emphasized that effective human resource management requires public managers to identity different types of employee commitment and to encourage them effectively.

CREATING AND MAINTAING HIGH QUALITY OF WORK LIFE

Productive human resource management in the 21st century must mean an increased attention to the physical surroundings in which people work, as well as to the concerns and crises that may arise in employees' work lives or personal lives. Making the workplace safe and healthy, and making workstations ergonomically sound, are challenges for productive organizations. Accidents, diseases, and hazards such as stress generally result in low productivity and inefficiency, high turnover, absenteeism, and medical claims. When there is a deliberate effort by the workplace to reduce the incidence of these, both the agency and the employee benefit. There is greater productivity, a healthier workforce, and a better quality of work life.

Crises in employees' personal lives typically affect their performance at work. When organizations help employees overcome these problems, they in all likelihood improve employee morale and loyalty and avoid incurring costs to the organization. The employee assistance program launched by the City of Memphis is a case in point. The program was "set up in response to estimated losses of $3,500,000 per year in reduced efficiency, absenteeism, and accidents as a result of untreated personal problems and disorders. The city established a broad-based effort designed to address various counseling, rehabilitation, and crisis-intervention needs, reducing losses by twenty-five percent" (Holzer and Callahan, 1998). Another employee assistance program, in Buena Park, California, helps employees deal with a range of problems: family and marital crises, stress, alcohol and drug dependency, job problems, child and spousal abuse, legal problems, care of and issues relating to elderly and infirm relatives, death, dying, and money and credit management. This program has led to $2 million in savings. In terms of problem prevention, wellness programs that provide employees with information and in-house facilities that encourage them to lead active and healthy lifestyles are integral elements of human resource management programs for the 21st century (Holzer and Callahan, 1998).

CREATING QUALITY WORK RELATIONS VIA COOPERATION

Creating Teamwork Spirit

Agency leadership, managers, and human resource managers will be required to build and sustain teams in the interest of quality of work life and agency productivity in the 21st century. Productive human resource management addresses cooperative work relations as well as the importance of a high quality, diverse workforce, and the quality of work life. Work relations in productive agencies require effective communication between employees and employers, and a working partnership between the two so that employees are aware of their rights, their obligations and employers' expectations, balancing employee and organizational needs. In this context, it is becoming apparent that productive organizations get work done through teams that work cooperatively rather than through individuals competing with each other. Teams typically provide a supportive ethos for their members. Teams typically accomplish more than a single individual would. In one jurisdiction in California employee teams have cut costs of public works services while increasing productivity. They accomplished this through involvement in generating work standards, performance targets, and work scheduling. As a result of this Shared Savings Program (SSP), Pittsburg, California, linked performance incentives with efficient use of equipment, supplies, and labor resources, significantly reducing the cost of public services (Holzer and Callahan, 1998).

Toward Labor-Management Cooperation: Building a Collaborative Culture

Many scholars in the public sector agree that a harmonious labor-management relationship is the key to improving productivity (Coleman, 1990; Grace and Holzer, 1992; Herrick, 1990; Hodes, 1991). The importance of labor-management cooperation is also reflected in the fact that Vice President Gore's National Performance Review changed its name to the National Partnership for Reinventing Government (National Partnership for Reinventing Government, 1998).

Traditional approaches to management, as Holzer and Callahan (1998) point out, "often assume a tension between employer and employee. Tight rules, systems, and supervision are necessary to limit counterproductive indiscretion, dishonesty, and laziness. Employees view the organization as the enemy, and vice versa; work is merely an interruption in their leisure time, and a great deal of energy is wasted attempting to sidestep these constraints. Organizations can be minimally productive under such assumptions, but almost never produce at high levels of productivity and quality."

As the regulative function of government becomes more developed, this tends to limit the scope for employers and employees to negotiate and compromise in a free spirit of collective bargaining. Obviously the tension exists between labor and management because of difficult workplace relationships, impasses, or other conflicts. Labor management cooperation tends to reduce the tensions between employer and employee. Adversarial relations between labor and management are a "no win" situation. Munroe (1992) advocates the development of partnerships in place of adversarial relations and cooperation in place of antagonistic work systems. He points out that building partnerships is likely to be a difficult task that requires patience and determination, time, and tact. Although Munroe advocates Employee Involvement Programs for the Caribbean, his ideas have merit and applicability elsewhere. He points out that these programs are likely to arrest workforce demotivation, mobilize the human resource base for urgent problem solving, and develop productivity to the point of coping with the demands of the 21st century.

The key to a successful partnership, as Holzer and Callahan (1998) point out, is a "collaborative labor relations program based on mutual trust and respect. Marion County, Oregon, and its largest union developed such a partnership—negotiating wages and benefits within a cap on the employer's future expenditures. The Model Program for Capping Wage and Benefit Expenditures defines the employer's maximum future personnel service costs while giving the union flexibility to bargain changes in salaries, insurance and other employee benefits."

Research by Holzer and Lee (1999) maintains that labor-management tension is likely to occur where each side sees the other as an outgroup, and harmonious labor-management partnership could be achieved through the metaphor change from "conflict" to "partnership." This metaphor change is made through open communication, provision of success stories, and top management support. A variety of open communications will also help both sides understand their mutual problems. Providing success stories on labor-management partnerships will lead to positive beliefs between labor and management sides. Finally, top management leadership and support will credibly transmit the vision of partnership in organizations.

Although labor-management cooperation is a backdrop for productive public management, obviously tension exists between labor and management because of difficult workplace relationships, impasses, or other conflicts. It should be noted, however, that partnerships between both groups are possible. The labor-management partnership could be achieved where these three factors are working at the same time. For example, a case from the Department of Public Works in the City of Portland, Maine, shows that the labor-management partnership was very successful and could be achieved by these three factors. Despite severe budget constraints and a difficult winter, labor-management cooperation in construction of a baseball stadium enabled the department to complete its job at a cost of only $2.5 million and in record time. First of all, in order to utilize open communication devices the City Manager formed a twenty-six-person labor-management committee that included an equipment operator, a working foreman, an assistant city manager, a secretary, an arborist, an engineer, and the head of the department as well as the president of American Federation of State, County, and Municipal Employees (AFSCME) Local 481. Second, through this success story, many employees now say that there is no longer an "us" and "them." They also feel that they have been able to move away from an adversarial relationship to more of a team concept. Finally, this success was also a function of a strong backing of the mayor (U.S. Department of Labor, 1996).

As indicated above, labor-management tension can be overcome and transformed to partnership by open communication, provision of a success story, and top management support. Public managers should realize the importance of labor-management partnership and focus on these three factors for productive human resource management in the future. That is, productive human resource management does not exist without a harmonious labor-management relationship.

In addition, good working relationships are not limited to relations between employer/employee. Relations between agencies and citizens they serve are also important. Effective work relations with internal and external customers are important to avoid problems that may emerge between either party. Quality work relations are required to ameliorate problem situations that may mushroom into conflict and become the subject of litigation. It is important, therefore, for public managers to emphasize the importance of this relationship to employees

CONCLUSION: PRODUCTIVE HUMAN RESOURCE MANAGEMENT AS A COMPREHENSIVE ART

This chapter examined the overall strategic context of, and a range of strategies for, productive human resource management for the 21st century. Overall, productive human resource management should be understood in an open system where internal and external factors are effectively connected. As people are the key to improving productivity in the public sector, it is important to be aware of how to manage public employees effectively in their organizations, and to identify what factors are likely to motivate these people toward productivity enhancement. Managing people effectively is always a critical issue in public personnel administration.

From these perspectives, this chapter suggests a variety of strategies based on the following three categories: (1) creating and maintaining a quality, diverse workforce, (2) creating and maintaining a high quality of work life, and (3) creating quality work relations via cooperation.

In relation to creating and maintaining a quality, diverse workforce, in fact attracting the best and the brightest is the starting point for productive human resource management. The next step will then be providing these people with training and development so that they might effectively work in a turbulent environment. At the same time, public managers should be aware of a variety of factors affecting employees' motivations. In addition to general factors such as rewarding personnel (using material as well as psychological rewards), public managers must also identify different types of motivational bases among public employees and recognize a multidimensional construct of employee commitment. Understanding different types of employee commitment is especially important because people may also be differentially committed to their supervisors, work group, unions, top management, and customers beyond their organization. This multidimensional view of employee commitment helps managers identify what type of employee commitment serves as a major motivational mechanism in their organizations. Employee commitments also vary with regard to organizational culture.

The second category that should be addressed is "creating and maintaining a high quality of work life." Considering the importance of the physical surroundings in which people work, making the workplace safe and healthy, and making workstations ergonomically sound, are challenges for productive organizations. Accidents, diseases, and hazards such as stress generally result in low productivity and inefficiency, high turnover, absenteeism, and medical claims. In order to deal with these problems, it is necessary to have a variety of employee assistance programs. When the organization reduces the incidence of these problems, both the agency and the employee benefit.

Finally, the importance of the culture of cooperative workplaces for the 21st century should also be addressed. Considering that no productivity improvement is a product of a single employee's efforts, creating a teamwork spirit helps employees achieve higher levels of performance and productivity. Furthermore, as the labor-management partnership is a backdrop for everything that is going on in governments at all levels (Holzer and Lee, 1999), productive human resource management should also be based on a collaborative culture at the workplace. In this regard, we also suggest three ways of converting existing labor-management tensions to partnerships. The keys to labor-management partnership are open communication, provision of success stories, and top management support and leadership. Although partnerships are difficult, they can be achieved when these three factors are working at the same time.

Considering the dynamic context of human resource management, it should also be noted that productive human resource management is possible when all strategies mentioned in this chapter are working at the same time. As an effective public sector exists when internal and external factors are effectively interrelated, productive human resource management for the 21st century should be designed to effectively respond to the demands of a turbulent environment as well as to the demands of employees.

REFERENCES

Angle, H.L., and J.L. Perry. (1981). An Empirical Assessment of Organizational Commitment and Organizational Effectiveness. *Administrative Science Quarterly*, 26: 1–14.

Balfour, D.L., and B. Wechsler. (1991). Commitment, Performance, and Productivity in Public Organizations. *Public Productivity & Management Review*, 14: 355–368.

Balfour, D.L., and B. Wechsler. (1996). Organizational Commitment: Antecedents and Outcomes in Public Organizations. *Public Productivity & Management Review*, 19: 256–277.

Bateman, T.S., and S. Strasser. (1984). A Longitudinal Analysis of the Antecedents of Organizational Commitment. *Academy of Management Journal*, 27: 95–112.

Becker, T.E. (1992). Foci and Bases of Commitment: Are They Distinctions Worth Making? *Academy of Management Journal*, 35: 232–244.

Becker, T.E., D.M. Randall, and C.D. Riegel. (1995). The Multidimensional View of Commitment and the Theory of Reasoned Action: A Comparative Evaluation. *Journal of Management*, 21: 617–638.

Clegg, C.W. (1983). Psychology of Employees' Lateness, Absence, and Turnover: A Methodological Critique and an Empirical Study. *Journal of Applied Psychology*, 68: 88–101.

Coleman, C.J. (1990). *Managing Labor Relations in the Public Sector*. San Francisco, CA: Jossey-Bass.

Cooper, P.J. (1998). *Public Administration for the Twenty-First Century*. Fort Worth, TX: Harcourt Brace.

Golembiewski, R.T. (1995). *Managing Diversity in Organizations*. Tuscaloosa, AL: The University of Alabama Press.

Grace, S.L., and M. Holzer. (1992). Labor-Management Cooperation: An Opportunity for Change. In M. Holzer (Ed.), *Public Productivity Handbook*, pp. 487–498. New York: Marcel Dekker.

Guy, M.E. (1992). Managing People. In M. Holzer (Ed.), *Public Productivity Handbook*, pp. 307–320. New York: Marcel Dekker.

Herrick, N. (1990). *Joint Management and Employee Participation: Labor and Management at the Crossroads*. San Francisco, CA: Jossey-Bass.

Hodes, N. (1991). Achieving Quality Through Labor-Management Participation in New York State. *Public Productivity & Management Review*, 15(2): 163–168.

Holzer, M. (1991). Attracting the Best and the Brightest to Government Service. In C. Ban and N. Riccucci (Eds.), *Public Personnel Management: Current Concerns—Future Challenges*, pp. 3–16. White Plains, NY: Longman.

Holzer, M., and K. Callahan. (1998). *Government at Work: Best Practices and Model Programs*. Thousand Oaks, CA: SAGE.

Holzer, M., and S-H. Lee. (1999). Labor-Management Tension And Partnership: Where Are We? What Should We Do? *International Review of Public Administration*, 4(2): 33–44.

Holzer, M., and J. Rabin. (1987). Public Service: Problems, Professionalism, and Policy Recommendations. *Public Productivity & Management Review*, 11: 3–13.

Isaacs, H. (2003). Non-Monetary Incentives and Productivity. In *Encyclopedia of Public Administration and Public Policy*, pp. 830, 834. New York: Marcel Dekker.

Isaacs, H. (1996). *Personnel Management and Industrial Relations MS488 Study Guide*, pp. 1, 52, 59–66, 213–214. UWIDITE, The University of the West Indies, Kingston, Jamaica: University Printers.

Jurkiewicz, C.L., T.K. Massey Jr., and R.G. Brown. (1998). Motivation in Public and Private Organizations: A Comparative Study. *Public Productivity & Management Review*, 21: 230–250.

Lewis, J.R., and J.R. Raffel. (1996). Training Public Administrators to Work with Legislators. In M. Holzer and V.Gabrielian (Eds.), *Case Studies in Productive Public Management: From the Public Productivity and Management Review*, pp. 301–309. Burke, VA: Chatelaine Press.

Mathieu, J.E., and D.M. Zajac. (1990). A Review and Meta-Analysis of the Antecedents, Correlates, and Consequences of Organizational Commitment. *Psychological Bulletin*, 108: 171–194.

McDonald, N. (1995). The Importance and Role of Performance Appraisal. In *Personnel Management and Industrial Relations Readings*, pp. 71–72. UWIDITE, University of the West Indies, Kingston: University Press.

Meyer J.P., N.J. Allen, and C.A. Smith. (1993). Commitment to Organizations and Occupations: Extension and Test of a Three-Component Conceptualization. *Journal of Applied Psychology*, 78: 538–551.

Mills, O. (1994). Leadership and the Culture of Change. In *Personnel Management and Industrial Relations Readings*, pp. 133–137. UWIDITE, University of the West Indies, Kingston, Jamaica: University Press.

Minzberg, H. (1996). Managing Government, Governing Management. *Harvard Business Review*, 74: 75–83.

Mowday, R.T., L.W. Porter, and R.M. Steers. (1982). *Employee-Organization Linkages: The Psychology of Commitment, Absenteeism, and Turnover*. New York: Academic Press.

Mowday, R.T., R.M. Steers, and L.W. Porter. (1979). The Measurement of Organizational Commitment. *Journal of Vocational Behavior*, 14: 43–77.

Munroe, T. (1992, September). Partnership in Labor Relations. *Caribbean Labour Journal*, 3(3): 27.

Naff, K. C. (1993). Human Resources Management Support. In P. Cooper (Ed.), *Public Administration for the Twenty-First Century*, p. 285. Fort Worth, TX: Harcourt Brace.

National Partnership for Reinventing Government. (1998). *Vice President Gore's National Partnership for Reinventing Government Summary of Accomplishments: 1993–1998*. Available at http://www.npr.gov/accompli.

Perry, J.L., and L.R. Wise. (1990). The Motivational Bases of Public Service. *Public Administration Review*, 50: 367–373.

Rainey, H.G. (1997). *Understanding and Managing Public Organizations*. 2nd ed. San Francisco, CA: Jossey-Bass.

Reichers, A.E. (1986). Conflict and Organizational Commitments. *Journal of Applied Psychology*, 71: 508–514.

Reichers, A.E. (1985). A Review and Reconceptualization of Organizational Commitment. *Academy of Management Review*, 10: 485–476.

Report of Task Force on Work Attitudes to the Right Honorable Edward Seaga, P.C. Prime Minister of Jamaica, March 1983, 11–12.

Romzek, B. (1990). Employee Investment and Commitment: The Ties That Bind. *Public Administration Review*, 50: 374–382.

Schein, E.H. (1988). *Organizational Culture and Leadership: A Dynamic View*. San Francisco, CA: Jossey-Bass Inc.

Steers, R.M., and S.R. Rhodes. (1978). Major Influences on Employee Attendance: A Process Model. *Journal of Applied Psychology*, 63: 391–407.

Stone, C. (1983). *Findings of the Stone Survey*. Kingston, Jamaica: JIS Press.

U.S. Department of Labor. (1996). *Working Together for Public Service*. Washington, DC: Government Printing Office.

7

"Strategic Planning" as Fakery: Government Does It While Pretending It Does Not

FREDERICK THAYER

Schools of public and/or business administration have in recent decades included courses, perhaps several of them, training future executives in "how to DO strategy." This activity supposedly involves "integration" and "holistic thinking" dedicated to the health, growth, success, and sustainability of individual public sector agencies or individual corporations and nonprofit organizations. Yet an entire nation-state needs a truly comprehensive plan to mobilize, equip, and train a huge military force to fight and (hopefully) "win" a long war against one or more enemy nation-states, or perhaps guerrilla and insurgency forces, and to then manage such aftermaths as the occupation of those combat areas. In October 2005, for example, the U.S. special inspector general for Iraq reconstruction concluded that "the U.S. government had no comprehensive policy or regulatory guidelines in place" for post-hostilities Iraq, and that "systematic planning was insufficient in both scope and implementation" (Kirchgaesser, 2005). "Strategic" planning, therefore, can easily fall short of what is needed, even by the nation-state. The larger point is that individual corporations and public agencies are incapable of strategic planning, and we all should stop pretending otherwise.

Many of the concepts and the language of nonmilitary strategy are borrowed from military experience. I begin this critique of theory and practice in strategic planning by noting that both corporate and public agency concepts involve the bitter and intense competition and conflict that have in the past included the use of military force. Economic "trade" has often been conducted by military forces capable of imposing and enforcing "agreements."

I then explain how strategic thinking suddenly became important to the U.S. private sector in the early 1980s, during the deepest economic recession since the Great Depression of the 1930s. The United States became fascinated with the exploding Japanese economy and that country's seeming dedication to long-term thinking and central planning. I look next at the use and problems of strategic planning in U.S. corporations and the U.S. public sector.

I then try to explain how governments at all levels within the United States and in other countries have taken over strategic planning while pretending not to do so. Government policy decisions initiate all important trends in corporate and public agency planning, not the publicized but irrelevant "visions" of corporate leaders, and not the "needs assessments" of public agencies presumably dedicated to solving public policy problems. While government decisions are not always coordinated with each other, as in decisions by independent U.S. courts and the Federal Reserve Board, all such decisions have enormous authority. Strategic planning is as much a governmental function everywhere else as it ever was in say, the former Soviet Union, and it is folly to pretend otherwise as the United States does. I will look at some specific examples of that folly. Finally, I will look at the implications for public personnel planning or, as it is often labeled these days, Human Resources Management.

Three additional points should be made at the outset. The first is that when strategic planning became important in the United States in the early to mid-1980s, the ambience of corporations and public agencies was vastly different than it became by the end of the 20th century. The nature of the change was from relative stability, despite the deep recession of the early 1980s, to an everincreasing instability of organizational existence, employee job security, and expectations of comfortable retirement for both private and public sector employees. To put it mildly, instability creates widespread fear among all those affected by strategic planning. The second point is that the massive changes became threatening enough to corporate leaders to incite widespread corruption, as in intentional misreporting of financial results that has misled investors and governments, overcharged government agencies when performing contracted public services, and increased the need for politicians to reward campaign contributors with contracts that are lucrative enough to permit future contributions. The third point, a natural follow-on, is that textbooks about strategic planning cannot possibly keep up with everincreasing turbulence. Students and professors have little choice but to pay close attention to day-to-day reports of unpredicted changes in supposedly long-term strategic plans. Even a 3-year-old textbook had become woefully obsolete by 2004.

MILITARY PLANNING: WAR, FOREIGN POLICY, AND LYING

To develop a military strategy is to create a "vision" of "winning" a very tough contest that also creates "losers." The success of a country at war does not mean that all the noncombatant citizens of that country will survive and prosper. Casualties of all kinds are likely and unpredictable in number. Many of those who engage in combat will be mentally and/or physically disabled for life. National leaders are unlikely to reveal all the elements of their strategy because they cannot risk having enemies learn about that strategy. Lying to their own citizens, including those likely to be killed, becomes a basic part of the strategy itself. Leaders may indeed command subordinates to kill innocent noncombatants, including children, to make the war as brief as possible. Massive and repeated firebombing of major cities, and the use of nuclear weapons, were parts of U.S. strategy in the latter stages of World War II, events that might have been labeled war crimes if the United States had lost the war. There is little doubt that some "detainees" captured in Afghanistan or during and after the invasion of Iraq in 2001–2005 have been tortured and/or killed (Mayer, 2005).

Strategic principles hold that it is more important to win than to worry about what must be done in order to win. It can be helpful to be cold and impersonal about enemy casualties, but it can also help to hate or despise an enemy, no matter how untruthful the instruments of such motivation may be. It is impossible to overstate the implications of war-fighting strategies. By mid-2005, the United States was supporting approval of the first draft of a new constitution for Iraq, and approval could indeed become significant. The United States, however, popularly celebrates the July 4, 1776, Declaration of Independence as the founding U.S. document even though the U.S. Constitution was not ratified until the late 1780s. The Declaration remains a statement of abstract principles while the original Constitution included provisions to preserve slavery that Americans now prefer to avoid reading.

The Declaration proclaimed the "inalienable rights" of humans to "life, liberty, and the pursuit of happiness." Leaving aside all issues except the connection of "rights" with "strategy," it is obvious that a "Right to Life" has never played a part in nation-state strategy. When a national government can draft its citizens to fight and die for the preservation of the nation-state, there can be no "Right to Life." Recent debates about such issues as abortion and stem cell research, therefore, are examples of reductionist and inaccurate thinking. Why "save" the unborn from "murder" if government later compels those children to fight and die for the sake of national survival?

If lying is inevitable in the conduct of foreign and security policy, observers can only speculate about its extent. Nobody can expect "transparency," that is, the ability to look inside a government and clearly ascertain what policies are being pursued and why. There is no reason to assume that any speech by a national leader is entirely truthful, especially when matters of war and peace are involved.

The need to lie is also an all-encompassing principle of management in hierarchical organizations. When a leader decides to act, subordinates are expected to support that decision. If they believe the decision is erroneous, they are expected to pretend they endorse it. Those at the bottom must believe that the orders have the full support of everyone above them. When intermediate levels of the chain of command express their support for a decision, therefore, who can know if they are being entirely truthful? Strategic planning and its implementation in any type of organization, therefore, must assume that at least some expressions of support for the decisions of organizational leadership are at best insincere and, at worst, lies.

The chief advantage of the military version of strategic planning is that it encompasses all the human and materiel resources that a national government has decided to bring to bear in a particular war. The other forms of strategic planning to be mentioned here (by individual corporations and public agencies) are much narrower in scope, and are usually so relatively minor as to be unworthy of the label "strategic." The scope of U.S. military involvement in World War II was indeed huge, amounting to something between 11 and 15 million members of the armed services. Even so, the size of such an operation relative to the perceived power of a nation-state can be so misleading in appearance as to hide the disadvantages that can more than overcome the advantages of scope.

In recent years, U.S. strategic planners believed that invading Iraq, toppling an authoritarian regime, and establishing a "new democracy" would be a relatively easy task. The planners minimized the possibility that a post-invasion insurgency would involve the United States and some "coalition partners" in urban guerrilla warfare that always results in extensive civilian casualties. When the United States toppled the regime in South Vietnam in 1963, the post-regime military conflict ultimately involved some 500,000 members of the U.S. military before the United States retreated in chaotic conditions in 1975. The Korean War that began in 1950 had not been officially ended by 2005, remaining in an armistice negotiated in 1953 after the United States was compelled to pull back from its attempt to "unify" North and South Korea. Most Americans do not realize that their continuing celebration of the U.S. invasion of Western Europe in 1944 ignores the fact that the Soviet-German land war was 400 percent larger than the Western front, thereby giving the Soviets post-war control of Eastern Europe. Americans who now celebrate the Civil War as one that "saved" or "created" the Union, largely Northerners, do not understand why many Southerners still label that conflict as the War of Northern Aggression.

No matter how broad the scope of strategic planning, it cannot expect to control outcomes once the planning is implemented. Many enemy reactions will be unanticipated, compelling revisions to strategic planning on virtually a daily basis. Decisions made in big or small wars will be debated for years as to their logic and effectiveness. Americans still debate whether the United States should have tried to enter Berlin ahead of the Soviets in 1945, and whether the United States should have dropped nuclear bombs on Japan later that year. Even at the level of the total nation-state, the broadest strategic planning imaginable can control only a fraction of the important factors that will affect long-term outcomes. The "unknowables" are far too many.

THE EMERGENCE OF STRATEGIC PLANNING IN THE 1980s

The sudden prominence of strategic planning in the 1980s should have been a reminder that economic strategies owe much to concepts of military strategy. As the United States suffered a steep recession, with annual unemployment rates rising to 9.9 percent (just short of the 10.0 percent that is the unofficial indicator of serious depression-like downturn), the United States appeared to be losing its dominant position in the world economy to its 1940s enemy. The Japanese economy was fast expanding, buying into other economies around the world, and seemingly demonstrating new managerial and manufacturing techniques that might revolutionize economies everywhere. In retrospect, the fears were overdone, if very real at the time.

The United States needed a U.S. "victory." Americans had to adopt and adapt to Japanese practices, then outdo them at their own game. Some observers credited the Japanese with superior national planning by the Ministry of International Trade and Industry (MITI). While U.S. corporations were accused of giving too much attention to "short term" planning, 3 months at a time, MITI appeared to have master plans based upon helping industries to increase Japan's long-term global dominance, especially in consumer electronics and automobiles. The United States also accused Japan on numerous occasions of selling television sets and steel in the United States at prices that were below production costs, the typical "dumping" accusation that accompanies "trade wars." The United States said it was averse to creating a "planned economy," but did help automakers, especially Chrysler, temporarily recover from the Japanese automobile invasion. In actuality, the Arab-OPEC embargoes of the 1970s had caused Americans to look for smaller autos, a necessity in overcrowded Japan, so that Japanese central planning to export autos in the United States had little to do with auto sales.

Americans credited the Japanese with miraculous increases in quality control, especially in automobiles, an improvement that became known as Total Quality Management (TQM). Ironically, Japan did not invent TQM, donated to Japan as part of U.S. post-World War II foreign policy during the cold war with the Soviets. The United States made Japan a part of a containment strategy aimed at a presumed alliance of the Soviet Union and Communist China. The United States exported the management and quality control expertise of Western Electric, a subsidiary of AT&T, but later chose to de-emphasize American contributions because AT&T was broken up during the "deregulation fever" of the United States that began in the 1970s. Japan, a country without an excellent system of higher education and research, was given too much credit for what turned out to be its temporary ascendance. Indeed, U.S. business interests chose to blame American public schools for a "failure" to adequately prepare workers, a well-mounted campaign that initiated the movement for public school "reform" in this country.

An important aspect of Japanese industrial expansion remains overlooked even now. Not long after World War II, the Japanese (with U.S. approval) replaced Communist control of labor unions by guaranteeing the jobs of about 30 percent of the workforce, principally those in major industries. The job security of Toyota employees, a typical example, made them wholly receptive to TQM innovation. When in the later 1980s and early 1990s, TQM was brought back into U.S. industry, TQM expert W. Edwards Deming listed as one of its major requirements the need to "remove fear" among employees afraid of losing jobs. U.S. manufacturers who used TQM then promised workers they would not lose their jobs, an impossible guarantee. In this first decade of the 21st century, most "innovations" seek to reduce wages and eliminate jobs, thereby reducing employee morale.

STRATEGIC PLANNING AND CORPORATIONS: GROPING IN THE DARK

Strategic corporate planning suffers from a schizophrenia that, once understood, makes such planning at the level of the individual firm an impossible dream. This schizophrenia bounces corporate planners back and forth in ways that make wholly accidental any relationship between planning and outcomes. Corporations actually react to the "hidden hand" policies of uncoordinated planning by national and subnational governments, a sort of non-Soviet version of Soviet thinking that has the effect of compelling firms to constantly change direction. Planning and basic economic concepts contradict each other.

Americans do not study in depth the consequences of the principles of economics. In a paradigmatic free market, for example, the competitive ideal is that no single producer can be powerful enough to influence prices and industry-wide output. A firm's "strategic plan," therefore, cannot be a blueprint for that firm's desired "results" because the firm cannot in principle control those "results." A free market (local, national, or global) is a form of economic anarchy (unrestricted competition) that cannot be expected to move toward equilibrium, yet this is another doctrine of free market operations. These economic principles are little discussed in business school courses on strategic planning or management.

Long-term intellectual disputes are almost forgotten. Historians once successfully argued that the cause of major economic collapses was "overproduction," an overall definition that included "excessive competition," "redundancy of output," and "overinvestment/overcapacity" in the production of consumer goods that created an inevitable surplus of consumer goods and services relative to effective demand for those goods and services. Economists, conversely, have now successfully argued that chronic overproduction is impossible because according to Say's 1802 Law of Markets, supply always creates its own demand. As recently as the early years of the Great Depression in the 1930s, the historians' view prevailed in U.S. policymaking circles, but it gave way even in the late 1930s to the seeming precision of economic analysis. The dominant paradigm of free markets holds that the unrestricted or unregulated production of consumer goods and services is generally self-correcting and without massive disruption of social stability.

Antitrust laws prohibit individual corporate managers from engaging in multifirm planning because that would constitute "collusion" or "conspiracy in restraint of trade." This doctrine also established the fiduciary responsibility of corporate managers to protect and advance the financial interests of their shareholders, a requirement that compels managers to keep all important information about future plans wholly secret from competitors. Individual firms develop strategic plans without knowing what their competitors plan to do, otherwise describable as "planning in the dark." Globalism, conversely, ultimately threatens to require global designs that will have to abandon all contemporary approaches to strategic planning. Without some form of agreed global planning, nation-states are likely to revert to historic patterns of military competition for control of important resources.

In a globally competitive market, all producing countries follow the rules of competition that are the same for all ideologies. The global economy is not a "capitalist" economy. Multinational corporations can operate in many countries regardless of the stated ideologies of those countries. "Socialists" must attract buyers by ensuring that their workers earn very low wages, quietly abandoning the socialist dogma that workers are in control.

The schizophrenia of strategic planning is also demonstrated by the pretense that the success or failure of a corporation is a byproduct of the "vision" of its top leadership. Jack Welch, the now retired CEO of General Electric, was still lionized in 2005 as the most effective corporate chieftain in memory, but others honored earlier (the CEO of Enron, for example) were later identified as having cheated or having been duped by subordinates. This American pretense requires that corporations and especially their CEOs be identified as having real control over their destiny. Jack Welch typified in 2005 how corporate planning had suddenly changed for unexpected reasons. During a book tour with a stop in London, Welch faced 638 business executives who had paid $350 each for a 1-hour question period (Sanghera, 2005). He casually mentioned the famous management concept of the "old" Welch, and then added a concept of the "new" Welch.

His original "20–70–10" concept divided employees into a "top" 20 percent group, paid lavish bonuses for their performance, a "middle" 70 percent urged to do more, and a "bottom" 10 percent to be quickly terminated instead of keeping them around until a "downturn" forced them out when they were no longer employable. The "new" Jack Welch added that in responding to Chinese competition, "just trimming costs by 4 percent is not enough!" Declaring this a "road to suicide," Welch added, "you need to think about taking out 30 to 40 percent!" His audience responded with loud applause (Sanghera, 2005). To cut costs by 30 to 40 percent would require the "new" Welch to drastically cut wages and benefits while dumping pensions for perhaps 80 percent of his workforce, perhaps more than that.

The "old" Jack Welch was known as "Neutron Jack" when he took over at GE near the end of the steep recession of the early 1980s. His first task was to reduce the workforce and institute a yearly program of terminating managers he thought substandard. While this strategic plan emphasized job security for the top 20 percent of employees, the "new" Jack Welch plan would be much more drastic if he were in a position to implement it. What he did not tell his audience was that his hypothetical plan actually was a response to U.S. government guidelines designed to help businesses survive in a bitterly competitive world, at whatever costs to the jobs and income of workers.

It is not possible to outline in detail a number of examples of the strategic plans designed by individual corporations because such plans do not meet a "transparency" test. The details of such plans are not publicly released, nor are the data that lead to specific decisions. Any single-firm plan is developed in the blind, so to speak, except when government guidelines form the basis of the plan. The word "transparency" is in wide circulation these days, but corporations are very opaque organizations except for financial reports subject to detailed auditing by regulatory agencies.

STRATEGIC PLANNING AND PUBLIC ADMINISTRATION

The concept of strategic planning for nonmilitary public agencies has always included the desirability of long-term stability in planning, legislative authorization, appropriations for human and material resources, and implementation. There have been dreams of multiyear federal budgeting, perhaps as long as 5 years, but U.S. policymakers have shied away from the Soviet example of 5-year plans (*Gosplans*). Worse yet, U.S. principles on how to manage public affairs and, by definition, the teaching of these principles in the academic field of Public Administration are mired in the textbook principles of economics and even Biblical principles, neither of which is ever reexamined. I shall briefly outline a few of these principles, then show how they have affected such recent and important policy problems as welfare "reform," the national response to such disasters as the 2005 hurricane-related flooding of the Gulf Coast in Louisiana and Mississippi, and the Medicaid health care program for those living in poverty.

A fundamental principle of economics is that because prosperity and progress depend upon the health of the private economy, government spending should be kept as low as possible so as to not to "deprive" the private economy of the resources it needs. Essentially, economics teaches that government spending on public goods produces only "waste" because such goods are not sold in the marketplace. The production of private goods and services, conversely, creates "wealth." The building and equipping of a brewery is officially considered an "investment," but the public bridge necessary to travel to and from the brewery is not so counted. Even when public spending is considered necessary and unavoidable, this doctrine encourages underfunding that is then publicly labeled as "adequate" even when it is obviously insufficient.

A second principle holds that if government borrows money to incur deficits (spending exceeds revenues) and an increased national debt, the borrowing and spending "crowds out" the private sector from borrowing the capital it needs for the creation of "wealth" and, by increasing the competition for the funds available from "savings," pushes up interest rates and causes inflation. This remains a standard argument, but it has been obsolete for decades, since the United States abandoned commodity-based currency (gold standard) in favor of a fiat monetary system. Put simply, there cannot be a shortage of available capital in a fiat economy because the money supply is not limited by the amount of gold at Fort Knox, Kentucky. It is indeed extraordinary that arguments of this sort still dominate U.S. policy discourse.

A third and related principle is drawn from the *Bible*. In 2 Thessalonians 3:10 (*Paul's Second Letter to the Thessalonians*), the principle is stated as "He who does not work shall not eat." Taken literally, the principle condemns any and all "handouts," "entitlements" or other financial rewards except in return for work actually performed. The principle assumes that the only bar to work is an individual's willingness to do so. Paul's command includes no list of mitigating circumstances such as disability, age (old or young), health, or childraising. The principle was widely quoted by advocates of welfare "reform" in the 1990s, a "reform" that also demonstrated the bipartisan power of such principles. Ironically, the same principle appeared in the Soviet Constitutions of 1918 and 1936, advertised as a "socialist" principle that would compel "capitalists" to perform work themselves rather than having their money "work" for them. The principle may have been introduced into Russia about a 1,000 years ago when the Prince of Kiev imported Byzantine priests to operate labor camps. It was and is amazing that a single sentence of this sort can be successfully used to ignore all the complexities of poverty and unemployment (Thayer, 1995a). I turn to three examples of strategic planning and public policy deeply affected by such principles.

Case: Welfare "Reform." Many Americans believe that jobs are always available for those who exert the effort needed to find them. While most Americans agree that it is legitimate for those who can afford it to pay "nannies," cooks, or maids for child care and household work, many do not think it legitimate for society as a whole, acting through government, to pay single parents for performing all those tasks when also holding full-time jobs. While the initial "reform" debates of the 1990s included references to "Boys' Town" and other orphanages of the miserable 1930s, this did not become a popular argument. Two very real problems were almost ignored in the furious attempt to "save" a relatively few dollars by throwing people off welfare rolls. The first was that everyone admitted that a comprehensive "reform" would have to include job training and child care programs financed and supervised by government. The "reform" ultimately did not include such comprehensive programs because they would have violated the principle of "spend as little as possible."

The second problem, totally ignored in "reform" debates, was that the federal government already had in place a long-term policy to make sure that the overall unemployment rate was always high enough to discourage those who had jobs from demanding higher wages because they were afraid of being replaced. This unemployment rate was known as NAIRU (Non-Accelerating Inflation Rate of Unemployment), and has long played a part in Federal Reserve interest rate decisions to "stimulate" or "cool off" the economy. The policy was endorsed in the yearly economic reports of all presidents from the mid-1960s onward. The standard view was that a 6.0 percent rate would prevent wage increases from causing inflation. At a time when welfare "reform" was a hot issue, President Clinton's chief economist wrote in the *New York Times* that she and her fellow presidential economic advisers believed that a 5.9–6.3 percent unemployment rate was necessary to prevent wage-push inflation (Tyson, 1994), a declaration that amounted to a Clinton policy statement. The rates for minorities and young people were much higher, even up to 30 percent in some cases, a condition that had been in effect since the mid-1970s. In effect, NAIRU was and still is a policy of compulsory unemployment because the "desired" unemployment rate has been a target of public policy. It should have been obvious that many poor and young single parents would not be able to find jobs, training, and child care. Throwing them off the welfare rolls, however, removed them from the database, a normal 19th-century method of pretending that a problem does not exist.

The concept of welfare for single parents originated about 1910, and the original thought was that those on welfare would not be expected or required to work outside the home. That, too, was a form of strategic planning, as the country gradually began to understand that church-operated orphanages and nongovernment programs to ship urban orphans to farm states where they could be supported in return for working could not do the job, and that it made sense to pay poverty-ridden single parents for taking care of their children. At the turn of the 20th century, the United States had suffered through two major economic collapses in the past 25 years, with poverty and homelessness everywhere.

As the United States approached the 21st century, however, there had been no truly major economic collapse since the 1930s. It was easy to return to the traditional and Biblical view that the poor were to blame for their predicament and that both adults and their children should be punished by forcing the parents to look for nonexistent full-time jobs. It was easy to ignore the NAIRU policy of compulsory unemployment and not even mention it in the same breath as welfare "reform." Sadly, this "reform" was wholly bipartisan.

Case: Katrina and the New Orleans Levees, 2005. The key factor for New Orleans was the breaching of levees by a hurricane that strategic planning had not officially anticipated. Proposals to refurbish the levees had been considered in the Army Corps of Engineers annual analyses for some years, but the primary reason for repeated rejections should be included in any course that looks both at strategic planning and such analytical tools as cost-benefit analysis.

Katrina arrived at New Orleans as a "Category 4" hurricane, one below the maximum of Category 5. Past legislation had authorized protecting the city against Category 3 storms. The issue was and is how the Army Engineers perform their cost-benefit analyses when looking at particular natural disasters that may recur only once in every 50, 100, or 200 years, very critical for a city that is subject to flooding because it is below sea level. Overall spending on public infrastructure amounted to about 3 percent of GDP from the mid-1950s until the end of the 1960s, and it began declining to less than 2 percent in the 1980s and 1990s (recall that such spending is considered economically "wasteful").

The assistant secretary for the army who supervised civil works spending, John Paul Woodley, acknowledged that when the "benefits" are compared against the "costs" of proposed improvements, short-term "benefits" take precedence over "benefits" that may only be realized at some unpredictable time in the distant future. Another Army spokesman stated, "it's not economically feasible to protect against a 500-year storm." An expert in coastal research asserted that "in order to know what a 100-year storm is, you probably need 1,000 years of data" (Uchitelle, 2005; Strauss, 2005). Cost-benefit analysis, therefore, becomes more a gamble or a lottery than a scientific method. Conceivably, refurbishing of levees might never be approved with contemporary cost-benefit concepts.

Whether the potential problem is one of national disaster, terrorist attack, or some other responsibility of the Department of Homeland Security (DHS), the basic requirement is for wholly integrated federal, state, and local plans that would include the specific details of what every agency at every level of government would be expected to do in the event of each foreseeable event that might arise, and prospective private contractors would have to be involved in the planning process and paid for that participation, a need that might not be compatible with procurement practices. This large library of strategic plans would have to be updated very frequently, at least annually or whenever new and important information became available. A strategic plan for DHS alone, or a plan for FEMA alone, would be irrelevant.

Contrast this requirement with the White House Office of Management and Budget (OMB) evaluation of some 1,300 individual federal programs for their planning and performance. Each evaluation is separate from any of the other 1,299 programs that might affect the evaluated program. Even when an agency has "outsourced" mission performance to private contractors, the performance of contractors is not reviewed as part of the evaluation. Strategic planning, that is to say, is usually treated in a fragmented and reductionist fashion, one program at a time or one agency at a time. While management "overlap" is widely condemned as an indication of waste, especially by loud politicians who scream about "bloated bureaucracies," overlap is virtually automatic in the performance of most public functions, even at low levels of government. Safe drinking water always must combine at least the functions of public works and health, and their performance must be integrated.

Case: Medicaid. An outgrowth of the "War on Poverty" initiated in the 1960s was the federal program to provide health care for the poor. After spending 16 months at the Morris Heights Health Center in New York City's Borough of the Bronx, a journalist began a lengthy 2005 report by outlining the case of a fifth-grade girl with an irregular heartbeat. The primary physician told her parents that the girl could not get an appointment with a cardiac specialist for almost 6 months, one of several such examples. Reimbursements managed by the state were so low that many specialists were refusing Medicaid patients. Many poor citizens have little education and are not very familiar with the English language.

They cannot cope very well with six-page applications for enrollment that they must submit every year, along with extensive documentation that proves their eligibility. A former health law chief of the Legal Aid Society said, "the state looks at each applicant as a potential criminal." The president of United Hospital Fund, a research group, added "we look upon Medicaid as a welfare program, so it's given grudgingly." At any time, more than one-fifth of those eligible in the state were not enrolled because their annual re-enrollment had not been completed. Because Medicaid is handled by states through HMO systems, primary physicians often must battle insurers to get permission to refer patients to specialists. (Perez-Pena, 2005). It has long been known that the administrative costs of HMO systems are enormously high relative to the classical contrary example of Medicare, principally because of the extensive arguments and negotiations between physicians and insurers over what treatment is needed, case-by-case. Medicaid patients and primary care physicians generally are not well equipped to fight the HMO systems in which they are trapped.

The Bush administration approved in October 2005 the first of what it hopes will be many drastic changes in how states administer Medicaid. Based upon individual medical histories, the state of Florida will "cap" the amount of money available for each individual, with such decisions to be made largely by HMO managers (Pear, 2005). While children under 21 and pregnant women will be exempted, others will suddenly find themselves with "medical savings accounts." Medical histories, recent or long-term, are not necessarily useful enough to predict what will happen to each individual in the next few years, so this becomes another example of gamble with lotteries advertised as careful analysis of the needs of the poor. What will happen with individuals if and when their yearly "caps" have been exceeded? A senior researcher at Georgetown University's Health Policy Institute labeled the new system "radical," in that decisions will be made by private health plans "out of public view." The objective of the HMOs, of course, is to increase their profits.

The ostensible purpose of Medicaid is to provide whatever medical treatments are needed by the poor. The purpose of the Florida system, intended to be used as a "model" elsewhere, is to reduce health care spending even if this adds health risks to Medicaid "customers" by denying them services that would raise total costs above the "caps" that vary from person to person. A corollary and unemphasized objective is to help Medicaid providers cover their big administrative costs while also making significant profits from reducing the delivery of health care that might have been necessary. Some poor people will die because their medical support will be "capped." Studying Medicaid alone, of course, is misleading. The number of Americans living below poverty level was increasing as of 2005, and so was the number of Americans who have no health insurance at all.

U.S. health care has been attacked in recent decades as encouraging excessive use of available care by physicians who order too many tests of their patients, and individual consumers who avail themselves of health care they really do not need.

Such arguments amount to claiming that if I have an annual physical examination, and if the examination shows that I am in excellent health, this demonstrates that the examination wasn't really needed. Yet neither the physician nor I knew before the examination that nothing was wrong with me ("preventative" care is not cheap). The classic case of such fallacious thinking involved then President George H. W. Bush more than a decade ago. A recently completed annual examination had found him in excellent health. Shortly thereafter, he suddenly felt bad enough to be checked for particular symptoms, at which time he was found to have a significant thyroid problem. A test for this problem had been removed from his annual examination because the probability of a negative result was as low as having Katrina breach levees in New Orleans. The fact that any test ordered by a physician finds no problems does not mean the test should not have been ordered. The fact that the U.S. president was not given a test he should have been given indicates that his examination was less thorough than it should have been.

It is worth noting that the only public purpose that has been adequately funded in my lifetime was World War II. The resolute prohibition of full funding for other public purposes comes from an economic ideology that is all-pervasive in the United States, but is never reexamined despite powerful evidence that it is totally wrong. This is as good an entry point as any for introducing how strategic planning in the private, public and nonprofit sectors is controlled by a collection of decisions made by U.S. government agencies that do not formally coordinate decisions that are made independently of each other.

IDEOLOGY AND GOVERNMENT AS THE REAL STRATEGIC PLANNERS

Following President Clinton's prediction that a steady diet of federal budget surpluses would totally wipe out the national debt in 12 years, Democratic candidate Al Gore endorsed the forecast that this would be the first such celebration since President Andrew Jackson had paid off the debt in 1835–1836. Republican candidate George W. Bush set his target at 15 years, and Americans were advised to look forward to sustained prosperity. Ideology was so embedded in American thinking that nobody even noticed the record of history.Table 7.1 lists the only five great economic depressions of U.S. history. Each depression occurred immediately following a multiyear sustained reduction in the national debt through budget surpluses. After 14 consecutive paydown years, Andrew Jackson left office with virtually no debt left behind. Sadly, a 6-year major economic slump immediately followed. Massive debt paydowns immediately preceded the other four economic collapses. Reducing the national debt has never led to sustained economic prosperity, but just the opposite. Depressions used to occur with some frequency, but it has been 60+ years since the Great Depression ended with World War II, and deficit spending has been chronic throughout that period. Deficits and the national debt never seem to have damaged the economy. These relationships may all be coincidences of history, but why is it automatically assumed that federal spending and deficits harm the economy? Why must the federal

TABLE 7.1.

BUDGET SURPLUSES AND MAJOR DEPRESSIONS

---

1. 1823-36: In 14 years, the debt was reduced by 99.7 percent, to $38,000 (virtual zero). The major depression began in 1837, lasting until 1843. Americans still celebrate this payoff of the national debt, ignoring the collapse that followed.
2. 1852-57: In six years, the debt was reduced by 59 percent, to $28.7 million. The major depression began in 1857, ending only with the Civil War.
3. 1867-73: In seven years, the debt was reduced by 27 percent, to $2.2 billion. The major depression began in 1873, lasting until 1878. A bleak Centennial celebration and disastrous presidential election struggle occurred in 1876.
4. 1880-93: In 14 years, the debt was reduced by 57 percent, to $1 billion. The major depression began in 1893, lasting until 1898 and casting a pall over the "Gay Nineties."
5. 1920-30: In 11 years, the debt was reduced by 36 percent, to $16.2 billion. The Great Depression began in 1929, ending only with World War II in 1941. According to standard economic principles, the annual deficits and national debt caused by that war damaged the economy, but there is no evidence to support that conclusion. The national debt reached about 125 percent of GDP during the war (by far the highest in our history), ended the depression, won the war, and nobody said these outcomes were too expensive.

There have been no major collapses since the Great Depression, but deficit spending has been almost continuous since then. All "recessions" have immediately followed sustained deficit reductions relative to GDP. The most recent downward cycle, just after the 21st century began, followed that pattern.

Source: (Data from Historical Statistics of the United States, available in all libraries). Adapted from Thayer, 1995a.

government always underfund important public services because economic ideology holds that public spending is dangerous? Those who develop strategic plans in public agencies know full well that such plans are likely to be underfunded, the single exception having been World War II.

The evidence does not "prove" that a cause-effect relationship exists between federal budget surpluses and paydowns of the national debt on the one hand, and major economic collapses on the other hand. History shows only that truly significant reductions in the national debt have never sustained economic prosperity. The record does suggest, however, the necessity to bring to the surface and analyze the likely falsehoods embedded in what American policymakers say about the public purposes they seek to fulfill. Concepts and slogans such as "needs assessment" and "zero-based budgeting" have been used to imply that the first step should be an honest analysis of what must be done to achieve a desirable public purpose. The word "need" suggests that an obvious "need" should be totally fulfilled, but economic ideology says otherwise.

The point is that almost without exception, elected political leaders at all levels of American government come to office with the express intention of spending as little as possible on the delivery of public services. The belief is wholly bipartisan, and either of the two major parties in the United States can be counted upon to criticize the other if it appears that spending is higher than it need be. Deficit spending is almost always subject to attack, with the single and unusual exception of World War II. Even Franklin Roosevelt promised to balance the federal budget during his 1936 campaign, at a time when the unemployment rate was 17 percent. Immediately following a landslide victory, he promised to do immediate budget balancing, and drastically cut spending and deficits, at which time an economy already in deep depression collapsed once again.

Let me summarize other major guidelines that the informal American system of governmental planning imposes upon private, public, and nonprofit sectors:

1. The NAIRU policy, mentioned in connection with welfare reform, keeps unemployment high enough to depress wage increases. The primary method of implementing the NAIRU policy is for each presidential administration to implicitly endorse the Federal Reserve Board's decisions to change interest rates from time to time so as to control inflation, mainly by "slowing" job creation so that wages will remain stagnant or decline. Decisions in the White House and Congress to not push for increases in the minimum wage and have reduced the purchasing power of that wage to much less than it was in 1968. The Federal Reserve Board is an independent agency, but interest rate changes and inaction on the minimum wage give every appearance of being coordinated policies that have significant bipartisan support. The overall effect is to create massive unemployment among minorities and young people. High and compulsory unemployment has served to almost destroy collective bargaining and union strength. The union movement has begun to splinter as other union leaders complain that the AFL-CIO president is not performing well, but in point of fact, unions are essentially powerless. The most astonishing aspects of the NAIRU policy are that it compels decision makers to fear full employment and to deny forced unemployment

2. U.S. companies find it difficult to compete with companies based in low-wage countries. This has caused desperate searches for cost cutting, as in the remarks Jack Welch made to British business executives. The Supreme Court, in a unanimous 1984 decision, said that companies in financial trouble could abrogate labor contracts, and neither employees nor unions have found a way around that decision. Bankruptcy courts follow this guidance by approving wage and benefit cuts along with the dumping of pensions that were once an important part of planning for all firms. Indeed, bankruptcy became by 2004 the widely understood and frequently used "tool" for making massive cuts in labor costs (Nocera, 2005). Frank Lorenzo, then CEO of Continental Airlines, was seen as a cruel manager when he tore up union contracts a few years after airline deregulation in 1978 but after unanimous Supreme Court approval in 1984 of what he had done, bankruptcy gradually became the accepted method for "busting" union contracts involving wages, benefits, and pensions. Many retirees, too young for Medicare and Social Security, have lost company benefits once promised them for life.

The pension crisis is perhaps the best example of how supposedly uncoordinated decisions can come together to create a unified policy. Frank Lorenzo was the airline president who was later widely condemned for the decisions he made, but his tactics have become unacknowledged public policies. The Supreme Court unanimously endorsed the decisions he made without negotiating with unions (Greenhouse, 1984), and Congress followed by endorsing the same processes so long as bankruptcy court judges approved them. As of 2005, Professor Elizabeth Warren of Harvard, an expert on bankruptcy law, concluded that "There's no business in America that isn't going to figure out a way to get rid of [these promised benefits]" (Delaney, 1992; Barlett and Steele, 2005). The special irony of the pension crisis is that there is in reality a cohesive and integrated policy that has been changed only trivially from Lorenzo's first decisions. He abandoned labor contracts, and the Supreme Court, Congress, and White House ultimately agreed. None of them would acknowledge if asked, however, that it was responsible for a cohesive and integrated policy. As of 2006, there is no way to predict how many elderly people will be driven into poverty by the pension crisis, and what government ultimately may feel compelled to do about it. Decisions to make it possible for corporations to terminate labor contracts and dump pensions are about as "strategic" as can be imagined, but government opened doors that business executives could not have opened by themselves.

3. State and local governments must intensely compete with each other to persuade businesses to move into their states and cities. The vehicle for doing this is tax abatements and other financial breaks that give companies a "free ride" for some specified period of time such as 5 years. When it comes time to begin paying local taxes, the companies move elsewhere. This has caused communities all over the country to drastically raise property taxes, and elderly people on small incomes are likely to lose their homes in large numbers. Local politicians are widely seen as incompetent, but they are trapped in a system of competitive bidding that compels them to provide big subsidies for new businesses.

4. Because public spending is considered wasteful, bipartisan public policy increasingly supports the notion that as many public services as possible should be "outsourced" or "contracted out" by all levels of government. One effect is to substitute a contractor's motivation for profit for the public's interest in service delivery. The corollary notion that private businesses are innately more efficient than government is a matter of ideological faith, there being no real evidence to support the belief.

The list of strategic planning decisions and actions by U.S. governments at all levels comprises a form of strategic planning that cannot be so identified because that would be a confession that "central planning" is in vogue. Decisions made by national policymaking bodies (Federal Reserve, Federal Courts, Bankruptcy Courts, Congress, and White House), along with those made by state and local governments, have created a system that compels planners to obey its guidelines. In effect, America's hidden but real "central planning" has simply endorsed global market pressures on lifetime pensions that were themselves earlier strategic plans that must now be abandoned by edicts from new central planners. The fact that market conditions and new decisions by U.S. policymaking bodies have forced corporations to effectively cancel those strategic plans demonstrates yet again that there is no basis for strategic planning at the level of the individual firm or public agency. Strategic planning requires steady jobs, steady incomes, and 30-year mortgages. It was widely understood by the end of the 20th century that these conditions could no longer be met. The pension crisis demonstrates that strategic plans can be quickly cancelled by central planners who, in the American system, need not accept responsibility for doing so.

Meanwhile, of course, various state attorneys general and such national agencies as the Securities and Exchange Board do their best (within funding limitations) to unearth the false corporate financial statements that are designed to mislead investors by keeping as many false statements away from those who have legitimate interests in "transparency" and "accuracy." Corporate executives cannot be blamed for doing what they can to ensure survival of their firms. It would help, however, if government officials did not constantly pretend that "transparency" is a normal condition of doing business in highly competitive situations. It is not.

SPECIAL CONSEQUENCES FOR PUBLIC SECTOR PLANNING AND MANAGEMENT

In the November 2005 issue of PA Times, a monthly newspaper of the American Society for Public Administration (ASPA), President Don Menzel had this to say (Menzel, 2005):

> Once upon a time, not so long ago, a giant chorus sang with gusto-hosannas to efficiency, effectiveness and economy. Government should be run like a business, so another refrain went. Today the singing continues but new refrains have been added—hurrah to entrepreneurialism, get me results, just do it, pay me for performance, contract out, competition needed, satisfy our customers, outsource the work and more. This is the language and siren music of managerialism. Hard to resist. You betcha. . . .
>
> Privatization as a form of public-private managerialism has become even more pernicious in the ongoing effort nationwide to deconstruct, some would say destroy, the non-partisan civil service system that has served the nation well for more than a hundred years. Civil service systems characterized by non-partisanship, merit advancement, impartiality, life-time security are steadily being replaced by "employment at will" arrangements. . . .
>
> The irony, of course, is that civil service as we knew it came about as a result of at-will employment, i.e., patronage government. In the U.S. government, the Transportation Security Agency uses at-will employment and the Departments of Homeland Security and Defense are moving headlong in that direction. . . .
>
> I believe we have a very serious problem on our hands—the continuing evisceration of the civil service in the United States—that bodes ill for the nation. Governance will be infected by political favoritism and the likelihood of ethical lapses or worse (corruption) are inevitable.

This is the first such statement that I had seen by that time, and I think it significant that the president of ASPA used such words as "deconstruct," "destroy," and "evisceration" in describing current trends. This brief institutional statement understandably did not spell out in detail how the civil service had been created in 1883 to prevent elected politicians from succumbing to the normal and direct political pressures to personally reward their followers with lucrative contracts to deliver public services (Thayer, 1997). The move toward "at will employment" is designed to make all employees instantly subject to termination without appeals, giving political executives complete authority to fire those who ask questions. The return of a 19th-century "spoils system" is already underway, but a second problem is perhaps even more dangerous.

The "revolution" in civil rights of the 1960s was important in helping to ensure that minority citizens, particularly African Americans, would face fewer obstacles to voting in elections. It was perhaps more important that they would have help never before available to find jobs and promotion opportunities. Programs for affirmative action, equal employment opportunity, and diversity in the make-up of private and public organizations promised that minority citizens would be more welcome in the totality of American social, economic, and cultural life. The federal government has always led the way in such efforts, even though it has taken much longer than a century to make significant progress, as in the formal integration of the armed forces that was decreed after World War II. As public service delivery becomes more and more "privatized," governments at all levels will ignore their responsibility for the enforcement of the employment rights that were included in the civil rights laws of the 1960s. As noted earlier, the NAIRU policy to maintain high unemployment for purposes of controlling inflation has led to high jobless rates for young people in the 16–24 age groups, with young minorities having much higher rates than young whites. These disparities cannot be attributed solely to job qualifications that are difficult to measure, but to the intense competition for jobs when those seeking jobs far outnumber the jobs that are available.

The United States is in grave danger of retreating from some of the progress it has made since the Civil War of the 1860s, especially the progress that did not even begin until the 1960s. The destruction of the civil service is not only an invitation to runaway corruption, as Menzel pointed out, but also a revived denial of civil rights for minorities. Ironically, the responses of the Department of Homeland Security and its subsidiary Federal Emergency Management Agency to the hurricanes that ravaged New Orleans and the Gulf Coast were widely acknowledged as "incompetent," in part because most politically appointed senior managers had no background or training for their jobs. As of January 2005, a *Washington Post* headline announced that "Civil Service System on Way Out at DHS" (Lee, 2005). As of February 2006, the situation in New Orleans could indeed be labeled as one of widespread "evisceration."

REFERENCES

Barlett, Donald, and James B. Steele. (2005, October 31). The Broken Promise. *Time*, 35–47.
Delaney, Kevin J. (1992). *Bankruptcy: How Corporations and Creditors Use Chapter 11 to Their Advantage*. Berkeley, CA: University of California Press.

Greenhouse, Linda. (1984, February 23). Unions Lose as High Court Backs Companies in Bankruptcy. *New York Times*, A1.

Kirchgaesser, Stephanie. (2005, October 31). U.S. Lacked Postwar Iraq Plan. *Financial Times*, 1.

Lee, Christopher. (2005, January 27). Civil Service System on Way Out at DHS. *Washington Post*, A01.

Mayer, Jane. (2005, November 14). A Deadly Interrogation: Can the C.I.A. Legally Kill a Prisoner? *New Yorker*, 44–51.

Menzel, Donald C. (2005, November). Public-Private Managerialism: What's to Be Done? *PA Times*, 16.

Nocera, Joseph. (2005, October 15). The Hammer of Bankruptcy at Delphi. *New York Times*, C-1.

Pear, Robert. (2005, October 20). U.S. Gives Florida a Sweeping Right to Curb Medicaid. *New York Times*, 1.

Perez-Pena, Richard. (2005, October 17). At Clinic, Hurdles to Clear Before Medicaid Care. *New York Times*, 1.

Sanghera, Sathnam. (2005, October 29/30). He's Got the Power … And So Has She. *Financial Times*, W3.

Strauss, Robert. (2005, September 11). Storm Warnings. *New York Times*, 14NJ; column 1.

Thayer, Frederick C. (1995a, Spring). The Comic Opera of Welfare Reform. *Social Policy*, 17, et.seq.

———. (1997). The U.S. Civil Service: 1883–1993 (R.I.P.). In Ali Farazmand, *Modern Systems of Government: Exploring the Role of Bureaucrats and Politicians*, pp. 95–124. Thousand Oaks, CA: Sage.

Tyson, Laura D'Andrea. (1994, April 15). Inflation: Myth and Reality. *New York Times*, A31.

Uchitelle, Louis. (2005, September 11). Disasters Waiting to Happen. *New York Times*, 3–2.

———— 8 ————

Innovations in Strategic Human Resource Management: Building Capacity in the Age of Globalization

ALI FARAZMAND

PROBLEMS AND SOLUTIONS

The world has changed dramatically during the last 20 years, and the dawn of a new form of civilization has emerged as the new millennium begins. In this age of rapid, unexpected, and unpredictable changes with far-reaching consequences, the role of governments, citizens, organized groups, nation-states, and societies is changing rapidly as well. Public and private organizations, and management systems, are being transformed by either choice or pressure and the necessity of adaptation for survival.

Along with governmental transformation, citizens are also transforming from the traditional passive or receptive role to one that is highly demanding, challenging, and participating. New technologies and organizational networks are enabling citizens to play a more active and powerful role in the governance and administration processes that affect their present as well as their future lives. Obviously, inequality persists and in fact widens rapidly between the rich and the poor, and between the rich nations of the industrialized world and those of the developing and less developed countries. All nation-states are challenged by the forces of rapid globalization and their governments' sovereignty is being eroded by the new norms and organizations of the world order. There is also a widening gap between the few powerful nations that are home to globalizers, and those of the rest of the world that are being globalized and affected by the consequences of globalization and the new world order. Therefore, the challenges—positive as well as negative—facing the governance, administration, and management of developing nations are far more serious and more demanding than those in industrialized nations (for a detailed discussion of globalization, see Farazmand, 1994, 1999, 2001a,b, 2002a, and forthcoming).

These challenges present opportunities as well as severe constraints to the governments in these nations that are making efforts to develop their economies, to utilize and manage their resources, to promote the social welfare of their citizens, to advance in science and technology, and to improve their capacity in both governability and service delivery to their citizens. To counter and meet these challenges, all governments are forced to rethink the philosophy of government, to reconsider the modes of governance, and to redesign new systems and organizations of public administration and management. To accomplish these multiple objectives, a new vision is required that strategically places *human resources development and management* as a key strategic instrument in meeting and managing the challenges of globalization.

This new future-oriented and anticipatory strategic vision is especially needed to assist countries toward rapid development and enhanced capacity for sound governance and democratic administration. Strategic planning and management is central to accomplishing developmental goals, but strategic human resources development and management is key to the design and implementation of developmental plans as well as to the operation of a sound governance and administration of Iran. To this end, capacity building and enhancement must be established in all areas of governance and administration, and this can be accomplished only through innovation. To meet the challenges of globalization and to ride the rapid "waves of change" (Morgan, 1995), the future managers—both generalists and human resource specialists—have no choice but to be effective human resource managers with high qualities. They must be intelligent, knowledgeable, skilled in human resources management and organizational behavior, able and willing to learn and lead learning organizations, and capable of creating human capital and work with people on an equal basis, not as authoritative leaders over them (Farazmand, 2002e).

This paper addresses innovation in strategic human resources development as a capacity building strategy to not only cope and meet the challenges of core national development programs in the age of rapid globalization, but also to move beyond by developing an anticipatory and future-oriented capacity that can foresee potential challenges and devise strategic "choices" to control destiny in the highly uncertain global environment. First, the importance of capacity building and strategic innovation is briefly discussed, followed by a more detailed discussion, in Section Two, of innovation and its multiple meanings. Then, areas of strategic innovations are presented as strategies to human resource capacity building in government and public administration. Finally, several suggestive approaches are outlined, without elaboration, for implementation and transformation of the ideas into action, followed by a brief conclusion and call for further research and writing on this important subject.

CAPACITY BUILDING IN STRATEGIC HRM

The key words or concepts of innovation, capacity, and strategy or strategic human resources management used in this paper require some explanations. First, innovation is considered as a strategic instrument for building and enhancing capacity in government and public administration.

Second, the strategic human resource management is central to all development plan and programs and their implementation, as no plan or program can be designed and implemented effectively without strategic thinking. Strategic human resources development is essential to the governance and management systems of all organizations of public, private, and nonprofit sectors, regardless of the nature of the political and economic systems. Thus, both strategic human resources development and strategic capacity building in human resource management are used interchangeably in this paper.

Third, capacity building here refers to the development of institutional, organizational, managerial, technological (both soft and hard), cultural, and individual abilities, capabilities, skills, and knowledge of a government and public administration system to not only manage today but also tomorrow. Such a capability enables government and public administration to not only cope with and manage ongoing current challenges of governance and administration but also to act well beyond by performing through anticipation, effective visions, proactive knowledge and skills, and self-corrective organizational behavior. Capacity building is mainly an internal, local, or domestic matter, and it is directly related to sustainable development and enhancement; it means building and developing national or local capabilities to conceive, develop, promote, and manage policies, programs, and projects with excellence and toward desired goals and missions.

Capacity building also means developing abilities to build and control the future, and this means "choice" of strategies to control events and build future by developing an anticipatory capability in public management and governance. The United Nations Development Program (UNDP) defines capacity-building as "the process by which individuals, groups, organizations, institutions and societies increase their abilities to: (1) perform core functions, solve problems, and define and achieve objectives; (2) understand and deal with their development needs in a broader context and in a sustainable manner" (quoted in UNDP, 2002, 68). While very helpful, this definition is limited in scope as it only points to the development capacity building, while the concept capacity building is a much broader one, as noted in my earlier definition and explained throughout this paper; it covers well beyond the ability to perform "the core function," and entails future-oriented and anticipatory capabilities as well as abilities to govern and manage.

Capacity building and enhancement in strategic human resources management, therefore, refers to building and enhancing a cadre of highly qualified, highly able, and highly motivated human resources at all levels of government, public administration, and management that serves the country in her pursuit of not only coping and managing the challenges of the day, but also of making strategic choices and decisions that can control her destiny tomorrow in the rapidly changing global environment under globalization of corporate capitalism. In this respect, building strategic human resource capacity also includes human resource capacity in private business as well as nonprofit, nongovernmental organizations, and self-governing organizations of the cooperative sector.

Human resource capacity building and development in Iran is critically needed both horizontally and vertically. The first focuses on domestic capacity building strategies, while the latter stresses capacity development in international relations and in effective functioning as a nation in the global community; both are directly related to national sustainable development capacity building.

The domestic area of capacity building innovations address all sectors of the economy, society, and politics as well as administration: in the heavy infrastructure development, diverse industries, agriculture, tourism, social services, transportation and communication, urban and rural governance and administration systems, and in the management of all organizations in public, private, and nonprofit sectors. Innovation in domestic human resource capacity building requires new as well as established skills in technical as well as nontechnical areas. This is essential to running and managing a dynamic economy, to promote opportunities for political and social involvement and participation of not only employed people but also ordinary citizens who can take part in the governance and administration processes through various forms of partnership-based and network-based organizations.

Innovations in domestic strategic human resource capacity building also promotes the enabling role of the government by providing it with the highest levels and types of skills and cutting edge knowledge that are not only essential but also critical to the effective functioning of the government. The skills and knowledge required to prepare through education and training are crucial to obtain on an up-to-date basis. The search and effort must be endless, for advancement in science and technology, and in human and social sciences, is fast and the changes in domestic and global environments are so rapid that no time can be wasted. Thus, domestic-oriented human resource capacity building is a first step toward accomplishing the objectives of an effective vision for tomorrow's Iran as a historic nation with a glorious past and a promising future. Domestic capacity building is a stepping stone, a priority to establish a sound governance and management system to gain international and global confidence and respect among fellow nation states in the international or global community. This domestic capacity building must be done both horizontally (through technical and operative personnel and managerial or organizational leaders as well as generalists and professionals at the same levels of organizations), and vertically at different levels of organizations in government, nonprofit, and private sectors.

Capacity building and enhancement in international or global areas of skills and knowledge are formidable tasks and most demanding, especially in the age of dramatic change and transformation, and accelerated globalization (Farazmand, forthcoming-a). The global environment has turned during the last two decades into a highly turbulent and uncertain state, causing unpredictability, anxiety, and chaotic development (Rosenau, 1990), and leading to a long-term future world that is inconceivable to our current mode and capability of thinking and acting (Farazmand, 2003). Most governments and political officials in both industrially advanced countries of the West and developing or less developed nations lack the necessary and effective capacity to cope with and mange the rapid changes that globalization is posing on them (Dror, 1994).

The capacity to govern and manage uncertainties requires new, anticipatory skills, flexibility in action and innovation, and creativity on all fronts. The kinds and levels of skills and knowledge essential to building international capacity must be acquired and mastered through new education and training programs well integrated with the rest of the overall national plans.

Capacity building in external international arena requires a set of strategic human resource skills and knowledge that are different from domestic human resources capacity building. For example, preparing and developing strategic global managers, and global civil as well as political and military executives require significant attention to public investment in education and training in the areas of technical, behavioral, managerial, organizational, linguistic, and diplomatic knowledge and skills. However, both domestic and international capacity areas must be well coordinated and they must complement each other, as there is a high degree of interdependence between what the nation does domestically, on the one hand, and how it relates and functions in the international community, on the other.

Building and enhancing capacity in strategic human resource management, or building and enhancing strategic capacity in the process of human resources development, requires a new vision that places human resource management at the apex of Iranian strategic plan in an effort to not only meet the challenges of globalization, but also to be effective; such a strategic human resources management vision must meet several criteria. Specifically stated, the effectiveness of a strategic vision (1) is compelling and satisfying; (2) it poses clearly stated goals and challenges; (3) it serves as a guidepost on the terrain of uncertainties; (4) its achievement requires the creation of substantial capacity or capability for implementation; (5) it honors the past and lives in the present; (6) it requires the development of serious commitment; and (7) it demands innovation on all fronts, especially in science and technology, managerial and organizational behavior, design and implementation, and administrative capacity. These criteria of effectiveness will provide an assurance of success in the processes, structures, and cultures of strategic human resource capacity of Iran, and align it with other keys of strategic plans and management of the country. But, such a vision must also be sustained and updated on a continuous basis.

INNOVATIONS IN HUMAN RESOURCE DEVELOPMENT AND MANAGEMENT

Innovation is the key to progress, development, and sound governance and public administration. Innovation is also the key to invention and reinvention in all spheres of life, society, science, technology, and administration. Through innovations, inventions, and reinvention, survival and dynamic continuity can be assured with high certainty, though the latter is subject to various environmental contingencies.

Through innovations, environmental contingencies can be tamed, predicted to a degree, and anticipative strategies can be utilized toward achieving the goals of effective visions. In the case of strategic human resource management, anticipative capacity building is the key to prepare and develop domestic and international cadres of strategic personnel for all sectors—public, nonprofit, and profit. Innovation is also the key to learning organizations with learning leadership capacity that must lead and manage those organizations for high performance and productivity (Argyris and Schon, 1996; Schein, 1985) As noted earlier, in our treatment of the subject, the idea of strategic innovation in human resources management is used interchangeably with the phrase innovation in strategic human resources management capacity building and development.

Innovation: Definition and Function

Innovation refers to novelty in ideas, approaches, methods, processes, structures, behaviors, attitudes, and cultures, as well as in technologies and skills. It also refers to the knowledge base that is used to produce new products and deliver services, to govern and administer societies, and to manage organizations of all types. This broad definition is obviously not conclusive but it covers the main realm of the innovation concept. Generally speaking, innovation may be viewed, among other things, to serve several functions as follows:

1 *Innovation as a concept.* Conceptualization is a useful way of expressing creativity through modeling and establishing frames of reference that serve as guideposts to observation and experiential as well as metaphorical phenomena. Innovation as a concept serves as a guide to explanations, but it also serves as a transition to reality, to practice, and to future actions. Conceptualizing innovations in human resources development and management is both helpful and necessary, as it is a building block to strategy formulation and development for capacity building and enhancement in governance and administration. This is an absolute necessity for Iranian development process.

2 *Innovation as a response to needs or problems:* The old notion that "need and necessity lead to creativity and invention" holds true in the case of innovations. Domestic and international environmental pressures, constraints, and uncertainties dictate a need for innovations, creativity, and self-reliance, which itself serves as a key impetus for further innovations to promote capacity enhancement in all areas of science, governance, management, and administration. Innovation is an answer to constantly challenging problems and changing needs and expectations, obligations, and responsibilities governments face all the time, especially in the age of rapid globalization. To be responsive, it is imperative to innovate.

3 *Innovation as progress and advancement.* To innovate means to invent, to create the means of progress and advancement. Examples include invention of new weapons

systems, new computer software, and new rocket systems to carry spacecrafts into orbit. This is an innovation of staying on top and being dynamic.

4 *Innovation as a mind-set:* Treating innovation as a mind-set is like navigating in an ocean with full alert senses, radar systems, and the capacity to create and find new ways of breaking through storms and barriers as well as clear and calm realms of the sailing process. Having a campus is not enough for the captain of a ship; what is more important is a restless and creative mind-set that is always seeking new ways of naval operation. Innovation as a mind-set allows strategic human resource management to guide the human dimensions of organizations to monitor and advance beyond routines and predictable outcomes. It provides the strategic human resource managers and, indeed, all organizational leaders to stay on top and manage organizations with confidence through an anticipatory capacity system (ACS) that cuts across the four areas of innovation: human, technological, organizational, and managerial. With a mind-set of innovative management, innovation will become a key strategic instrument of progress, development, high performance, and organizational and system legitimacy.

Areas and Issues or Subjects of Innovation

There is no limit to the areas of innovation in human resources development and management. These areas may be grouped into three categories: (1) human resources or personnel area, including general management and leadership; (2) technological and financial resources necessary to sustain and promote strategic human resources; and (3) organizational area, which include structure, process, and value system or culture.

The first, or human resource management category for innovation, is a constant search for the needed personnel, for the right person for the right position, and for the right position or job for the right person. This is a challenging job that can and should be accomplished through careful planning, recruitment, education, and training all the time. This includes the challenge of recruiting, educating, and training the highly competent managerial and leadership personnel for strategic and operational levels. These are the people whose knowledge and skills are indispensable for leading and managing large and complex organizations in all sectors.

Second, technological innovation is central to strategic human resources development and capacity building, but it can only be made possible through the availability of necessary financial resources that finance and support it. Without necessary financial support, innovations can and do occur but may not reach the developmental stage. The third category of innovations in strategic human resources development and management is directly related to the first two, and all three complement each other. Organizational setting provides structure through which processes of innovation take shape, and the norms and values that develop within the organizational structure and process help shape a system of organizational culture that can promote or hinder strategic innovations.

Once institutionalized, the new culture of innovation can help shape and reshape the process and structure of the organization. Institutionalization is key to the legitimacy and support systems that innovative ideas can enjoy as a strategic instrument toward capacity building and enhancement in human resources development and management (Farazmand, 2004b, forthcoming). It is this institutionalized organizational culture of learning and learning to learn for adaptation, change, and transformation that the strategic human resource management in particular, and all-level managerial leadership, in general, can raise its quality standards of performance by means of strategic capacity building and enhancement. Examples of this sort include postrevolutionary Iranian government's efforts to build and develop capacity for self-reliance in many areas, including in warfare and scientific technologies that even the Western powers have long considered a monopoly of their own (Farazmand, 2001d).

Another example includes the postrevolutionary shape and institutionalization of macrolevel cultural values of independence, respect for other people's views and ideas, and eagerness to share knowledge and expertise with other developing nations in the international community. Still another example is the creative foreign policy of conciliation, peace, and dialogue of civilizations of President Khatami that has helped institutionalize a new value system within Iran and has gained for Iran a good degree of respect and recognition in the international/global community. Effectiveness of the visionary government system will be evaluated against the seven criteria identified earlier.

Aside from these three broad areas of strategic concern to build and develop capacity, there are a number of areas or subjects that demand innovation and present both challenges and opportunities for strategic human resource management in Iran.

REALM OF STRATEGIC INNOVATION IN HRM

Identifying and explaining a comprehensive list of strategic realms of innovation in human resource development and management is beyond the scope of this short chapter. The following highlights of some of the key strategic areas or realms of innovation to build and enhance capacity in human resources as human capital in public administration. The list is suggestive, and by no means an exhaustive one.

1. *Information Technology:* Information technology is the central intelligence of strategic human resource management. It is a strategic tool for collecting, processing, and managing strategic data and information in order to make strategic decisions for forecasting, planning, recruiting, promotion, evaluation, and developing key human resources at all levels of organizations. This includes technical, professional, managerial, scientific, leadership, and administrative functions in public and private sectors (Davenport, 1992).

   Innovations in IT programs must be consistent with current and future overall plans and programs of national development, management, and governability capacity building. Such strategic IT programs can be developed through a multitude of methods and approaches that include, for example, internal and external schemes, in-house and outsourced programs, training and education modules, and public-private partnerships. They can also be developed through international assistance agencies affiliated with the United Nations. Finally, it can be developed through regional and international or global partnerships with other governments, corporations, and universities. Needless to say, IT programs must be provided adequately through both hardware and software systems that are most up-to-date and recognized as the state of the art worldwide.

2. *E-Governance and E-HUMRM*: The age of red tape, long line waiting, and time-consuming procedural processes are passing rapidly and becoming bureaucratic features of the past, though it takes time to totally eradicate them. What is coming of age is the new generation of organizational capability and capacity tools that enable governments in general, and human resource management systems in particular. These tools enable governments to formulate, develop, and communicate public service delivery messages that are routine and strategic, essential and informative, and required as well as suggestive. Through E-governance and electronic systems, governments, and human resource managers can identify, locate, place, and train key strategic personnel all over the country, and provide maximum capacity to various agencies and organizations in need of such personnel (Cladow, 1999).

   E-governance and E-human resource management can also provide two more functional capacities: First, they enable public organizations to provide public service information—from position and personnel needs announcements to assessment and report of the human resources status—to citizens as a way to inform people of what and how their government in general, and public organizations in particular, are performing. This function serves the citizens, who in turn may develop trust in their government. The second capacity function is even more important, and that is the electronization or automation of government-citizen interaction, eliminating or reducing time-consuming, red tape–oriented, and delay-prone activities of government organizational performance that has traditionally been the case for thousands of years (Davenport, 1992).

   Through E-governance and E-HRM innovations, citizens can interact with their government organizations and receive services in an efficient and effective manner, and public organizations can also cut on time, cost, and red tape, which burden governments all the time. However, strategic innovations in such E-governance and E-HRM programs require serious education and training in information technology as applied to such functions. It also requires training and educating the old as well as young citizen populations who can use such innovative technologies and techniques. Without training how to work with new technological systems ad programs, the most sophisticated technological systems will be of no use beacuse noone knows how to work with them. Despite the difficulties, E-governance and E-HRM systems are strategic answers to the future governance and human resources development challenges. In fact, E-government has been "virtual" government, and dealing with virtual bodies and virtual souls.

3. *Strategic Positions and Leadership Personnel*: A key strategic area of capacity building in human resource development and management is the innovation in identifying strategic positions and functions in public organizations of government, a task that is challenging. At the same time preparing and promoting exceptionally skilled and knowledgeable personnel for leadership and managerial as well as professional

functions of government organizations is essential for all managerial functions. The challenge is a great one, and so is the effort to meet it. Strategic human resources at all levels of organizations are core components of innovative human capital development. There are at least four major areas of attention, which may fall into two broad categories: one is preparation of "generalists" and another being "specialists."

Generalists must be educated and trained with utmost effort to master as well-rounded, highly developed executives who can lead as well as manage strategic posts of public organizations with the broad, long-term visions of anticipatory characteristics. Such strategic people are hard to come by, but Iran like most other countries, is full of such potential talents. Once trained and developed, these people can serve as able captains of the ships that can navigate under any circumstances and lead the ship to safety and reach the desired destination. However, retaining such a cadre of highly talented and extremely valuable strategic people in organizations requires significant motivational and institutional programs that serve as incentives within and outside the organizations in government and business enterprises. These strategic executives are the organizational assets that must be utilized most effectively across agency and interorganizational levels.

Many of these executives are specialists either by training or experience that provides public organizations with institutional competence beyond market values. These strategic people should be placed in key professional, managerial, administrative, behavioral, and technical functions of organizations where the proper "fit" is both desirable and necessary. Remember: these people are strategic leaders of the organizations in government.

4. *Strategic Motivation:* The old theories, ideas, and techniques of motivating people at work are still valuable, but to develop strategic human resource management capacity requires stepping beyond the traditional methods and approaches. Here, identification, recognition, and application of some of the most up-to-date, dynamic systems of motivation that can move people beyond their daily excitements and provide them with an extraordinarily high level of mission-driven purpose is a central task that must be adopted by an anticipatory and vision-driven organizational system.

Some of the examples of these high-road and visionary motivational forces include (1) creation and instilment of a "real purpose" of "public service" among strategic personnel; (2) promotion of trust with a promise of future career beyond the narrow notion of "careerism," a sense of belonging to the organization, to the cause they serve, and to their nation as well as to the faith they cherish; (3) maintaining a sound compensation system that is both equitable and efficient in order to not only prevent organizational brain drain but also attract the most competent talents to the public service; (4) create an interorganizational mobility and rotation system that would enable both organizations and strategic personnel to move freely without obstacles; and (5) promote the "knowledge and skill-base" of these strategic people periodically to keep them up to date and equipped with the cutting-edge knowledge they need to manage, and function, in the organizations in the information age. This can be done by in-service training programs, seminars, conferences, and workshops; nothing is worse than ignorance, and ignorance is the mother of many organizational anomalies in government, business, and nonprofit systems (Farazmand, 2004b).

5. *Strategic knowledge development and management:* Knowledge is the key to learning and understanding, without which no progress can be made. Strategic organizational adaptation and success require development and management of strategic knowledge, skills, and inventories, and this is an essential element of any management system, especially for human resource management (Milner, 2000). Cutting-edge knowledge is critical to the rapid progress of all organizations, and it can only be obtained through education, training, and development via university and technical as well as behavioral types and norms of inquiry. Knowledge inquiry is one task, and management of such knowledge is another, a more challenging one.

   Today's national and global changes demand acquisition of the latest knowledge and skills in information technology (IT), management information systems (MIS), dynamic data processing techniques (DDPT), human resource inventory and potential migratory resource analysis systems (HIPMRAS), and a host of other models and techniques that are necessary knowledge-based capacities that must be developed in the strategic human resource management. Also, acquiring the latest management systems borrowed from the private sector is another way of applying new benchmarks to promote organizational capacity. Finally, a key area of knowledge development and management is the new "organizational learning" and the "ability to learn," a requirement that must start from the top leadership of public organizations and develop throughout the organizations. Learning to learn enables organizational leaders and managers to transform human resources at all levels, but most importantly at the strategic levels (Argyris and Schon, 1996; Schein, 1985).

6. *Cultural innovation and transformation:* Most organizational problems and failures emanate from a creeping cultural dysfunction that generates from many organizational and environmental anomalies. Cultural anomalies, or what I would prefer to call "cultural diseases" are the most difficult barriers and obstacles to change, learning, and transformation. Without such change and transformation, organizational failure is almost guaranteed (Farazmand, 2004a,b; Senge, 1990). To transform, strategic human resources of organizations in government and business must learn to learn, change, and adapt, and this can only be done through cultural change and transformation.

   Such organizational culture change and transformation can also be accomplished in a variety of ways, utilizing a variety of techniques and approaches that range from behavioral or technical and managerial training and education. Ethics education is a key component of this process, so is the behavioral and human relations skills training, but above all is the training and change of cultural values that emanate from both the external and internal organizational environments. Strategic human resource leadership plays a key role in changing and transforming such an organizational culture that is characterized by results-oriented purposes, visionary missions, highly innovative energies, and quality commitment (Schein, 1995).

7. *Total Quality Management (TQM):* TQM is not a new technique or system of managing organizations. It has been around for over 3,000 years and its successful application can be traced to the administration of the ancient Iranian Elamite and Persian Empires, especially under Darius the Great, and Babylon under Hamurabi. However, what is new is the novelty of sophistication in techniques, ideas, and applications of the concept TQM with a multitude of different variants applied in private and public sectors around the world. The underlying assumption behind the TQM

is quality in production, service delivery, and simply performance in personal and organizational settings (Milakovich, 1995).

The old Iranian saying "do things right the first time in order to avoid duplication" is key to understanding TQM, and the concept comes in a variety of terms and titles, such as Quality Service, Quality Assurance, Quality Circle, and the like. Central to TQM is commitment to quality performance from the first step, followed and monitored all the way throughout the "process" to the end, and continue the process all over again.

Using TQM as a strategic innovation helps promote the goals and missions of strategic human resource management capacity building. Although pioneered in application by Japan, TQM has been used in various countries of the world and at different levels of government, with various degrees of success (Robertson and Ball, 2002). Public sector application of TQM is a fairly new development and still in progress, but its success in private sector organizations has been proven worldwide. Using TQM along with the "global quality standards" exposed by the International Standards Organization (ISO-2000, 2002, and more) is helpful in strategic human resource development of Iranian public and private sectors. In a nutshell, TQM is a strategic capacity building tool (Saner, 2002).

8. *Merit and Pay-for-Performance*: This strategy is not entirely new, but its novelty still works very well when applied properly and consistently. Merit system should award meritorious performance in government and private industries, and it is merit that can serve as a powerful motivator to keep and promote talented people in organizations. One of the big problems with the management of contemporary organizations is, and has always been, that they spend so much time, energy, and money to recruit and hire talented people, and even train them to the details, only to "lose them easily with mismanagement and carelessness." This is a problem that most organizations around the world practice: Attract the best and lose them to others or turn them into apathetic and unproductive people. This is a fundamental mistake, even a managerial stupidity. It is true that not everyone can be retained, but retaining, motivating, and promoting talented people in organizations is a challenge that is often ignored or overlooked because managers very often "take for granted" the most valuable people (Farazmand, 2004; Hays and Plagens, 2002).

Merit system builds trust and enhances capacity in organizations through credibility, quality performance, and "pay-for-performance" should be a key strategy to attract and retain quality personnel in government. It is a challenge that must be met by developing a comprehensive and consistent plan of pay-for-performance along with a system of merit protection in government, especially in the age of rapid globalization where border crossing and labor migration from one country to another is becoming easier and more attractive. Countries that can offer such a system more effectively are likely to attract some of the best talents globally, but strategic positions must be maintained by indigenous strategic executives at home (Farazmand, 2001a,b).

9. *Global executives:* Living in the age of rapid globalization requires preparation and adaptation to this new global challenge. Today, public as well as private organizations are rapidly interacting and doing business across national boundaries, and this new development demands a cadre of highly trained technical, professional, managerial, and cultural, organizational, and leadership knowledge and skills that can be moved across the globe from one location to another. These global managers

and executives are the change agents of the future; they are also the agents of cross-national organizational innovation and adaptability.

Iran is in a strategic position in the region, and with her potential capacity in scientific, technological, economic, and managerial areas, Iranian global managers and executives will be in a greater need tomorrow, and before it is too late to catch up, steps must be taken to prepare such a strategic human capital today. These global managers and executives can be trained both vertically and horizontally, and they will serve in both directions of home and abroad at the same time (Farazmand, forthcoming-b).

10. *Transparency, accountability, trust, and ethics*: Key to building and enhancing strategic capacity is trust in organization and government. The key words to building trust are credibility, fairness, transparency, and accountability, not just for the past actions but also for what should and should not be done now and tomorrow. Punishing one for past wrongdoing is too late to build trust; prevention is the answer. Transparency eliminates opportunities for corruption and closes the doors to secrecy and abuse, and proactive accountability mechanisms help serve as a strategic instrument in pursuit of excellence and trust, and hence legitimacy. Similarly, ethical training and ethical behavior in a public organizational setting promotes professionalism, organizational, and system integrity, and helps build trust in public organizations, managers, and administrators, whether civil servants or those contracted out to carry out the public's business (Davenport, 1992; Farazmand, 2001a, 2002c).

11. *Global labor migration and mobility:* The fate of labor and labor organizations in the globalization age is uncertain, but what is certain is the rapid movement of global capital and labor, as both organizations and labor forces find ways and motivations to cross borders—physically, intellectually, and virtually—around the globe. Labor means both white as wells as blue color employees and workers. Today, most of the transworld corporations' work is performed globally across the globe, breaking national borders. American, Japanese, German, and British corporations' actual work is performed in developing and less developed nations, and workers and employees in the latter countries never leave their home nations. Many people work at home and perform as virtual employees, and migrate through the cyber system. The global labor migration is a serious development that requires serious innovation strategies to keep and utilize talented people at home and local organizations. Through adaptation, Iranian government and private organizations can benefit from this new, global migratory workforce in the future.

12. *Management-Labor partnership building:* Management-labor contradictions will never disappear in capitalism; in fact, as globalization of capitalism increases rapidly, so do the degree and intensity of these contradictions. However, these contradictions can be and should be managed more effectively by utilizing innovative strategies, and one such approach is formation of various forms of partnership between management and labor/employees. These partnerships should be based on mutual understanding, trust, and cooperation, with mutual gains. They can be formed through various systems and approaches such as, for example, "productivity bargaining partnership," "productivity-based partnership," "interest-based partnership," "indigenous partnerships," "collective and individual partnership," and others (see Farazmand, 2004a)

13. *Reform and reorganization*: Reform and reorganization are two concepts directly related to each other. Reform aims to improve administrative, organizational, and

institutional capacity and it covers both structure and process as well as culture, while reorganization aims at structural rearrangements and reconfigurations, and it is mainly structural in nature. One example of strategic reorganization is privatization of government functions, another is consolidation of several government agencies and/or bureaucratic organizations into one or vice versa, and or internal reorganization of a particular agency by either flattening the hierarchy or vice versa. Strategic reform and reorganization programs within the bureaucracy and public service in general, and in human resource management, in particular, must be carefully designed and applied in order to increase the capacity to manage. This can involve a variety of human resource management areas, from recruitment to compensation and merit system to civil service system restructuring, and the like (Farazmand, 2002b,d).

14. *Benchmarking:* Benchmarking has been around for a long time, but its recognition as an effective innovative strategy is fairly new. Benchmarking can be used as a strategy by using best practices across (1) public organizations within one government; (2) organizations of different governments worldwide; (3) sectoral organizations such as industries, service sector, and around the world, and types or level kinds of products or services. Benchmarking requires standards of performance, and performance measurement becomes important as a key instrument to achieve the goals of benchmarking process (Keehley et al., 1997). Using best practices and case studies to promote excellence in performance is one of the key approaches to build and develop capacity in government and private management.

15. *Strategic civil service and public enterprise capacity:* Should all governmental functions be performed by government organizations? This is a key question of policy and politics as well as management. Policy because it hits the heart of how the society and economy be organized into public, private, and cooperative sectors. The Constitution of the Islamic Republic of Iran has already answered this question, but the legislature must deal with the details, because it involves politics of various kinds: interest groups politics, policy politics, organizational or bureaucratic politics, institutional politics, economic politics, and more.

It is also a management question because doing what government organizations do and must do matter most to the society. Here, a reorganization and restructuring of the government organizations is necessary to determine: what the right size of the civil service should be, what organizations and institutions can and should be consolidated or reorganized to eliminate duplication, and what government enterprise should or should not remain under direct public management. No matter what the decision, strategic innovations should be addressed at running public organizations and enterprises with utmost adaptability, efficiency, and effectiveness that include fairness as well. Should there be a core of strategic civil servants with different forms of privatization at the side? Should outsourcing and contracting out be key strategies to freeing the government from nonstrategic functions? If yes, what should the new contract management be like? (Farazmand, 2001a; forthcoming-a).

16. *Strategic public enterprise management:* Governmental functions will never disappear, the state is here to stay, and market cannot replace core government functions. Historically, many public enterprises (PEs) have served strategically the core functions of government and contribute to national economic development worldwide (Farazmand, 2001a). But, inefficiency, lack of accountability and transparency in many

enterprises have caused a major problem of legitimacy, therefore making them ripe for privatization. What is needed is a new philosophy and way of thinking about public enterprise management, and as a public asset, public enterprise management must be strategically revisited. PEs require specialized personnel, training, and expertise. There should be special educational and training programs and projects to prepare public enterprise managers with academic degrees, certificates, and recognition. A competent public enterprise management will be a desperate need of tomorrow when the market failures will begin to surface one after another as a result of sweeping privatization; therefore, preparation must begin today (Farazmand, 2002a,b; UN, 2000; Wettenhall, 2003).

17. *Contract management capacity:* The rush to privatization during the last two decades has caused a major institutional crisis worldwide in the ways that privatization, contracted out programs, and outsourced projects are managed (Farazmand, 2001b). Most governments, including the ones in advanced industrialized nations, lack the capacity to manage and monitor contracted out and outsourced projects performed by private sector organizations. They simply do not have trained and qualified personnel to manage contracts. As a result, many, including the U.S. Federal and many local/state governments have been hiring private contractors to manage and monitor contracts— what a silly thing! It is like "asking a fox to watch over the henhouse full of chickens" Governments should prepare, through general and specialized training, a large number of "contractor managers" to effectively manage and monitor outsourced and contracted-out services and projects. The ultimate responsibility of all public service functions rest on the shoulders of government, and it would be irresponsible to shirk that responsibility, a fact that will come back and haunt the government.

18. *Human capital:* Considering human resources as human capital should be considered as a way of strategic capacity building. Strategic innovations in human capital development includes restructuring human resource management at all levels and across organizational divisions and units. One such restructuring is the removal or elimination of the old staff-line demarcation or distinction. A dynamic management system requires the knowledge and skills in managing human resources in all units and departments, in engineering, production, sale, and so on. At the same time, the specialized human resources located in such specific departments must focus on core functions unique to that organizational requirements. Their function is to enable all other departments and units to manage their own human resources; and this should be done through specialized capacity-building programs and methods.

There are several strategic challenges to human capital management, and these challenges range from organizational to cultural and communicational, but the most important challenges may be viewed in three categories of structure, process, and values. Structural challenges deal with organizational command, decision making, control, and authority issues, as well as levels and degree of complexity of the organization. Process challenges include techniques, methods, and programs used to process tasks and inputs into outputs, and the ways they are used by human resources. Here, innovation in technology and methods is key to meeting the challenges of human capital development (Farazmand, 2004b).

Cultural or value challenges are most important to overcome as they run deep into the value system of the organizations; they are the basic assumptions of the organization in which human resources operate. These challenges can be overcome through training, development, and learning to learn, a process that must start from the top leadership (Schein, 1995).

19. *Team building and development:* Team building has been a feature of some countries such as Iranian culture and administrative systems since ancient times. Much of the public works projects and programs, from building roads and highways to irrigation systems and housing development, have traditionally been performed through team structures, collective cultural values, and cooperative spirit. Team spirit must be reinvigorated inside and outside the administrative systems, but using it as a strategic innovation will boost the character and performance of the public sector organizations (Farazmand, 2001a; 1989).

Sharing power, responsibility, expertise, and skills as well as knowledge promotes the ability as well as capability to manage the diverse workforce of Iran and contributes to a high level of capacity building and sustainable development. Team spirit as well as formal structural team arrangements must be promoted among all human resources, but most importantly at the supervisory, managerial, and leadership levels; this is where genuine team spirits can translate ideas into action.

20. *Council system of management:* Closely associated with the team management system is the concept of council system in human resource management. Countries like Iran have a long history of council management system. Promoting this novel system of management serves as a strategy to improve morale and a sense of organizational belonging, builds trust and contributes to participatory management, raises the level of democratic administration and governance, and promotes motivation to work and productivity. No organization can operate or function without competent human resources, and participatory council forms of human resource management contributes to the effectiveness of organizational visions and strategic capacity building in public management.

21. *Enabling role capacity:* Government has a central enabling role in society; it must enable all sectors, institutions, and organizations of the society to develop and grow. The enabling role of the government is most essential for building and enhancing capacity in human resources of the public, nonprofit, cooperative, nongovernmental, and private sectors. It also must create the opportunities for such growth and sustainable development. Using the strategy of government as an enabling force to develop and manage human resources at all levels in order to meet the challenges of globalization (Farazmand, 2001c; forthcoming; 2002a).

Privatization and other alternative approaches to service delivery do not replace the role of government, and it is the government or state that must always shoulder responsibility of what happens in society, economy, administration, and politics. In the age of globalization of corporate capitalism, unfortunately, many governments have rushed to wash their hands of the responsibilities they traditionally have performed and by privatization have transferred the burden of social and economic tasks on citizens who lack the ability or capability to function in society. This problem is not unique to developing countries. In fact, it started out in the advanced nations of the West and was forced upon the governments in developing nations so subject to the influence of the former ones. Global sweeping privatization and structural adjustment programs imposed on developing nations by the International Monetary Fund and World Bank are but two examples of this externally imposed pressures that have served as powerful strategic instruments of implementing globalization of corporate capitalism worldwide (see Farazmand, 2002b for more details on this issue).

With the rapid privatization, the enabling role of government must be enhanced to promote self-governing organizations in all sectors. The old Persian question that "we salt whatever that tends to get rotten, but what happens when the salt itself gets rotten?" applies here to the washed-off hands of the state or government worldwide. Unless governments retake their role in society and citizens reclaim their rights and roles in economy, society, and governance systems, public administration, and human resource management cannot and will not succeed, and their capacity will diminish rather than enhance, especially in the age of rapid globalization and global integration (UN, 2000).

22. *Thinking globally and performing locally:* Thinking globally and acting locally is a strategy that must be utilized to change the old traditional organizational culture of localism and parochialism. Localism is good as long as a worldview is in the picture. Global thinking requires global knowledge and information, and strategic human resources must be trained and educated accordingly. Globalization is demanding new skills and knowledge that local managers must be able to respond to, and local demands also need to be addressed in this globalizing world of interdependence.

This whole thing requires new challenges that rapidly growing uncertainties and complexities pose to public management. Uncertainties and complexities dictate that managers "think unthinkable," "think unlikely, and do unreasonable" (Handy, 1998). To do so, strategic innovations are needed in all areas of human resource management to build capacity and prepare an anticipatory government that has the capacity to govern, and public management that has capacity to manage chaos and complexity, and manage. globalization at home while being globalized itself (Farazmand, 2003; Stacey, 1992).

APPROACHES TO IMPLEMENT INNOVATIVE CAPACITY BUILDING IN STRATEGIC PUBLIC PERSONNEL MANAGEMENT

This chapter has posited that in order to develop the human resource management strategicaly, innovative strategies must be designed and applied as strategic capacity for an anticipatory and dynamic system of management and governance that not only functions well today, but also helps control the future destiny of the country.

To accomplish this visionary end, governments need to build and enhance their human resource capacity strategically as well as operationally. Over twenty such innovative strategies are suggested in this chapter to achieve the goals of strategic human resource management capacity. Several approaches can be used, either separately or in combinations, to approach and carry out the innovative strategies suggested above. Strategic innovations are essential to building capacity for an anticipatory public management system that can ride the waves of change now and in the future.

These approaches include (1) reform and reorganization of the public sector institutions and organizations, especially the bureaucracy at large; (2) a comprehensive civil service reform along with creating more flexibility in managing human resources; (3) incremental reforms and changes in organization and management of the civil service and bureaucracy; (4) institutional reforms to meet the goals of reaching a balance between equity and fairness on the one hand, and efficiency on the other in society by addressing the public, private, nonprofit, and cooperative sectors properly; (5) privatization and outsourcing as an option; (6) increased public investments in infrastructure development, including in human capital capacity development; (7) partnership building in various forms, with domestic private, nonprofit, and cooperative sectors; (8) partnership building in various forms, with foreign and international organizations of public and private sectors; (9) direct training and development through universities and educational and training institutions; and more. Unfortunately, space limitation precludes discussion in detail of these approaches and related issues here. Such a discussion has to be done in another manuscript.

CONCLUSION

This chapter has addressed innovations in strategic human resource management as key instruments for capacity building and enhancement in the age of accelerated globalization of corporate capitalism and rapidly changing global environment that challenge governance and public management worldwide. Such capacity building enables the governments and public managers to not only perform the functions of today, but also move beyond by using strategic choices that control destiny through capabilities of an anticipatory and future-oriented system of governance and public management. Necessity of strategic innovations in human resource development and management is a necessity that no organizations can afford to overlook.

Defining innovation, a number of key strategic innovations have been suggested here for implementation toward achieving high excellence and visionary goals of national development of today and tomorrow, and various approaches for implementation are suggested. The paper concludes that essential to national development, to sound governance and public administration is the dire need to innovate in strategic human resource management that serves as capacity building to meet the challenges of globalization of corporate capitalism. No organization can function without competent and cooperative people, and strategic human resource management is central to the development and enhancement of sound governance and public management. Further research and writings are needed in this critical area of globalization, especially in less developed countries. Today's managers need the cutting edge information of tomorrow.

NOTE

This is a revised version of the paper originally presented at the International Conference on Human Resource Management and Development held in Tehran, Iran, in

December 2003, and subsequently published as "Innovations in Strategic Human Resources Management: Building Capacity in the Age of Globalization," in Kluwer Academic Publishers, *Public Organization Review*, vol 4(1)/2004: 3–24. Published with kind permission of Springer Science and Business Media.

REFERENCES

Argyris, Chris, and Don Schon. (1996). *Organizational Learning II*. New York: Addison-Wesley Publishing Co.

Cladow, J. (1999). *The Quest for Electronic Government: A Defining Vision*. IBM Corporation, Institute for Elecronic Government. Washington DC.

Davenport, T. H. (1992). *Process Innovation: Reengineering Work through Information Technology*. Cambridge, MA: Business University.

Farazmand, Ali. (forthcoming-a). Managing Globalization and Globalizing Management. *Public Organization Review*.

———. (forthcoming-b). *Globalization, Governance, and Administration*.

———. (2004). *Sound Governance: Policy and Administrative Innovations*. Westport, CT: Praeger.

———. (2003). Chaos and Transformation Theories: A Theoretical Analysis with Implications for Organization Theory and Public Management. *Public Organziation Review: A Global Journal*, 3(4): 2003: 339–372.

———. (2002a). Globalization, Privatization, and the Future of Modern Governance: A Critical Assessment. *Public Finance and Management*, 2(1): 125–153.

———. (2002b). Privatization and Globalization: A Critical Analysis With Implications for Public Management Education and Training. *International Review of Administrative Sciences*, 68(3): 355–371.

———. (2002d). *Administrative Reform in Developing Nations*. Westport, CT: Greenwood Press.

———. (2002e). *Modern Organizations: Theory and Practice*, 2nd ed. Westport, CT: Praeger.

———. (2001a). *Privatization or Reform: International Case Studies*. Westport, CT: Greenwood Publishers.

———. (2001b). Global Crisis in Public Service and Administration. In Ali Farazmand (Ed.), *Handbook of Crisis and Emergency Management*. New York: Marcel Dekker.

———. (2001c). Globalization, the State, and Public Administration: A Theoretical Analysis with Implications for Developmental States. *Public Organization Review: A Global Journal*, 1(4): 437–464.

———. (2001d). Bureaucracy and Revolution: The Case of Iran. In Ali Farazmand (Ed.), *Handbook of Comparative and Development Public Administration*, 2nd ed., revised and expanded. New York: Marcel Dekker.

———. (1999). Globalization and Public Administration. *Public Administration Review*, 59(6): 509–522.

———. (1994). The New World Order and the Global Public Administration: A Critical Essay. In Jean-Claude Garcia-Zamor and Renu Khator (Eds), *Public Administration in the Global Village*. Westport, CT: Praeger.

———. (1989). *The State, Bureaucracy, and Revolution in Modern Iran: Agrarian Reform and Regime Politics*. New York: Praeger.

Handy, Charles. (1998). *Beyond Certainty: The Changing Worlds of Organizations.* Cambridge, MA: Harvard Business School.

Hays, Steven, and Gregory Plagens. (2002). Human Resource Management Best Practices and Globalization: The Universality of Common Sense. *Public Organization Review: a Global Journal,* 2(4): 327–348.

Keehley, Particia, Steven Medline, Sue McBride, and Laura Longmire. (1997). *Benchmarking for Best Practices in the Public Sector.* San Francisco, CA: Jossey-Bass.

Milner, E. M. (2000). *Managing Information and Knowledge in the Public Sector.* Routledge.

Morgan, Gareth. (1995). *Riding the Waves of Change.* San Francisco, CA: Jossey-Bass.

Robertson, Robert, and Rob Ball. (2002). Innovation and Improvement in the Delivery of Public Services: The Use of Quality Management Within Local Government in Canada. *Public Organization Review: A Global Journal,* 2(4): 387–406.

Saner, Raymond. (2002). Quality Assurance for Public Administration: A Consensus Building. *Public Organization Review: A Global Journal,* 2(4): 407–414.

Schein, Edgar. (1985). *Organizational Culture and Leadership.* San Francisco, CA: Jossey-Bass.

Senge, Peter. (1990). *The Fifth Discipline: The Art and Practice of the Learning Organization.* New York: Doubleday.

Stacey, R. D. (1992). *Managing the Unknowable: Strategic Boundaries between Order and Chaos in Organizations.* San Francisco, CA: Jossey-Bass.

United Nations. (2000). *New Millennium, New Perspectives: The United Nations, Security, and Governance,* Ramesh Thakur and Edward Newman (Eds.). New York: United Nations University Press.

United Nations Development Program (UNDP) (2002). *Capacity For Development,* Sakiko Fukuda-Parr, Khalid Lopes, and Khalid Malik (Eds.). New York: UN Publications.

Wettenhall, Roger. (2003). The Rhetoric and Reality of Public-Private Partnerships. *Public Organization Review: a Global Journal,* 3(1): 77–108.

PART II

BUREAUCRACY, CIVIL SERVICE, AND POLITICS

9

Politics and Strategic Public Personnel Management: The Least Bad System?

ROBERT MARANTO

Democracy is the worst form of government except all those other forms that have been tried from time to time.

—Winston Churchill

S trategic public personnel policy in America evolved along with American public administration concepts, which to a considerable degree aimed to separate "politics" from the administration of public business. Indeed the merit system and the academic field of public administration developed in part as a reaction to the perceived excesses of party based "spoils" personnel systems of the late 19th and early 20th centuries. In a widely quoted 1887 essay, Woodrow Wilson gave the best short summary of the proper relationship between politics and administration:

> The field of administration is a field of business ... [A]dministration lies outside the proper sphere of politics. Administrative questions are not political questions. Although politics sets the tasks for administration, it should not be suffered to manipulate its offices. (Wilson, 1887, 10)

For Wilson and other Progressive reformers, administration should become a science whose methods are equally useful for "monarchies and democracies" since each "have in reality much the same business to look to" (15). Similarly, Theodore Roosevelt wrote in 1890:

> Once admit that it is proper to turn out an efficient Republican clerk in order to replace him with an efficient Democratic clerk, or vice versa, and the inevitable next step is to consider solely Republicanism or Democracy, and not efficiency, in making the appointment. (Schiesl, 1977, 39)

Frank Goodnow, Dorman Eaton, and other reformers agreed (Maranto and Schultz, 1991, 63–69). Indeed, in their rejection of messy, decentralized, and often self-interest-based political interactions in favor of seemingly rational expert decision making, Ostrom (1974) finds Wilson and other classical public administration theorists more akin to Hobbes than to the *Federalist Papers*. Lindblom (1959) and Wildavsky (1969) make similar, though less blunt arguments.

In this essay I argue that the classical reformers were wrong. After making the case that both partisan and "small p" nonpartisan politics are inherent to public personnel management, I will summarize the Hult and Walcott (1990) framework for evaluating the likely "politicization" of a public bureaucracy. I will then present a brief history of federal personnel reform, noting how the twin political forces of ideology and self-interest shaped the system. Finally, I will speculate about the near-term future of public personnel systems. In a time of rapid change, to speculate further would be foolhardy.

IN PRAISE OF POLITICS

In a democracy, regime and party politics define the playing field for public management. Inherently political decisions of the legislature, executive, and courts determine what are inherently governmental functions, a matter of much import today when many government services are being completely privatized, or performed by private contractors under varying degrees of public oversight (Gore, 1993; Kettl, 1993; Savas, 1987).

Second, elections assure that each public bureaucracy will get new management each 4 or 8 years, with new executives reflecting the political agenda of the incoming president. Third, the political process sets the written and unwritten rules of government personnel systems, which tend to be far more complex, multipurpose, and (at least officially) open than those of private sector counterparts. The complexity of government personnel systems reflects the efforts of Congress to limit the control presidents wield over the permanent bureaucracy, and to control favoritism. Complexity also reflects the successful efforts of government unions to protect members (Anechiarico and Jacobs, 1996; Johnson and Libecap, 1994).[1]

Fourth, the desire of politicians to please constituencies forces regular management reform upon government bureaus. Though the private sector also faces constant change (e.g., Micklethwait and Wooldridge, 1996), a clear "bottom line" (profit) makes the success of businesses relatively clear. In contrast, government organizations often have multiple goals with no clear criteria of success, making their operations more subject to reasoned (and other) political judgments (Allison, 1984; Hult and Walcott, 1990).

Finally, and most important, as part of a representative government in an open society, politics in the bureaucracy mirrors that in society. Such social movements as the labor movement or the civil rights movement affect public bureaucracies just as they do business, the media, and the clergy. Political decisions by the three branches of government prioritize government programs. As Downs (1967) writes, newer organizations such as NASA in the 1960s (or EPA in the 1970s) represent the most pressing political priorities. As through much of our history, the major political parties today have different priorities. Currently, Republicans are more supportive of the military with Democrats more supportive of the social welfare and regulatory missions. Bureaucrats reciprocate, with federal employees in the Defense Department voting Republican, while those in social welfare and regulatory agencies tend Democratic. Similar relationships probably occur in states and localities, with police supporting Republicans and educators Democrats. In short, parties link to the institutions of the state, and supposedly neutral bureaucracies often have strong emotional and material stakes in elections (Holsti, 1997; Johnson and Libecap, 1994, 166–169; Maranto, 1993a,b). Such links may be even stronger for state and local public sector employees, since their greater numbers make them a more potent voting block and since the relative weakness of state and local merit rules makes political outcomes more important to public personnel management. State and (especially) local government employees are more likely to vote than are their federal counterparts (Johnson and Libecap, 1994, 128–138). While some lament the ties between agency and party ideals, believing in the missions of their agencies motivates government employees. Values based motives are particularly important given pay compression and job security (Downs, 1967; Maranto, 2005), and are endorsed by modern leadership theory (Blank, 1995; Peters and Waterman, 1982).

Despite its necessity in a democratic system, both classical public administration and the public itself tend to eschew "politics." As surveys and focus groups confirm, most Americans love the Constitution *in theory* because the separation of powers prevents the concentration of power. At the same time, most Americans detest the separation of powers *in practice* because of partisan bickering and extended process. The public is unaware that its expectations of constitutional government are unrealistic and that contentious, divided government actually does get things done (Hibbing and Theiss-Morse, 1995; Mayhew 1991). In short, despite the seeming success of Madisonian democracy, Americans long for the sort of nonpartisan action by experts embraced by classical public administration theory (and the likes of Ross Perot). Further, some of the public's business is in fact noncontroversial and highly technical, and can be dominated by experts. Indeed, in the decades of Progressive civil service reform, the most pressing work of local government, providing safe water and fighting infectious diseases, was of this nature (Scheisl, 1977).[2] For better or worse, the work of government, particularly the federal government, is no longer so noncontroversial.

The most sophisticated presentation of the role of politics in organizations is the Governance Model developed by Hult and Walcott (1990) and applied to the White House by Walcott and Hult (1995). Hult and Walcott see politics not as maladaptive, but as fundamental to all organizations. Organizations cope with uncertainty and controversy through *political* governance structures that make decisions and allocate scarce resources (such as jobs). Different governance structures are suited to different decision settings. An organization's goals *and* technologies can be characterized by consensus, by uncertainty (under which actors are not sure), and/or by controversy (under which different actors *disagree* on desired goals or appropriate techniques). Technical and particularly goal controversy make the job of a public manager more difficult.[3]

Different organizational structures are suited to different policy types. When goals and techniques are certain, as in supplying safe water or fighting infectious diseases, conventional bureaucracies are suitable. On the other hand, when goals and technologies are uncertain, Hult and Walcott suggest allowing decisions to emerge from the decentralized "unguided interplay of key actors" (106): competition between government organizations free to experiment. As controversy (either goal or technical) rises and becomes polarizing, confrontational or quasijudicial organizational structures (often with appeals to presidents or agency chiefs) are more appropriate to clarify choices and promote policy closure. Such structures have been used in such diverse environments as the Eisenhower National Security Council and the Reagan Environmental Protection Agency. The latter included interest representatives in modifying pesticide policy (74–75). When goals or technologies are relatively uncertain, Hult and Walcott advocate diverse teams to develop and explore alternatives. The teams should be dominated by career technical experts if technologies are uncertain. My informants suggest that such teaming is becoming more common in government, with diverse teams often employed as part of reengineering work processes. In contrast, as *goals* become uncertain or (especially) controversial, teams should include increasing numbers of political appointees or group representatives. It is interesting to note that political appointees in the federal government concentrate in agencies with controversial missions (Maranto, 1993b). American presidents and former British Prime Minister Margaret Thatcher increased the numbers of political appointees in organizations they wanted to change, but used more conventional civil service systems when the status quo was acceptable (Maranto and Schultz, 1991; Stelzer, 1992, 29–30). *In short, as an organization becomes more controversial, its personnel management inevitably becomes more political.*

Before the New Deal, the scope of government was relatively limited and public administration, once a statute was passed, was relatively noncontroversial. It was thus suitable to leave administrative questions to technical experts. In contrast, since the New Deal and especially Great Society expansions of governmental responsibility, the existence, scope, and operation of much of government have become matters of ideological controversy (Lowi, 1979). Accordingly, the recent history of American public personnel management shows a gradual politicization of public administration theory, and of public personnel systems.

A SHORT HISTORY OF FEDERAL PERSONNEL REFORM

Government by Gentlemen

As Kaufman (1956) points out, through American history the key political concepts driving public personnel management were representation, executive leadership, and neutral competence. In the Revolutionary period and the era of the first six presidents, or "Government by Gentlemen," as Mosher (1982) calls it, representation was the guiding concept of American public administration. This reflected a reaction against the perceived tyranny of British rule. Indeed, Wilson (1976, 101) argues that the American Revolution was fought largely to protest the Crown's attacks on an independent judiciary and the use of royal patronage at colonial expense: thus "almost all of their complaints involved the abuse of *administrative powers*." Fearing a strong executive, the Continental Congress even attempted to manage the war against the British, with predictable results. As Michael Nelson (1982, 750–751) writes:

> John Adams found himself working eighteen-hour days just to keep up with the business of the ninety committees on which he served. In one typical case, Congress formed a three member committee "to prepare a plan for intercepting two [enemy supply] vessels" that were enroute to America.... This form of decision-making doubtless comforted British sea captains, but it exasperated almost everyone else.

Government by Gentlemen was characterized by strong legislatures and weak executives, whether on the national or state levels (Mosher, 1982). Save to some degree under Washington and Jefferson, the national government as a whole was fragmentary and weak, with high turnover in the legislative branch and low congressional voting cohesion. At the political level, the executive branch was similarly fragmented. Cabinet secretaries often feuded with each other, in part since the ill-defined limits of departments led to jurisdictional disputes and in part because secretaries saw each other as rivals for the presidency. Presidents of the era had little control over a secretary's personnel, and one-third of secretaries lasted across administrations. Often presidents were stuck with secretaries they would rather dismiss, but had to keep to mollify congressional factions. Cabinet secretaries sought favor from congressional committees that appropriated their funds, and from congressional caucuses that determined presidential nominations until 1824 (Young, 1966).

For both executive branch and congressional politicians, public service could be an ugly experience. In tones that could be repeated today, Young (p. 52) quotes four politicians of the era who lamented that their profession meant:

> ... perpetual and malignant watchfulness with which I am observed in my open day and my secret night, with the deliberate purpose of exposing me to public obloquy or public ridicule;
> ... every man, in a high public station, must become fire-proof and bullet-proof, in his own defense;
> ... a certain loss of money [and] a very *uncertain* gain in reputation;
> ... abandonment of our professions or occupations, and the consequent   derangement of our private affairs.

As Young notes, the weakness of both the executive and legislative branches reflected a republican distrust of strong national power, and discouraged some talented Americans from pursuing public service. This distrust of centralized power continues today (Devine, 1976), and continues to make public service difficult (Carter, 1994).

Yet this is not the whole story. While turnover at the political levels was high, there was considerable stability among executive branch officials below the cabinet level. These officials often served for life and were succeeded in office by their sons. Departments were hierarchically structured and could be considered the only institutions in Washington. As today, career bureaucrats complained about their salaries and attitudes of their political bosses. They also had a distinct culture and community, with its own benevolent society, and such regular social activities as an annual parade that mocked the pretensions of political superiors (Young, 1966, 213–217). Further, this early administration was bureaucratic in its emphasis on standard procedures, record keeping, rationality, and use of statistics (Van Riper, 1958, 18–19; Nelson, 1982).

The Spoils System: Ideology and Self-Interest

By the 1820s, the nation was larger and had become even more populist in its view of the national government. An uncritical faith in elections brought an expansion of suffrage and an explosion in the number of elected offices on the state and local levels. Unified political parties developed to sort out ballot complexity and provide coherence to government. To win office, parties needed an army of workers. The patronage of government jobs helped motivate these partisans, and maintained some discipline once a party won office (Kaufman, 1956; Knott and Miller, 1987, 17). This ushered in a second era of American public administration, termed by Mosher (61–70), Government by the Common Man—the Spoils System. Starting on the state level, the movement to spoils was expressed on the federal level through the 1820 Tenure of Office Act, which created the machinery for a clean sweep of the bureaucracy by making the tenures of many positions coincident with presidential terms (Hoogenboom, 1961, 5).

Using government offices to reward successful partisans has always appealed to the self-interest of election-winners. The use of patronage for reward has always been most common in regions dominated by individualistic political culture, where politics is viewed as a tussle for material gain rather than an expression of ideals (Freedman, 1994; Maranto and Schultz, 1991, 46–50). Indeed, political boss George Washington Plunkitt declared that the people would not bother to vote, much less work in politics unless there is something in it for them: jobs and payoffs (Riordon, 1963, 15). Conversely, such moralistic politicians as President John Quincy Adams refused the widespread use of appointments to reward supporters and even retained men openly aligned with the opposition (Van Riper, 1958, 26).

Yet there are also idealistic reasons to support patronage. These were best expressed in the first inaugural message of Andrew Jackson, who is usually thought of as the father of spoils:

> There are, perhaps, few men who can for any great length of time enjoy office and power without being more or less under the influence of feelings unfavorable to the faithful discharge of their public duties. . . . Office is considered a species of property, and government rather as a means of promoting individual interests than as an instrument created solely for the service of the people. Corruption in some and in others a perversion of correct feelings and principles divert government from its legitimate ends and make it an engine for the support of the few at the expense of the many. (quoted in White, 1954, 318)

Jackson's observations accord with modern organization theory (Downs, 1967) and are echoed by certain modern writers (Maranto, 1998; Peters, 1979). Jackson's next observations are more doubtful, though certainly more accurate in his day than in ours:

> The duties of all public officers are, or at least admit of being made, so plain and simple that men of intelligence may readily qualify themselves for their performance; and I cannot but believe that more is lost by the long continuance of men in office than is generally gained by their experience. (White, 1954, 318)

Ironically, on the national level spoils increased bureaucratization. Many government jobs were in fact not so simple that anyone could do them. Yet if the government did not perform such basic services as mail delivery, voters would hold the ruling political party accountable. To cope, government managers under Jackson and later spoils presidents reorganized government, defining and simplifying jobs. They developed accounting and monitoring units to control corruption, and stressed unity of command to increase accountability; thus spoils bred bureaucracy (Crenson, 1975, 42–52; Nelson, 1982, 760–761).

Indeed, at least on the national level, turnover under the spoils system was not so great as many suppose. Jackson replaced well under 20 percent of federal officials. With the exceptions of Polk, Buchanan, and Lincoln (who purged southerners), later spoils presidents had similar records (Maranto, 1993b, 10–12). As White (1954, 349) notes, a career service was saved "by the hard necessities of administration, by the sheer need to get things done.[4] The necessities of administration also led parties to seek qualified political appointees. Though arguing that spoils decreased efficiency and increased corruption, White (1954, 343) nonetheless admits that "both Whigs and Democrats looked for character and competence among their partisans, and often found these qualities." The need to get things done also led spoils managers to develop such personnel reforms as civil service examinations to assure minimum competence, official pay grades, the employment of women as clerks and administrators, statistics to measure productivity, antinepotism rules, and even rules against sexual harassment in the workplace (Aron, 1987; Maranto, 1998; Maranto and Schultz, 1991; White, 1954, 1958). As with any American administrative innovation (e.g., Ingraham, 1995; Light, 1997), these practices were introduced ad hoc by individual political entrepreneurs, without a guiding plan for reform.

At the level of the political system, increased party discipline under spoils helped bring coherence to a larger nation and more fractious political system. As Young (1966, 253) writes:

> ... Jacksonian democracy seems to have been the only alternative to the disintegration of the only institution which could hold the nation together: the Washington community. At the very least, Jacksonian democracy bought time enough—another three decades—for the polity to have a fair chance of surviving in the face of open insurrection.

Though spoils today lacks legitimacy, executive leadership still requires the ability to appoint fellow-partisans to policymaking positions (Maranto, 1993b, 2005; Weko, unpublished, 1995).

The Slow (and Partial) Death of Spoils

Though the spoils system was popular for most of the 19th century, the causes of its eventual demise were numerous, and were linked both to material interests and to changing ideas. As Irish American politicians increasingly ran American cities and rewarded their constituents with jobs, Protestants came to oppose spoils (Callow, 1965; Riordon, 1963). More importantly, business interests resented the corruption of some services, and found American public service less efficient and effective than European counterparts. This was particularly true of mail delivery, tax collection, and Union military performance in the Civil War (Hoogenboom, 1961; Skowronek, 1982). These comparisons led American academics to advocate a merit-based public service, often importing European ideas (Van Riper, 1990).

More important were the beliefs and interests of politicians. As Johnson and Libecap show, as the size of government increased, the ability of presidents and congressmen to select and monitor patronage employees decreased, making a merit system more attractive to politicians (1994, 12–41). Short-term forces were also important. As supporters of the party of Jackson, Democrats had traditionally favored spoils. Republicans, representing business and academia, were more skeptical. For many upper-class moralists spoils politicians replaced slave owners as a devil to be fought. Yet the experience of losing each presidential election from 1860 to 1884 weakened Democratic support for spoils. The 1881 assassination of President Garfield by an insane position seeker blackened the name of spoils. After losing the 1882 midterm elections, Republicans saw that they would lose the 1884 presidential race and joined Democrats in passing the Pendleton Act. The Act set up a small merit system, which was then expanded by presidents through executive order until the Hoover Administration, by which time over 80 percent of federal employees were under a merit system and very few of those outside it could be considered endangered (Maranto and Schultz, 1991, 44–59, 80). The Pendleton Act did not address removal, since reformers reasoned that there would be no temptation to remove officials politically so long as selection was not political (Ingraham, 1995, 27).

Spoils appointments continued on the state and local level, and when presidents staffed new agencies, such as the many New Deal organizations created by Franklin Roosevelt. As noted above, to some degree spoils is necessary to assure executive leadership. Still, the Pendleton Act marked an intellectual defeat for spoils from which it never recovered (Freedman, 1994; Maranto and Schultz, 1991). The moralist opposition to spoils caused Mosher (1982, 64) to call the period after the Pendleton Act Government by the Good.

Government by the Efficient

Regulating hiring might limit corruption, but was insufficient to manage the larger bureaucracies of the era. Accordingly, reformers paid increasing attention to improving the capacity of public bureaucracies, in part by forging links with universities and businesses. Indeed, as noted above, Wilson, Roosevelt, and other reformers believed that public administration should be considered a field of business apart from politics. This business focus prompted Mosher to call the 1906–1932 period Government by the Efficient. In personnel policy, the period emphasized rationality, planning, specialization, quantitative measurement, and standardization of work reflecting the belief that there existed "one best way" to perform any task. This Scientific Management based personnel philosophy, as well as the decreased ability of politicians to monitor the growing federal establishment, led Congress to pass the Classification Act of 1923, which classified and graded federal positions according to five occupational services and established the principle of equal work for equal pay. A near science of efficiency ratings and job testing was developed in order to depersonalize personnel decisions to the extent possible, and remove politics from personnel (Johnson and Libecap, 1994, 85–87; Mosher, 1982, 70–79; Taylor, 1916). Given that most of the work of government was noncontroversial, this could be defended. Even today, many career bureaucrats support a strict separation between politics and administration, believing the latter to be the realm of career experts (Maranto, 1993b, 117–126).

This was the heyday of classical public personnel management. In the era of "normalcy" public bureaucracies on all levels were relatively respected and stable. Yet certain policies undermined principles of merit-based personnel management. The veterans' preferences in hiring introduced after the Civil War remained in force, as they do today (Ingraham, 1995, 40–41). The 1912 Lloyd-LaFolette

Act granted federal employees the right to organize and petition Congress, even though union agreements could undermine merit-based compensation and promotion. As Ingraham (43) writes, "[m]erit itself had been essentially redefined by political reality, by veterans' preference, and by unions." Notably, under the postspoils regime there were fewer political influentials in the federal bureaucracy. Perhaps for this reason, Congress let federal pay lag, though (save at executive levels) federal compensation remained ahead of most private sector alternatives thanks to lobbying by civil service unions (Johnson and Libecap, 1994, 108–119).

A much more nefarious political attack on merit came under Woodrow Wilson. Under the examination-based merit system, small but significant numbers of African Americans had attained middle and upper level government positions by excelling in civil service examinations. By the Wilson administration, increased racism nationwide and the Democratic dependence on southern white voters jeopardized their positions. The Wilson administration made candidate photographs mandatory for job and promotion seekers, and used the "rule of three" (allowing selection of any of the top three candidates rather than the high scorer) to block the path of promising African Americans. Wilson political appointees segregated the civil service, in part to assure that African Americans would never supervise whites. The Republican presidents of the 1920s failed to undo these policies (King, 1995, 43–58).

Government Gets Big and Controversial

Relative consensus could not last. In the 1930s and 1940s all levels of public service, but particularly the federal service expanded to confront the calamities of depression, world war, and later the cold war. As never before, the federal government played a key role in managing the economy, providing jobs and entitlements, building housing, assuring the civil rights of workers to form and join unions, and maintaining a permanent military (Galambos, 1987). The growth of government made the goals of government agencies more controversial. Before the New Deal, each political party supported the missions of most federal agencies, though Republicans were traditionally more supportive of federal bureaucracies than were Democrats. After the New Deal, Republicans opposed the missions of many domestic agencies, particularly those representing labor unions or with entitlement-based missions (Agriculture, HEW, and Labor). Political controversy complicated personnel management. Traditionally, presidential transitions led to some demands on bureaucracies for patronage. Efforts on the part of political appointees to substantially reorient the work of agencies were unusual, however, and normally linked to cleaning up corruption or increasing efficiency. The New Deal changed this. By the 1950s, old style (reward) patronage was less common than that intended to enhance presidential control of administration; thus the Republican presidential transition of 1953 had unusual levels of conflict between career executives and political appointees (Lowi, 1979; Maranto, 1993b, 1998;

Somers, 1954; Van Riper, 1958). As he confided to John Foster Dulles, Eisenhower suspected that:

> Almost without exception [career executives] reached these high administrative offices through a process of selection based upon their devotion to the socialistic doctrine and bureaucratic controls practiced over the past two decades. (Brauer, 1986, 42–43)

To put his stamp on the sprawling post–New Deal federal executive, Eisenhower inaugurated the "Schedule C" personnel category to increase the numbers of political appointees. Schedule C's exist to this day, and are still resented by federal careerists (Maranto, 1993b; Maranto and Schultz, 1991, 111–13).

The more political nature of public personnel management was reflected in changing concepts of public administration. Increasingly, the separation of politics and administration championed by classical reformers was questioned. Such academic/practitioners as Paul Appleby (1949), Norton Long (1962), and Marver Bernstein (1958) saw political savvy as key to administration. As one federal executive (quoted in Bernstein, 43–44) said:

> You would not be able to recruit top executives for a strictly nonpolitical job. That kind of job is without flavor. It is not the sort of job that a man with spunk would live with, and he couldn't even if he wanted to. The facts of life in Washington just wouldn't let him. The career executives must have policy commitments, and these commitments must be of the stature to attract and hold men of dedication and capacity.

While formally neutral, skilled public executives would have to work with rather than avoid politics and politicians (Maranto, 2005). They would have to judge the success of their agency in part by political viability, rather than mere efficiency. This was reflected in the passage of the Administrative Procedures Act of 1946, which outlined the rule-making and adjudicative powers of federal agencies (Maranto and Schultz, 1991, 110). In part to allow greater responsiveness to political leadership, the Second Hoover Commission proposed a 3,000-member Senior Civil Service that would be careerist and politically "neutral," but also transferable to assure accountability to political leadership. This proposal languished for many years, but eventually inspired the 7,000-person Senior Executive Service developed by the Civil Service Reform Act of 1979. The shift from an efficiency emphasis to a broader management emphasis led Mosher (1982, 79) to call the new era a Government by Administrators.

The greater size of the public sector and more political nature of public administration led Congress to weaken presidential control of the bureaucracy. In 1939, in response to President Roosevelt's efforts to use patronage to control Democratic congressional nominations, Congress passed the Hatch Act banning political activity by federal employees. Hatch remained substantially unchanged until 1993, when President Clinton and a Democratic congress essentially repealed the law. (The "unHatching" of federal employees has seemingly done the civil service no damage.) The evergreater size of the civil service in this era made federal employees still more difficult for political leaders to monitor. In response, Congress passed the Ramspeck Act of 1940, which brought New Deal agencies under the merit system and made it easier for congressional staff to join the executive. In 1949, Congress modified the classification system and extended it to field offices (Johnson and Libecap, 1994, 100; Van Riper, 1958, 332–343). As always, broad political and social movements affected the civil service. The 1960s represented the peak of labor union influence. In 1962, President Kennedy's Executive Order 10988 gave federal employees the right to bargain collectively and the Federal Salary Reform Act introduced the principle of comparability with private wage scales. The 1970 Federal Pay Comparability Act gave federal unions direct input to the methodology determining pay comparability. In the long run, union influence and case law also made it extremely difficult to terminate civil servants for cause (Johnson and Libecap, 1994, 104–118; Maranto, 1999, 2002). Similarly, the civil rights movement affected the civil service. The 1964 Civil Rights Act prohibited discrimination in federal agencies, and President Johnson's Executive Order 11246 established affirmative action as the method to attain equal opportunity. By the 1980s, federal courts ruled the most commonly used civil service examination discriminatory towards minorities; by consent decree the PACE exam was discarded (Maranto and Schultz, 1991, 136–137).

Republican party skepticism about federal intrusion grew after the Great Society further expanded the missions of the federal government to include the protection of civil rights for minorities and women (the Equal Employment Opportunity Commission, the Civil Rights Division of the Department of Justice, and other organizations), environmental protection (the Environmental Protection Agency), protection for workers (Occupational Safety and Health Administration), subsidies for the Arts (National Endowment for the Arts), and for the regulation of such state and local services as education (U.S. Department of Education). Some conservatives saw these and other public bureaucracies as institutionalized liberalism. At the same time, their skepticism about the cold war in general and the Vietnam War in particular led liberal politicians to question the funding and operation of the Pentagon with increasing vehemence. Naturally, bureaucrats reciprocated. Federal employees (and especially military officers) in the Defense Department now tend to vote Republican, while those in social welfare and regulatory agencies now tend Democratic. More than in the past, party politics link to the institutions of the state, and many supposedly neutral bureaucracies have strong emotional and material stakes in elections (Holsti 1997; Johnson and Libecap 1994, 166–169; Maranto 1993a, 1993b).

The expanded scope and increased controversy of federal missions made the role of political appointees in assuring White House domination of the executive branch more vital than ever before. Presidents Nixon and Reagan, in particular, used elaborate political criteria to assure that their appointees were ideologically correct. In social welfare and regulatory agencies, this made the career-noncareer relations under the Nixon and Reagan administrations particularly controversial (Maranto 1993b; Maranto and Schultz, 1991, 115–160) The increased import of political appointments led presidents from Nixon on to centralize political personnel mechanisms in the White House, rather than relying on the party national committees as had been traditional (Weko, 1995). In regulatory agencies, conservative presidents have also institutionalized in-house analytic units to assure that economic costs are considered in regulatory rule-making (McGarity, 1991).

Open Government

In the wake of Watergate and later scandals, Congress passed and successive presidents imposed increasingly onerous ethics rules for both political appointees and career federal executives. These were intended to increase public trust in government, but their actual impacts may have been to decrease trust by criminalizing trivial actions. New rules made both contracting decisions and hiring more cumbersome than in the past. The same occurred in state and local government (Anechiarico and Jacobs, 1996; Garvey, 1993; Kelman, 1990; Maranto, 2002). Further, a new culture of investigation changed how the media covered public affairs (Garment, 1992; Sabato, 1993). Combined with the increasingly ideological nature of political appointments, the open government regime has made the Senate confirmation more difficult than ever, as presidents struggle to find appointees who will not present even the appearance of scandal, and applicants go through ever more elaborate disclosure forms and background investigations. Each president from Kennedy to Clinton had a more difficult time than the president before in filling executive branch positions. It took President Clinton 8 months to get most of his Senate-confirmed appointees in government (Mackenzie, 1996), a record roughly matched by the George W. Bush administration (Maranto, 2005). The new culture has had its greatest impact on the political ranks, but has also affected how career civil servants perform more routine functions of government, including hiring and promotion.

The Recent Past and Near Future: A New Government by the Efficient

As always, changing public ideas have influenced the civil service of the post-Watergate period. The ascendance of conservative and neoliberal ideas since the mid-1970s led Presidents Carter, Reagan, Clinton, and George W. Bush to seek to make the civil service operate more like business. Persistent deficits driven by entitlement spending led both Democratic and Republican politicians to seek ways to increase the efficiency of the civil service. After the fall of the Soviet Union discredited central planning, the pace of reform picked up both in the United States and abroad (Gore 1993; Maranto, 1993b, 36–37; Savas, 1987; Schwartz, 1992; Yergin and Stanislaw, 1998). For New Democrats like President Clinton and Old Republicans like President G.W. Bush, increasing government efficiency could win votes, provide funds for new initiatives, and increase public trust in the government's ability to provide service (Gore 1993; Marshall 1997; Osborne and Gaebler 1992).

But increased efficiency and marketization is not the only goal of the new era. As government does more things involving both goal and technical controversy (such as ending welfare, redesigning education, and fighting acid rain), the increased use of consultative mechanisms as recommended by Hult and Walcott may find their way into public bureaucracies. Intellectually, Peters (1996) suggests that the old bureaucratic paradigm will be replaced by emerging models based on markets, greater participation by stakeholders (including bureaucrats), and increased flexibility and deregulation of the civil service process. None of these stresses such old-fashioned administrative values as stability, hierarchy, procedure, and the rule of law. Similarly, Barzelay (1992), Moore (1995), and most importantly, Vice President Gore (1993) describe the need to create stakeholders both inside and outside of government to allow public entrepreneurship to add value to government outputs, and to allow government to act quickly in an information age of turbulent technological and political environments.

An early example of market-based civil service reform was President Carter's Civil Service Reform Act of 1978, which introduced merit pay and collapsed the old career supergrades into a new Senior Executive Service (SES). SES members have rank-in-person rather than in position, and can be transferred by their political bosses with relative ease. Not surprisingly, this received criticism from some public administration scholars, who argued that merit pay and transferability would promote individualism and undermine a civil service ethic. Supporters claimed that bonuses would reward high performers, and that the SES could maintain competence while enhancing political leadership (Maranto, 1993b, 41–42, 46–48).

A second series of reforms decentralized and instilled more choice in federal personnel management. From the 1970s to the 1990s, hiring was increasingly decentralized so that by 1987 more than a third of new hires were conducted via more than thirty hiring authorities outside the regular merit system. This reflected the simple truth that centralized hiring was too slow to meet the changing needs of federal agencies (Ingraham, 1995, 55–63; Maranto, 2002). On the individual level, segments of the new federal retirement plans inaugurated in 1983 allowed federal employees to be vested in the retirement system immediately, and gave them considerable control over their individualized retirement investment accounts. This loosened the "golden handcuffs" of the old retirement system in which pensions were highly dependent on tenure and punished those who left government service to pursue other careers. In the long term, this will lead to less permanent government employment, decreasing institutional memory but also making government bureaucracies more representative of the society they serve.

The most far-reaching, and probably most successful set of civil service reforms came under the broad umbrella of Vice President Gore's Reinventing Government report, much of whose work has indeed continued under President George

W. Bush. As part of the "REGO" initiative, federal agencies had to justify why their activities should remain in-house rather than be contracted out. Core functions would be kept inside government, but actual service delivery could be contracted if that would result in savings. Those functions that would be provided by government would focus more on results and less on procedures. The new management ideal would be to set broad directions and specify measurable results (as through the Government Performance and Results Act) for whole agencies, and where possible, for individuals. Rather than regulation, employees and agencies would be motivated through values and incentives to do the right thing (Gore, 1993). In addition, the U.S. Office of Personnel Management increasingly allowed agencies to develop their own merit procedures, with oversight. The Clinton Defense Department worked on plans that in the long run would mean that most new hires will not have tenure. Rather they would sign 3- or 5-year contracts, with continued employment based on success in the job (Causey, 1998). More recently, the George W. Bush Defense Department and the new Department of Homeland Security have adopted such plans, and reformed pay to increase managerial discretion to reward high performers.

Enjoying popularity and significant intellectual support, even within the bureaucracy, reforms that emphasize efficiency and results in government personnel policy are likely to continue for some time. Indeed, similar reforms of government are taking place in many democracies (Kettl, 1997; Schwartz, 1992) and on the state and local level (Klingner and Lynn, 1996). Such reforms will mean that government personnel policies will focus less on procedure and more on hiring (and separating) employees as needed by workload demands. Government managers can expect more flexibility in hiring, compensating, and separating their employees. Politically, this will prove popular, at least unless scandals and lawsuits put an end to the new era of efficiency and lead to reregulation. How quickly—or indeed if—this will happen is anyone's guess.

While we cannot know the duration of the new version of government by the efficient, it is certain that for so long as American democracy continues, public personnel management will remain representation and political, with bureaucratic systems tempering but also reflecting the changing ideas and interests of the broader American polity. So near as we can tell, this politically driven system has indeed given the United States good public service, perhaps the best on earth. To paraphrase Churchill, political public administration is indeed the worst form known—except for its various alternatives, which have been tried from time to time.

NOTES

1. I say "officially" since in practice, the very complexity of public personnel rules often leads to complex end-runs around the official system. These shortcuts can be baffling to outsiders and may in fact make public personnel practices less open than those in the private sector. For some examples of federal personnel systems in practice, see Ban, 1995.

2. Similarly, one of my informants lamented that in the 1950s and the 1960s the Indian Health Service was fighting infectious diseases, a mission which required great dedication and technical skill but was not controversial. Today IHS must work to modify Native American lifestyles, a far more difficult and controversial mission.

3. Naturally, public managers attempt to shape perceptions of goals and technologies to define their desired actions as successful, for example, J. Edgar Hoover and Robert Moses.

4. This was not always true on the state and local level, where less competitive political systems gave political leaders more power to reshape administration (Maranto 1998, 636).

REFERENCES

Allison, G.T. (1984). Public and Private Management: Are They Fundamentally Alike in all Unimportant Respects. In Richard J. Stillman (Ed.), *Public Administration: Concepts and Cases*, pp. 453–66. Boston, MA: Houghton Mifflin.

Anechiarico, F., and J.B. Jacobs. (1996). *The Pursuit of Absolute Integrity: How Corruption Control Makes Government Ineffective*. Chicago, IL: University of Chicago Press.

Appleby, P.B. (1949). *Policy and Administration*. University, AL: University of Alabama Press.

Ban, C. (1995). *How Do Public Managers Manage?* San Francisco, CA: Jossey-Bass.

Barzelay, M. with B.J. Armajani. (1992). *Breaking Through Bureaucracy*. Berkeley, CA: University of California Press.

Bernstein, M. (1958). *The Job of the Federal Executive*. Washington, DC: Brookings.

Blank, Warren. (1995). *The Nine Natural Laws of Leadership*. New York: American Management Association.

Brauer, C.M. (1986). *Presidential Transitions: Eisenhower Through Reagan*. New York: Oxford University Press.

Callow, A. (1965). *The Tweed Ring*. New York: Oxford University Press.

Carter, S.L. (1994). *The Confirmation Mess: Cleaning Up the Federal Appointments Process*. New York: Basic Books.

Causey, M. (1998, March 26). Possible Shape of Things to Come. *Washington Post*: D2.

Crenson, M.A. (1975). *The Federal Machine*. Baltimore, MD: Johns Hopkins University Press.

Devine, D.J. (1976). *The Political Culture of the United States*. Boston, MA: Little, Brown.

Downs, A. (1967). *Inside Bureaucracy*. Boston, MA: Little, Brown.

Freedman, A. (1994). *Patronage: An American Tradition*. Chicago, IL: Nelson-Hall.

Galambos, L. (Ed.) (1987). *The New American State*. Baltimore, MD: Johns Hopkins University Press.

Garment, S. (1992). *Scandal: The Culture of Mistrust in American Politics*. New York: Anchor.

Garvey, G. (1993). *Facing the Bureaucracy: Living and Dying in a Public Amy*. San Francisco, CA: Jossey-Bass.

Gore, A. (1993). *Creating a Government That Works Better and Costs Less: Report of the National Performance Review*. New York: Times Books.

Hibbing, J.R., and E. Theiss-Morse. (1995). *Congress as Public Enemy*. New York: Cambridge University Press.

Holsti, O.R. (1997). A Widening Gap Between the Military and Civilian Society? Some Evidence, 1976–1996. Working Paper 13. Harvard, MA: Harvard University Project on U.S. Post-Cold War Military Relations.

Hoogenboom, A. (1961). *Outlawing the Spoils.* Urbana, IL: University of Illinois Press.

Hult, K.M., and C. Walcott. (1990). *Governing Public Organizations: Politics, Structures, and Institutional Design.* Pacific Grove, CA: Brooks/Cole.

Ingraham, P.W. (1995). *The Foundation of Merit: Public Service in American Democracy.* Baltimore, MD: Johns Hopkins University Press.

Johnson, R.N., and G.D. Libecap. (1994). *The Federal Civil Service System and the Problem of Bureaucracy.* Chicago, IL: University of Chicago Press.

Kaufman, H. (1956, December). Emerging Conflicts in the Doctrines of Public Administration. *American Political Science Review,* 50(4): 1057–1073.

Kelman, S. (1990). *Procurement and Public Management: The Fear of Discretion and the Quality of Government Performance.* Washington, DC: AEI Press.

Kettl, D.F. (1997). The Global Revolution in Public Management: Driving Themes, Missing Links. *Journal of Policy Analysis and Management,* 16 (3): 446–462.

Kettl, D.F. (1993). *Sharing Power: Public Governance and Private Markets.* Washington, DC: Brookings Institution.

King, D. (1995). *Separate and Unequal: African Americans and the US Federal Government.* New York: Oxford University Press.

Klingner, D., and D.B. Lynn. (1996). Beyond Civil Service: The Changing Role of Public Personnel Management. Presented at the Annual American Society for Public Administration meeting in Atlanta.

Knott, J.H., and G.J. Miller. (1987). *Reforming Bureaucracy.* Englewood Cliffs, NJ: Prentice-Hall.

Light, P.C. (1997). *The Tides of Reform: Making Government Work, 1945–1995.* New Haven, CT: Yale University Press.

Lindblom, C.E. (1959). The Science of Muddling Through. *Public Administration Review,* 19,(2):79–88.

Long, N.E. (1962). *The Polity.* Chicago, IL: Rand McNally.

Lowi, T.J. (1979). *The End of Liberalism,* 2nd ed. New York: Norton.

Mackenzie, G.C. (1996). *Obstacle Course.* New York: Twentieth Century Fund.

Maranto, R. (2005). *Beyond a Government of Strangers: How Career Executives and Political Appointees Can Turn Conflict to Cooperation.* Lanham, MD: Lexington.

———. (1993a). Exploring the Clinton Transition: Views From the Career Civil Service. Presented at the 1993 American Political Science Association Convention in Washington.

———. (1993b). *Politics and Bureaucracy in the Modern Presidency: Careerists and Appointees in the Reagan Administration.* Westport, CT: Greenwood Press.

———. (2002, Fall). Praising Civil Service But Not Bureaucracy: A Brief Against Tenure in the U.S. Civil Service. *Review of Public Personnel Administration,* 22(3): 175–192.

———. (1998). Thinking the Unthinkable in Public Administration: A Case For Spoils in the Federal Bureaucracy. *Administration and Society,* 29(6): 623–642.

———. (November 1999). Turkey Farm: Why We Can't Delay Civil Service Reform. *Washington Monthly,* 27–21.

Maranto, R., and D. Schultz. (1991). *A Short History of the U.S. Civil Service.* Lanham, MD: University Press of America.

Marshall, W. (Ed.) (1997). *Building the Bridge: Ten Big Ideas to Transform America.* Lanham, MD: Rowman & Littlefield.

Mayhew, D.R. (1991). *Divided We Govern.* New Haven, CT: Yale University Press.

McGarity, T. (1991). *Reinventing Rationality: The Role of Regulatory Analysis in the Federal Bureaucracy.* New York: Cambridge University Press.

Micklethwait, J., and A. Wooldridge. (1996). *The Witch Doctors: Making Sense of Management Gurus.* New York: Random House.

Moore, M.H. (1995). *Creating Public Value: Strategic Management in Government.* Cambridge, MA: Harvard University Press.

Mosher, F.C. (1982) *Democracy and the Public Service.* New York: Oxford University Press.

Nelson, M. (1982). A Short, Ironic History of American National Bureaucracy. *Journal of Politics,* 44(2): 747–778.

Osborne, T., and Gaebler T. (1992). *Reinventing Government: How the Entrepreneurial Spirit Is Transforming the Public Sector* Reading, MA: Addison-Wesley.

Ostrom, V. (1974). *The Intellectual Crisis in American Public Administration.* University, AL: University of Alabama Press.

Peters, B.G. (1996). *The Future of Governing: Four Emerging Models.* Lawrence, KS: University Press of Kansas.

Peters, C. (1979). A Kind Word For the Spoils System. In Peters and Nelson (Eds.), *The Culture of Bureaucracy,* pp. 263–67). New York: Holt, Rinehart.

Peters, T.J., and R.H. Waterman, Jr. (1982). *In Search of Excellence.* New York: Warner Books.

Riordon, W.L. (1963). *Plunkitt of Tammany Hall.* New York: Dutton.

Sabato, L.J. (1993). *Feeding Frenzy: How Attack Journalism Has Transformed American Politics.* New York: Free Press.

Savas, E.S. (1987). *Privatization: The Key to Better Government.* Chatham, UK: Chatham House.

Schiesl, M.J. (1977). *The Politics of Efficiency.* Berkeley, CA: University of California Press.

Schwartz, H. (1992). Privatizing and Reorganizing the State in Australia, Denmark, New Zealand, and Sweden. Presented at the Annual Meeting of the American Political Science Association, Chicago, IL.

Skowronek, S. (1982). *Building a New American State.* Cambridge, UK: Cambridge University Press.

Somers, H.M. (1954). The Federal Bureaucracy and the Change of Administrations. *American Political Science Review* 48(1): 131–151.

Stelzer, I. M. (1992, Spring). What Thatcher Wrought. *The Public Interest,* 117: 18–51.

Taylor, F. W. (1916). The Principles of Scientific Management. In J.M. Shafritz and P.H. Whitbeck (Ed.), *Classics of Organization Theory,* pp. 9–23. Oak Park, IL: Moore.

Van Riper, P.P. (1958). *History of the United States Civil Service.* Evanston, IL: Row, Peterson.

Van Riper, P.P. (1990). Administrative Thought in the 1880s. In Van Riper (Ed.), *The Wilson Influence on Public Administration: From Theory to Practice,* pp. 7–16. Washington, DC: American Society for Public Administration.

Walcott, C.E., and K.M. Hult. (1995) *Governing the White House from Hoover through LBJ.* Lawrence, KS: University Press of Kansas.

Weko, T.J. *A Good Man Is Hard to Find: Presidents and Their Political Executives.* University of Minnesota: Unpublished Ph.D. Dissertation.

Weko, T.J. (1995). *The Politicizing Presidency: The White House Personnel Office, 1948–1994.* Lawrence, KS: University Press of Kansas.

White, L.D. (1954). *The Jacksonians: A Study in Administrative History*. New York: Macmillan.

Wildavsky, A. (1969). Rescuing Policy Analysis from PPBS. *Public Administration Review*, 29(2): 189–202.

Wilson, J.Q. (1976). The Rise of the Bureaucratic State. In N. Glazer and I. Kristol (Eds.), *The American Commonwealth*. New York: Basic.

Wilson, W. (1887). The Study of Administration. In J.M. Shafritz and A.C. Hyde (Ed.), *Classics of Public Administration*, pp. 3–16. Oak Park, IL: Moore, 1978.

Yergin, D., and J. Stanislaw. (1998). *The Commanding Heights: The Battle Between Government and the Marketplace That Is Remaking the Modern World*. New York: Simon & Schuster.

Young, J.S. (1966). *The Washington Community, 1800–1828*. New York: Columbia University Press.

10

Ending Civil Service Paralysis: Emerging Practices and Trends in State Human Resource Management

SALLY SELDEN

I n the 1990s, governments at all levels were interested in reforming, reinventing, and reengineering their human resource (HR) practices. Unlike in the 1970s, civil service was no longer viewed as the solution to the problems in the 1990s; rather, it was perceived as being the problem (Ingraham and Eisenberg, 1995). In an effort to modernize their systems, many governments implemented changes to their civil service systems and human resource management practices in the 1990s. In the 2000s, government officials are still interested in reform, but the focus has shifted. The rhetoric has shifted toward creating high performing government workforces by treating employees as assets, by recognizing and rewarding employee performance, and by providing employees opportunities to excel (Leavitt and Johnson, 1998). At the heart of these efforts is the need to establish high standards of professional conduct and performance for government employees. Public organizations can employ different human resource management (HRM) tools such as performance evaluations, performance-based pay, and discipline to reinforce conduct and performance expectations. The extent to which states engage in practices that promote high performance varies depending upon the existing human resource management systems and state environment. Most states, however, realize that labor force demographics are changing and that about one out of five state workers will be eligible to retire in the next 5 years (see Figure 10.1). If states want to compete for high quality hires, they must create employment opportunities that are attractive to prospective employees, who may be considering both private enterprise and public sector prospects. To remain competitive, states are changing hiring regulations; utilizing technology to support hiring, training, and development; and developing training partnerships across government agencies.

This chapter presents information on trends and innovations in state human resource management using data collected from state governments in August 2004 as part of the Government Performance Project (GPP). The GPP administered the survey to a central point of contact in each state, typically in the state's budgeting office. The central state contact person then provided the director of the state's central human resource management agency access to the HRM section of the GPP survey. The director and his or her staff completed the online survey and detailed the state's discipline and termination policies. Forty-one states provided information for a response rate of 82 percent. The summary GPP research highlights five trends in state human resource management that emerged from the GPP study. Understanding these trends is beneficial to students and practitioners of public administration.

TREND 1: THE DEBATE ABOUT CIVIL SERVICE CONTINUES

The ascendancy of reform at the federal level has often influenced state leaders; many states have reorganized their public personnel systems based on federal reforms. After the passage of the Pendleton Act in 1883, many states followed the federal government's lead by designing systems to ensure stability and to insulate state employees from political influence. The debate continues over the future of civil service and whether any government body should provide employees certain administrative and legal due process rights before discharging them for cause (Wallihan, 2003). In the past, the rationale for providing such protections was to protect public sector employees from partisan pressure and removal (Mosher, 1968). Over the last century, however, our understanding of effective human resource practices has evolved, and today some civil service reformers are lobbying to do away with such protections (Kellough and Nigro, 2005b). Some states, such as Georgia and Florida, have shifted at least part of the legal basis of their employment systems from a civil service structure to an employment-at-will model.

In addition to activity at the state level, the debate continues at the federal level, with President George W. Bush promoting legislation that allows federal agencies to adopt employment systems like the Department of Homeland Security's (DHS) new personnel system (Lee, 2005). The new MaxHR system will allow DHS to focus on individual performance and accountability and offers a comprehensive approach to HRM, with new tools for recruitment and retention, training and development, and recognition of achievement through promotion and compensation (DHS, 2005). These tools, paired with at-will hiring practices, represent a new trend in government employment.

Employment-at-will typically connotes an employer's right to terminate an employee without a specified reason and an employee's right to leave when she or he elects (Baucus and Dworkin, 1998; Fulmer and Casey, 1990). Private sector

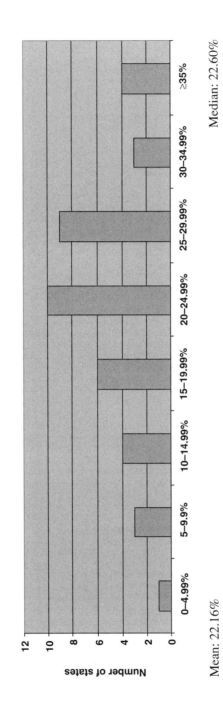

Mean: 22.16%   Median: 22.60%

FIGURE 10.1. Percent of Classified Employees Eligible to Retire in the Next Five Years

organizations in the United States have long adhered to this type of employment system. The right of employers to terminate employees has become an area of increasing litigation, with many wrongful discharge suits filed each year (Fulmer and Casey, 1990). Both federal legislation and state laws provide exceptions to the doctrine of at-will employment, including, but not limited to: participation in union activities, whistle-blowing, public policy, employer motivation, race, ethnicity, religion, national origin, sex, disabilities (Fulmer and Casey, 1990).

Some states are less receptive to the idea of wholly at-will employment. Montana, for example, is the only state that has passed legislation prohibiting employers from discharging employees without good cause (Falcone, 1999; Wallihan, 2003). In some states and organizations, just cause for discipline and discharge of employees is often an essential protection accorded to employees by a collective bargaining agreement (Abrams and Nolan, 1985; Stieber and Rodgers, 1994). Thus, all organizations, regardless of sector, have some constraints over their ability to terminate employees.

Many states are changing their employment paradigms but are not following the example set by Georgia and Florida in moving toward at-will employment. Rather than focusing on the elimination of civil service protections, these states are working on changing other Human Resource Management policies and practices to foster a high performance culture.

The Washington State Model

The Washington State Legislature enacted the Personnel System Reform Act (PSRA) of 2002, which reformed the state's 40-year-old civil service system. The new system is focused on enhanced outcomes and fewer rules. Specifically, the PSRA includes three principal components:

- Collective bargaining: For the first time, state employees will be able to bargain for wages, hours, and other terms of employment.
- Competitive contracting: Most state services will be managed on a contract basis and state employees may now compete in the bidding process.
- A new civil service system: A streamlined job classification system and completely new rules now manage all aspects of HR.

The full implementation of PRSA will bring about changes in the following areas:

Classification:

- Consolidates 2,400 job classes into approximately 300 broad occupational categories.
- Places more focus on key skills and responsibilities needed for specific positions.
- Enhances mobility and career opportunities for employees.

- Provides flexibility to adapt to changing technology and economic, workforce, citizen, and organizational needs.

Compensation:

- Provides decentralized flexibility to make salary adjustments, such as: assignment pay for special skills and competencies, working conditions, and recruitment and retention issues; salary adjustments to address equity issues; and individualized adjustments to progression increases based on nature of work or training needs.
- Provides options for monetary performance recognition, including acceleration or deferral of progression increases based on performance, or lump sum recognition awards of up to 15 percent of pay.

Recruitment and Selection Changes:

- Emphasizes recruitment and screening based on position-specific competency needs, rather than job classification.
- Gives employers more flexibility in how they recruit and screen candidates.
- Gives employers the option to use the Department of Personnel's (DOP) online application and screening process or develop their own process.
- Allows applications to be accepted at any time.
- Gives employers a choice between using desirable qualifications rather than minimum requirements (except where a qualification is legally required).
- Contains few, if any, required written exams.
- Provides each candidate pool as an unranked list.
- Allows employers to choose whether and how to use promotional preference.
- Decentralizes the candidate referral process to the employer, allowing the employer to choose how many names to refer.

Performance Management:

- Cultivates a performance-based culture in state government.
- Establishes a new Performance and Development Plan (PDP) to replace old evaluation forms, putting more emphasis on clear performance expectations, both competencies and results.
- Mandates management training within 6 months of an employee becoming a manager or supervisor.
- Requires a formal Performance Management Confirmation before an employee's performance may be used as a factor in compensation or layoff
- Allows the DOP to provide centralized guidance, training, and tools to assist in implementing performance management systems.

Reduction in Force (RIF):

- Allows agencies to factor performance and competencies into layoff decisions, along with seniority.
- Requires employees to meet position-specific requirements for layoff (bumping) options.

- Provides for all RIF names, plus promotional names, to be referred for reemployment after layoff (in the past, a rule of 1 was imposed, where only the most senior laid-off employee was referred for reemployment).
- Allows employers to require a review period for any RIF appointee.

With the implementation of PRSA, many centralized HRM functions in Washington were decentralized to state agencies, with the central HRM office serving as a resource for those state agencies and their changing business needs. In addition, the Legislature authorized modernization of the state's antiquated personnel/payroll computer system, replacing it with a modern integrated Human Resource Management System (HRMS). The HRMS is essential to supporting the successful implementation of all aspects of the state's personnel reform.

Other Examples of Civil Service Reform

In 2003, Iowa revised its civil service system for the first time since 1969. The state created charter agencies that are given greater administrative flexibility to operate in more innovative, results-oriented ways over a 5-year period. Agencies receiving charter status can convert direct report managerial positions to at-will positions. For example, the Iowa Lottery converted seven of its key positions to at-will status.

While many states have not significantly overhauled their Civil Service systems, they have reconceptualized the relationship between the central Human Resource Management office and state agencies. Arizona, for example, has focused on building partnerships with its state agencies. The state recognized the need for decision-making authority to reside in the agencies, but wanted to provide consistent HRM practices across the state. The state put together a team from the central and agency HRM offices to review, refine, and draft appropriate policies. The central office also established the Planning and Quality Assurance Unit, who is tasked with ensuring consistent human resources practices are maintained throughout Arizona state government.

TREND 2: STATES DO NOT MANAGE EMPLOYEE PERFORMANCE AS WELL AS THEY COULD

Performance Appraisals

Performance appraisals are an important part of a government's performance management system, the set of activities adopted by an organization to enhance the performance of their employees (DeNisi, 2000). The GPP found that 87 percent of classified employees in state government are evaluated formally at least once a year. This number falls significantly for employees in the nonclassified workforce. Only 47.9 percent of nonclassified state employees receive a formal annual performance appraisal.

State
goals

Agency
mission and goals

Unit goals and objectives

Team performance goals and objectives

Individual performance goals and objectives

FIGURE 10.2. Aligning Goals in a Performance Management System

Government agencies typically develop performance management processes to motivate and control employees (Mathis and Jackson, 2005). The process can motivate employees by establishing expectations and providing feedback on an employee's progress toward meeting those expectations. Ideally, the agency can then target training to address the weaknesses or areas of potential growth identified. In addition, agencies can adopt compensation systems to reward the achievement of goals. According to den Hartog, Boselie, and Paaiwe (2004), the ultimate objective of a performance management process is to align individual performance with organizational performance; the process should signal employees about the organization's goals, priorities, and expectations (see Figure 10.2).

The GPP found that about 30 percent of states used a performance appraisal system that strongly aligns state, agency, job, and individual goals. For example, the Montana Department of Transportation's (MDT) performance appraisal system is used to contribute to the agency's implementation of its strategic plan. MDT's performance appraisal is divided into two sections. Part I contains a set of seven competences that all MDR employees are expected to demonstrate regardless of position: interpersonal skills, decision making, creative problem solving, adaptability/flexibility, leadership/mentoring, accountability, and ethics/integrity. Part II focuses on specific job elements, criteria, and targets designed to link individuals to the Strategic Business Plan.

Connecticut's Performance Assessment and Recognition System (PAR) is designed to establish clear, achievable, measurable, results-oriented performance objectives, consistent with each agency's priorities and mission. Maine's performance management system is intended to relate employee performance objectives to organization goals and objectives so employees understand how their jobs contribute to the success of the organization. In addition to a set of jointly developed objectives, Maine state employees are assessed on a set of seven core competencies: initiative, adaptability, planning and organizing work, decision making, customer service, teamwork, and interpersonal relations.

Approximately 66 percent of states surveyed included a formal development plan as part of their performance evaluation process. For example, in Washington state, the Performance and Development Plan includes a training and development needs/opportunities segment. This segment should include training and development needs required in order for an employee to achieve or sustain fully successful performance. In addition to development goals for an employee's current position, the state expects that the development plans should include training and development goals for an employee's career advancement.

Since many of the states encourage regular informal feedback as part of their policy, the numbers reported in this study may underestimate the extent of feedback provided to state employees. Almost 43 percent of states provide formal feedback to employees once a year; slightly more provide formal feedback at the midway point and end of the year (44.7 percent). Only a few states (8.7 percent) provide formal, quarterly feedback to state government employees, with 4.3 percent of states providing formal feedback three times a year.

New Mexico's Employee Development and Appraisal (EDA) system is designed to foster constructive and ongoing dialogue between a supervisor and employee. EDA requires that the employee and supervisor formally meet five times during the year. In addition to an initial and final meeting, supervisor and employee meet for three interim reviews. The initial session between a supervisor and employee is used to establish goals and performance expectations via job assignments. Job assignments originate in the state agency's strategic plan and each employee is expected to share some of the responsibility and accountability for the agency meeting its goals. For each job assignment identified, the supervisor and employee name specific skills or behaviors the employee must utilize in order to succeed in that assignment. The three interim performance discussions are critical to maintain communication, identify challenges, review job and agency objectives, and to provide formal feedback about current performance.

Incentive Pay Structures

The GPP found that most states do not use incentive or performance-based pay. Incentive pay practices provide a mechanism to financially reward employees for their organizational contributions without having to rely solely upon traditional practices of promotion and position reallocation. The GPP collected data about the percentage of state employees eligible to receive four types of incentive pay: pay-for-performance salary increase, individual bonus, group bonus, and gain sharing (see Table 10.1). Eligibility does not guarantee a reward will be given; it

TABLE 10.1.   Percentage of States Using Incentive Pay

	P-F-P Salary	Individual Bonus	Group Bonus	Gain-sharing
All employees eligible	11.6%	8.1%	8.1%	5.6%
Most eligible (50–99 percent)	11.6	16.2	2.7	25.0
Some eligible (5–49 percent)	11.6	16.2	8.1	11.1
No employees eligible	65.0	59.0	81.1	55.6

only indicates whether state employees have any chance of receiving one. Only 11.6 percent of states offer pay-for-performance salary increases to all state employees. Individual and group bonuses are offered to all employees in only 8.1 percent of the states responding to the survey. Some states use gain sharing as an incentive. Louisiana uses the Exceptional Performance and Efficiency Incentive Program to reward state employees with up to 20 percent of their annual salary for activities that result in cost savings or increased efficiencies. While the trend in the private sector is to rely heavily on monetary incentives to differentiate outstanding performers from average performers, this is not true of state governments (White, 2006).

Virginia's performance-based pay system has received considerable recognition in the past few years. The state recently implemented a sweeping revision of its 40-year-old employee compensation system. The new performance-based compensation plan was modeled after the most successful "best practices" used by major corporations and governmental entities on the national, state, and local levels. The compensation plan brought new pay practices, greater opportunities for career growth within state government, greater management flexibility and accountability, and new ways to recognize and reward employees for exceptional performance and acquired skills. Virginia's changes included:

- Moving from a traditional graded pay plan consisting of twenty-three salary grades to nine broad pay bands.
- Implementing competitive differentials for select jobs based on local market conditions, allowing agencies to pay higher salaries where justified.
- Streamlining the state's job structure from over 1650 job classes to 256 roles.
- Eliminating entitlements, such as across-the-board increases, and adopting variable pay.
- Promoting the concept of total compensation by using salary and benefit values to analyze labor market information and to base pay increases on performance.

TREND 3: STATES ARE BETTER ABLE TO REMOVE EMPLOYEES WHEN NEEDED

An important element of managing performance effectively is a government's ability to address behavioral and performance problems and to discharge those employees who are not willing or are unable to correct identified problems (Cottringer, 2003). Retaining underperforming employees may impact organizational performance because important positions are held by staff who lack the skill level to perform effectively. This study found variation in dismissal rates of state employees. Almost 29 percent of states reported involuntary turnover of *less* than one percent in fiscal year 2003. Approximately 38 percent of states fired 1 to 2 percent of state employees. The study showed that 19 percent of states dismissed between 2.1 and five percent of their employees. Finally, 14 percent of states fired more than 5 percent of their workers.

The GPP found that about a quarter of the states implemented changes to their discipline system in the past several years. The changes varied across states. For example, Arkansas passed a provision that allows agencies to carry out their own disciplinary procedures. Oregon adopted statewide discipline and termination policies for nonrepresented groups. Two other states shifted their disciplinary philosophies, adopting positive discipline or discipline without punishment approaches. Changes in Washington state were more extensive. The state adopted a just cause standard to replace a standard based on nine specific causes for action, approved a positive discipline approach, and accelerated its process for dismissing employees.

TREND 4: STATES CONTINUE TO IMPROVE THEIR HIRING PROCEDURES

As shown in Figure 10.3, the GPP found that, on average, it takes states about 48 days (median) to hire a new employee. Many states continue to struggle with retaining new hires. On average, states lose about 20 percent of employees during their probationary period. The GPP found that a number of states have modified parts of their hiring processes to improve their timeliness and quality of new hires. First, a number of states rely heavily upon electronic recruiting and hiring. For example, Minnesota reengineered its selection process from a traditional exam-based process to a skills-based resume scanning process. The state's time to fill requisitions has dropped over 50 percent. The state has moved to a virtually paperless system, allowing managers the ability to submit requisitions, review resumes, and track results online. In Wisconsin, an online application and testing system (WiscJobs) was implemented to manage the recruitment and selection process. The public interface portion of the site includes: job announcements with a variety of search tools; a "job cart" feature to allow applicants to track jobs and the application process; online applications and online examinations for certain jobs; an online resume tool; and other features.

Second, several states eliminated structural barriers in the hiring process. Washington eliminated its Rule of 7 and Iowa removed its Rule of 8. Hawaii

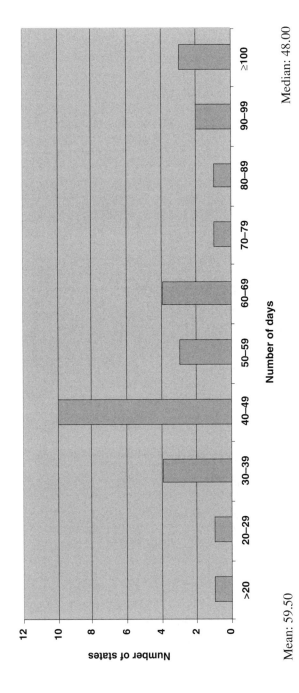

Mean: 59.50   Median: 48.00

FIGURE 10.3.   Average Number of Days to Fill Position in Fiscal Year 2003

changed its residency requirement, and Oklahoma provided direct hire authority to agencies. Third, states have changed their practices to reflect the realities of the job market for some fields. Connecticut now hosts hiring days for hard-to-fill positions. Over the course of a day, candidates complete an application, attend an orientation, and are interviewed. The state may then offer a candidate a conditional offer at the end of the day.

TREND 5: SOME STATES ARE INVESTING IN WORKFORCE TRAINING AND DEVELOPMENT

To cultivate a high-performing workforce that can meet the changing needs of citizens, governments need to invest in the training and development of their employees (GPP). On average, states spent about $274.10 per state employee on training in 2003. The GPP study found that five states spent over $500 per employee and six spent less than $50 per employee (see Figure 10.4). On average, state employees completed about 16 hours of training and managers finished approximately 21 hours of training over the year. About 68 percent of states operated a senior management leadership training program.

Arizona has focused its resources and efforts on creating a shared services training approach through Arizona Government University (AzGU). AzGU offers centralized administration for the training activities of 127 agencies, with a decentralized delivery system. A Board representing the state agencies has oversight for the direction of AzGU. Their mission is to create a workforce development program that delivers critical competencies and skill sets to enable employees to develop professionally. Courses are available to all trainers in executive agencies; a shared training calendar was developed to incorporate class offerings that are open to all employees. In addition, AzGU has developed a Web-enabled learning management system that maintains course descriptions, schedules training and meetings, tracks employees' training information and provides unlimited reporting capabilities.

Louisiana also realized it needed to build the skill levels of its current staff so they could be prepared to take on roles with greater responsibility. To help address the state's needs, Louisiana implemented a mentoring program pairing lower level, less experienced employees with more experienced employees and executive staff. This program is a central part of its succession planning effort.

In an effort to help state employees develop career plans allowing them to progress within state government, Ohio has created a three-level training program called the Pass Program. Level 1, which is a 12-week program, focuses on soft skills and technology courses designed to build and enhance core administrative skills and competencies. Levels 2 and 3, which can only be taken upon graduation from the previous level, help employees tap into leadership and team-based skills. Level 2 requires that class members develop and present a group project over 14 weeks of guided training. Level 3 focuses on skill building and personal management development. After completing all three levels, employees

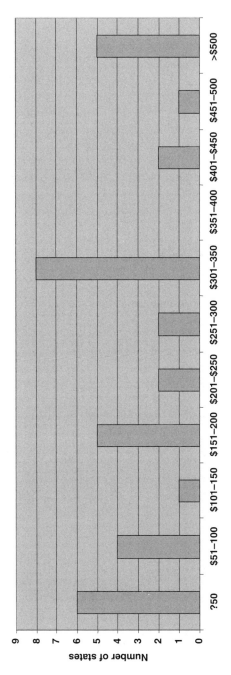

FIGURE 10.4. Training Expenditures Per Employee Fiscal Year

have developed their own career development plan and understand their role in guiding their own long-term development.

Lessons Learned through the GPP

In general, states are moving toward a more responsive and flexible human resource management model, although to varying degrees and with varied success. States must deal with somewhat conflicting objectives: adopting changes that provide greater flexibility to individual agencies and managers in administering human resource management systems while maintaining consistency across state agencies. A number of states are utilizing technology to improve their hiring and training processes. Most states still find it challenging to recognize performance with monetary incentives.

Looking at states that have more successfully implemented a culture of high performance, the GPP found a set of common characteristics. First, the central HRM office in these states took a proactive leadership role in developing practices that support high performance, and provided considerable support to state agencies during the implementation of new practices. Second, states that pushed for high levels of employee performance also engaged in a process of continuous improvement, even under strained budgets. Third, the central HRM office followed through on initiatives by providing adequate training and development, oversight, and consultation to state agencies. Finally, these states utilize technology more effectively, implementing systems to support existing processes, such as hiring, testing, career planning, and training.

States that find it difficult to shift toward a more innovative, performance culture will have to overcome their fear of changing the status quo. The government human resource management environment is changing as labor force demographics shift rapidly, and to remain an attractive employer, states must manage their human resources differently. Employing proven techniques such as decentralized hiring and promotion decision-making; monetary performance recognition; job-specific hiring and evaluation; and increased training and development throughout the government structure will help these states move ahead in an increasingly competitive hiring environment. Establishing these tools within an advanced technological framework will enable each state to develop the strongest workforce with the most efficient management system possible.

REFERENCES

Abrams, R.I., and D.R. Nolan. (1985). Toward a Theory of a Just Cause in Employee Discipline Cases. *Duke Law Journal*, 594.

Baucus, M.S., and T.M. Dworkin. (1998). Wrongful Firing in Violation of Public Policy: An Empirically Based Model of the Process. *Group and Organization Management*, 23(4): 347–361.

Cottringer, W. (2003). The ABC's of Employee Discipline. *Supervision*, 64(4): 5–7.

den Hartog, D. N., P. Boselie, and J. Paaiwe. (2004) A Performance Management: A Model and Research Agenda. *Applied Psychology: An International Review*, 2004, 53(4): 556–560.

DeNisi, A.S. A Performance Appraisal and Performance Management: A Multilevel Analysis. In K. Klein and S. Kozlowski (Eds.), 2000. *Multilevel Theory, Research, and Methods in Organizations*. San Francisco, CA: Jossey Bass.

Falcone, A. (1999). A Legal Dichotomy. *HR Magazine*, 44(5): 110–115.

Fulmer, W., and A.W. Casey. (1990). Employment At Will: Options for Managers. *Academy of Management Executive*, 4(2): 102–107.

Ingraham, P.W., and E.F. Eisenberg. (1995). Comparative Examinations of National Civil Service and Personnel Reforms. In Jack Rabin, Thomas Vocino, W. Bartley Hildreth, and Gerald Miller (Eds.), *Handbook of Public Personnel Administration*. New York: Marcel Dekker.

Kellough Edward J., and Lloyd Nigro (Eds.) (2005a). Classifying and Exploring Reforms in State Personnel Systems. *Civil Service Reform in the States: Personnel Policies and Politics at the Sub-National Level*, pp. 59–76. Albany, New York: SUNY Press.

Kellough, J. E., and L. Nigro. (2005b). Radical Civil Service Reform. In S.E. Condrey (Ed.), *Handbook of Human Resource Management in Government*, pp. 58–75). San Francisco, CA: Jossey-Bass.

Leavitt, W. M., and G. Johnson. (1998). Employee Discipline and the Post-Bureaucratic Public Organization: A Challenge in the Change Process. *Review of Public Personnel Administration*, 18(2): 73–81.

Lee, C. (2005, January 27). Civil Service System on Its Way Out at DHS. *Washington Post*.

Mathis, R. L., and J. H. Jackson. (2005). *Human Resource Management: Essential Perspectives*, 3rd ed. Canada: Southwestern.

Mosher, F.C. (1968). *Democracy and the Public Service*. New York: Oxford University Press.

Stieber, J., and R. Rodgers. (1994). Discharge for Cause: History and Development in the United States. *The Annals of the American Academy of Political and Social Sciences*, 536: 70–78.

Wallihan, James. (2003). The Politics of Employee Discharge: Triggering, Representation, and Venue. *The Policy Studies Journal*, 31(4): 625–642.

11

A Modest Proposal Regarding Political Appointees

WILLIAM L. MURRAY AND GARY L. WAMSLEY

The term political appointees has always struck us as a troubling one, because any term than can encompass both Deborah Gore Dean and Craig Livingston on the one hand and Gifford Pinchot and James Lee Witt on the other hand does not seem to be very useful.[1] What troubles us more, however, is our fields' tepid response to the proliferation of political appointees. There have been some notable and exemplary exceptions in Hugh Heclo (1977), Carolyn Ban (1987), James Pfiffner (1991), Paul Light (1995, 1997), and Patricia Ingraham (1993, 1987), but as a discipline political science, and public administration as an interdisciplinary field have been largely silent about, if not complicit in, the incredible proliferation of political appointees. For example, Richard Nathan argues for an "administrative presidency" in which management tasks can and should be performed by partisans (1983, 7) and Robert Maranto (1998a,b) argues that the tenure of career service administrators should be abolished, which most scholars feel would risk an even more dramatic increase in political appointments. Perhaps we have little reason to expect more from political science, but public administration owes its very existence to an outraged reaction to political appointees and their corruption, which had reached plague proportions in the late 19th century (Van Riper, 1958). It would seem reasonable to expect considerably more concern.

Today the nearest thing to outrage to appear in a scholarly journal was written by a retired Senior Executive of thirty-four years of experience, who had apparently been forced to endure one inept political executive too many (Cohen, 1998).[2] We had developed our "modest proposal" unaware of this, but we are delighted to find ourselves in agreement with someone who knows all too well at first hand whereof he speaks. Cohen is one of the few practitioner voices that has sounded the kind of alarm and outrage that we think the phenomenon warrants. A quote captures some sense of the depth of his concern:

> We entrust the administration of the largest "company" in the country—with the biggest budget and staff, the widest range of products and services, and the greatest impact on the life of every American—to a cast of well-meaning political loyalists with little or no management experience. They may be smart, committed, and high-energy, workaholics, but most have never run anything, except, perhaps, a political campaign. (451)

The current swelling of the ranks of appointees has so far involved relatively little or largely petty corruption, but it may be all the more serious for that reason. Greater corruption might at least provoke a response. Instead the current mushrooming of appointees has brought us blunders, minor scandals, and general ineptitude which is often blamed on "bureaucrats" or government generally, thereby tarring the career service and all those in public office, even legislators, with the same brush. All of this steadily and insidiously erodes public confidence in government and our ability to govern ourselves—a very serious matter for a democratic system. Absent the corruption that might fuel outrage and a broader reform movement, shouldn't our field, scholars as well as practitioner, still be in the forefront in examining the implications of the growth of political appointees, the consequences and possible reforms? We think so.

This chapter begins with a taxonomy of political appointees at the federal level, to sort out our thinking about them. It then offers an explanation for why political science, and more significantly public administration, has countenanced (if not encouraged) the growing number of political appointees. We conclude with a "modest proposal" about political appointees: greatly reducing their numbers and limiting their scope to the ranks *above* Assistant Secretary.

A TAXONOMY OF FEDERAL POLITICAL APPOINTEES AND THEIR DYSFUNCTIONS

While happy families may be all alike, this is not the case with political appointees. We first review the major types of political appointees at the federal level, weaving in some of the literature's observations about each. The reader is cautioned that these categories are not exhaustive and is referred to Light (1995) for the most complete mapping of political appointees. Nonetheless, for our purposes they can be reduced to three major types.

Presidential Appointed, Senate Confirmed Appointees

The highest ranking political appointees in the federal government are known as persons on the Executive Schedule or presidentially appointed, Senate confirmed (PAS) appointees.

These PAS appointees are compensated on levels I to IV of the federal executive schedule and were originally confined to occupants of key White House Staffers Cabinet Secretaries and agency heads. Unfortunately, the proliferation of such positions has extended them downward to division heads, and program directors in some agencies. In addition to cabinet secretaries and heads of independent agencies, the traditional titles carried by PAS appointees include: secretary, deputy secretary, undersecretary, assistant secretary, and administrator. Heclo's 1977 study of federal political appointees assumed an organizational structure consisting of a cabinet secretary, a deputy secretary, one or more undersecretaries, and several assistant secretaries. Even with this relatively simple executive structure, Heclo remarked on the growth of organizational complexity, commenting that a 19th century clerk would scarcely recognize his department—the impression of increased size and complexity due to general growth of course, but most assuredly due as well to the size and scope of the executive superstructure.

Pfiffner's work in 1991 and Light's 1995 study reveal a federal government becoming steadily and significantly more bloated with political appointees at the upper echelons of the departments. Light found that, while the absolute size of the civilian federal workforce remained relatively constant from 1960 to 1992, "the total number of senior executives and political appointees grew from 451 in 1960 to 2,393 in 1992, a "*430 percent increase.*" The four principal layers of political leadership identified by Heclo in 1977 had mushroomed to thirty-two layers in some cases (7). One manifestation of this increased layering of political appointees is the bewildering array of titles now carried by PAS employees. These include such mind-boggling titles as Associate Deputy Undersecretaries, and Deputy Associate Deputy Assistant Secretaries. (No, we did not leave out a comma; it is a real title.) These and many others would simply be funny if the implications were not so grave.

Light found that the growth of PAS appointees in absolute numbers was particularly pronounced at the lower echelons of upper management, at the deputy assistant secretary level. According to Light, the number of deputy assistant secretaries has increased from 77 to 507 from 1960 to 1992, meaning that in 1992 the federal government had more deputy assistant secretaries than it had political appointees of all ranks in 1960 (8). The growth in absolute numbers of political appointees is most pronounced at the deputy assistant secretary level, Light found that in terms of percentage increase, growth has occurred at all ranks of political appointees.

The growth in the number of PAS appointees has several consequences for public administration beyond the broader problem of the growth in total number of political appointees of all types (this would include noncareer SES and Schedule C positions in addition to PAS positions). We shall return to this point later. At this point, we need only say that a number of unfortunate trends have left agency leadership positions vacant for much of an administration's term. In August 1997, *Washington Post* ran a series of articles demonstrating that 30 percent of presidentially appointed positions in the federal government were vacant 8 months into the new administration. Moreover, very few of these latecomers will stay to the end of a President's term (Mackenzie, 1994).

Another consequence of the increase in PAS positions may at first glance seem counterintuitive: it has *reduced* rather than increased presidential influence over policy implementation. Upon closer examination the reasons for this are clear enough. Heclo points out that presidential appointees come with, or may develop, their own power bases and network of influence independent of the chief executive or the nominal agency head (1977). When we remind ourselves that PAS positions are not simply presidential appointments but also to a degree Senate appointments because it must confirm them, it becomes clearer why more PASs does not necessarily result in more presidential influence over policy and its implementation. Consequently, a President must nominate persons who are likely to survive the Senate confirmation process and this often means nominating someone with enough friends, allies, or advocates sitting on key subcommittees and committees. Such persons may not be of the same party as the president and in any event they are bound to have particularistic interests that differ with his or her interests.

Furthermore, if such potential fissures in the relationship between the president and his or her nominee were not already built in by the above calculus of potential confirmation, the process would itself produce such cracks. For the confirmation process is one in which behavioral contracts are made (to be enforced in future hearings, especially budget hearings). Interrogators in the confirmation process ply nominees with questions that seek to elicit responses committing his or her agency to future actions that serve the interest of the questioner or their district (Mackenzie, 1981, 156–170). Even if the nominee has been briefed well enough to give the cliché response—"I don't have the answer on that yet, but I'm looking forward to working with you on that, Senator"—they still have been put on notice and can be sure that question will come back again and again in future interactions with the Senator, the committee, or its staff (Reich, 1997).

The authors saw at first hand the consequences of an increased number of PASs and the lengthened confirmation process. The National Academy of Public Administration (NAPA) study team on which they served and the panel that reviewed the problems of the Federal Emergency Management Agency (FEMA) in 1993 took note of this phenomenon with the nine PAS appointees at FEMA, which is a very small agency of a little over a 1,000 employees. Of the nine PASs, the agency head (director) was the last to have been appointed.[3] All of his important executives or program heads had passed the confirmation gauntlet and been confirmed, having likely made such behavioral contracts as necessary to achieve confirmation. Even if the agency head had the confidence of the president, and this one apparently lacked this to some significant degree, he in effect had been given no say in the appointment of the agency's senior managers and thus no way of assuring that he could effectively implement presidential policy.[4] It was well-known in the agency that the director had the formal power but informally did not have the discretion to insist on the removal of any of the appointees in the agency, as all had their own political sponsors within the administration or Congress. Ironically, because political appointees, particularly PAS appointees, often have their own network of supporters, this makes them more difficult for other political executives to manage, not less. Heclo (1977) sums up the effect of the process nicely:

> To the normal confusions of pluralistic institutions and powers in Washington, the selection process contributes to its own complexities. . . . Political forces intervene from many quarters, and their interests in political appointments often bear little relation to presidential needs or to qualifications required for effective performance by public executives. (10)

A final consequence of the growth in PAS positions is that there are now many more layers of management between the President and the career administrators that the political appointees are nominally supposed to help the President manage. If there was ever a chance that personal or partisan fealty on the part of subordinates could give chief executives more effective control, it would have been when there were only one or two persons between him or her and the level of implementation. However, the National Commission on the Public Service (Volcker, 1990) noted that:

> . . .Presidents today are further away from the top career layers of government with 3,000 appointees than was Franklin Roosevelt 50 years ago with barely 200. From 1933 to 1965, during a period of profound expansion in government responsibilities, the number of cabinet and sub-cabinet officers appointed by the President and confirmed by the Senate more than *doubled* from 73 to 152. From 1965 to the present, a span when total employment and programs were more stable, the number more than *tripled* to 573. (17)

Ingraham (1987) also notes that the short average tenure of presidential appointees is just one of several reasons making them an imperfect instrument of presidential control. Similarly, Pfiffner (1987) argues that presidential mistrust of career bureaucrats is misplaced and that increasing use of political executives is counterproductive because of the inexperience and short tenure of political appointees. Heclo (1977) found an average tenure for political appointees of 2.5 years. Six years later, another study by the National Academy of Public Administration (1974) found that the average tenure of a political appointee had shrunk to *less* than 2 years. In addition, the Volcker Commission (1990) noted that the downward penetration of political appointees limits the career potential of federal employees and hence the attractiveness of a federal career by reserving ever more senior positions for political appointees. Many of these positions, particularly at the deputy assistant secretary level, were once largely filled by career personnel.

Noncareer SES

The authority for creation of the noncareer SES authority was brought about by the Civil Service Reform Act of 1978. The number of noncareer SES positions varies with the overall size of the SES, as the number of SES appointees is statutorily limited to 10 percent of the total SES. This also means that the number of them in any given agency may vary widely. The noncareer SES is the most recent type of political appointment created, and it is the only type of political appointment authority that has not grown demonstrably since its inception. Ingraham (1987) notes that, from 1979 to 1985, the number of noncareer SES positions ranged from 828 in 1979 to 688 in 1985. Light (1995) estimates that the SES had expanded to 8,130 by the end of the Bush administration, allowing for 813 noncareer SES appointments, approximately the same number as were available at the adoption of the Civil Service Reform Act in 1978 (58). The flat rate of growth tells us nothing, however, about the positive or negative significance of these political appointees. Especially problematic is their impact on the morale of the career staff.

Schedule C Appointments

Schedule C appointments are appointments on the general schedule without career tenure, that is, at *grade 15 and below*. Schedule C appointees have a wide range of potential assignments including staff assistant to a political executive, chauffeur, and secretary, initiated by the Eisenhower administration. According to Light (1995), this appointment authority initiated by the Eisenhower administration vested in cabinet secretaries' authority to appoint "positions of a confidential or policy determining nature" without regard to merit (45). Typical appointees are special assistants, but also such positions as secretaries and chauffeurs. The number of Schedule C appointees in the Eisenhower administration ranged from 868 to 1,128. By the end of the 1980s, according to Light, there were over 1,700 Schedule C appointees in the federal government (46). Ingraham (1987) found that in 1986 "there were more schedule C Reagan appointments at the GS 13–15 levels only (946) than there were in total of Schedule C appointments at *all* grade levels" (911).

While the Schedule C appointments were legally and by tradition the prerogative of agency heads and cabinet secretaries, in the Reagan Administration, these appointments became the province of the White House Personnel Office, although the secretary or agency head remains the formal appointing authority for the positions. According to Light (1995), the Reagan White House established a policy that all political appointments, including Schedule C appointments, would be subject to White House approval (56). Successive administrations have allowed the department to make such appointments, but only after review or clearance by the White House Personnel Office. In other instances the White House Personnel Office has made such appointments, but the Secretary of the department or agency director have been allowed to review them.

In addition to contributing to the overall politicization of the federal government, Schedule C appointees cause specific problems. The first is that many political executives have a tendency to become isolated by a phalanx of Schedule C aides. Schedule C appointees tend to act as gatekeepers of access and translators or distorters of information for more senior political appointees, and as such can screen political executives from needed interaction with career staff and exacerbate tensions and confusion.

Schedule C appointments are also problematic because they tend to magnify the problems noted previously with lower-ranking presidential appointees. The lower the rank of a political position, the more difficult it is to find a quality individual to fill the position and to justify why the position needs to be a partisan rather than career appointee. One of the authors interviewed a schedule C appointee serving as the secretary to President George H. W. Bush's cabinet, that is, she was not the Secretary of a department, but the secretary to the President's Cabinet. While it is true that the importance of the position depends on the significance a president attaches to his cabinet meetings, we think it fair to say that it was not a totally insignificant position and that at times has been quite important. This person was passionately partisan, her knowledge of government and its working bordered on tragicomic, for example, "there ought to be a law against Congress requiring all these studies of agencies," and her sole qualification seems to have been that she had organized one of the many inaugural balls. Incredibly, she had yet another schedule C appointee who served as her assistant. He was alert, young, eager, and as lacking knowledge of the government as she was. Matthew Holden (1991) describes some of these political birds of passage in this way:

> Errand-running falls to the young, who come equipped with enthusiasm, the zealous obedience born of ambition to rise, and school-taught techniques. The younger people will have had a relatively limited political experience. Sometimes their only experience will have been with the person who is now the chief executive. The professed loyalty to the chief is passionate. The tone toward all others, is preemptory. The ambitious youngsters are able to exert influence in the world by gaining a reputation for having access to the center. (66)

Thus when it comes to politicization, Schedule C appointees have a tendency to "out-Herod Herod." This is because many Schedule C Appointees, as Holden says, tend to be younger, zealous, campaign aides eager to win their partisan stripes. They are used to operating in the "no holds barred" atmosphere of campaigning. Whatever, the candidate seems to want, the campaign aide delivers—no questions asked. Holden explains some of the reasons for this:

> Life within the entourage is framed by the possibility of a fall from grace. The very powerful are also vulnerable. Personal dependence and the elements of trust that might be presumed impose a demand for loyalty to the incumbent of the office. Doubt about "loyalty" however grounded, is both a severe impediment and an instrument in the war of one advisor against another. Loyalty is judged on many criteria. Verification of one's own loyalty, to the satisfaction of others, is an ever-recurrent necessity. (1991, 66)

Thus, whatever or whoever threatens the candidate must be neutralized or destroyed. This may have an arguable functionality in the hurly burly of campaigning, but within government institutions and the processes of governance where politics takes on a much different guise and grammar, it can spell disaster and scandal.

For example a person such as a Craig Livingston, who held a schedule C appointment in the Clinton White House, and whose only qualifications were having worked as a campaign "advance man," may or may not have asked for the FBI background files on Republican politicians. But if such files fell into his hands his background meant it was unlikely he would be sensitive to the fact that a serious mistake had been made and needed urgent rectification. Indeed, his background meant it was likely he would consider it a stroke of good fortune to be exploited as fully as possible. Whether or not that was the case, the Filegate scandal that was created from the event dogged the Clinton administration through both terms. These relatively low-ranking appointees can therefore contribute significantly to the increased partisan conflict, faux pas, and scandals that hurt the political executive and his administration they are supposed to serve.

We are unaware of any close scholarly examination of their role, but our own experiences in government bring to mind many instances where we know or have every reason to believe schedule C appointees were the source of damaging or would-be scandals if they are ever uncovered. For example, we believe it was a schedule C appointee who diverted an Air Force transport carrying supplies for an emergency field operation thousands of miles to pick up the golf clubs of the political executive who was his superior. In another instance, an overzealous schedule C appointee precipitated the assignment of special Air National Guard tanker planes equipped to fight forest fires to an emergency for which they were totally unsuited. He then thought it would be good PR to arrange a photo-op of such a plane dropping water on a house to save it from being burned. He did not understand that such a drop would flatten the house like a matchbox. Only greater knowledge, experience, and political astuteness on the part of career officials at the scene saved the mission from becoming a political disaster for the agency and agency head. They persuaded the schedule C person to stage the drop for photographers, but not on a house. Typically, the problems created by persons in the schedule C positions are those resulting from lack of expertise combined with partisan zeal and an inability to recognize the difference between campaigning and governing. Lacking experience they are unaware that the politics of governing wear a different guise and unfold according to a different grammar. What is only "dirty tricks" in a campaign becomes illegal and even criminal in the institutional, legalistic, and highly transparent circumstances of governing. The Watergate Scandal in which a "third-rate burglary" brought down the Nixon presidency is only the most egregious example. Being zealous partisans, schedule Cs are quick to assume that all career officials are tainted with the partisanship of the opposition party. They are quick to amplify or distort and pass on to their partisan political superiors any real or imagined disloyalty of career officials. If there is no tension between their political superiors and the career staff, they tend to create it; if there is such tension, they exacerbate it. They are also prone to interfere and attempt to micromanage situations for the same reasons. Loyalty and confidentiality, the supposedly necessary qualities needed in these positions, become perverse and dysfunctional for the reasons discussed above.

OVERHEAD DEMOCRACY AND THE ADMINISTRATIVE PRESIDENCY

Some scholars like Paul Light (1995) have pointed to the increase in the total number of political appointees, their layering in federal agencies, and the problematic implications involved. Amazingly, other scholars like Maranto (1998a,b) call for an end to tenure in the federal civil service, something that a number of scholars believe will result in still more political appointees and unfortunate results (Durant et al., 1998).

Why has public administration, which seldom hesitates to indulge its reform impulse in such things as reorganization, budgeting, personnel, auditing, and other matters, held back until recently in doing more to raise questions about the remarkable increases in political appointees that have taken place in recent years? Why are some scholars, most notably Nathan (1983, 1985), Moe (1985), Knott and Miller (1987), and Maranto (1993, 1998a,b) taking positions that implicitly or explicitly justify an increase in political appointees? The reason lies, we believe in one of the central tenets in the ontology or core ethos of public administration and political science: "overhead democracy," a corollary doctrine to the concept of the "managerial or administrative presidency" (governor, or strong mayor), and a concomitant assumption that, regardless of the problems they create, political appointees are essential to the viability of both doctrines, and indeed the viability of democratic government. The doctrine of "overhead democracy" as originally developed, held that public administrators could be made democratically responsive and responsible by their subordination to *both* the legislative *and* the executive branches. Examined critically this is a logical impossibility, but tenets of political culture are not meant to be examined critically and much can be made to seem possible by verbal sleight of hand. Emmette Redford (1969) illustrates this beautifully in describing what became conventional wisdom among scholars in political science and both scholars and practitioners in public administration. According to Redford:

> Traditional literature on administration and politics gave us a model of how the administrative state ought to operate—a model that acquired orthodoxy in both administrative and democratic theory. It was a simple model of overhead democracy. It asserted that democratic control should run through a single line from the representatives of the people to all those who exercised power in the name of the government. The line ran from the people to their representatives in the Presidency and Congress, *and from there to the President as chief executive, then to lesser units, and so on to the fingertips of administration.* (71, emphasis added)

Scholars (with the notable and recent exception of David Rosenbloom (2000) and a few others) and practitioners of public administration had been and still are moving, sometimes consciously, sometimes unconsciously toward conceptualizing public administration and management as the instrument of the chief executive, and doing so to the diminishment of the constitutionally based role of Congress in administration and toward one of merely ratifying policy initiatives of the chief executive. Redford was critical of the trend, but to our mind did not go far enough in showing how far and how long scholars and practitioners had been pushing for a formula that they hoped would, in practice, center administration or management on the chief executive and limit the extensive constitutional role of Congress in administration to one of merely ratifying policy initiatives of the chief executive. Rather than trace the full history of it, let us begin with the rationale the Taft Commission on Economy and Efficiency of 1912 offers for an executive budget:

> The reason for urging that the budget should be submitted by the President is that *the President is the only person who under the Constitution is responsible for the acts of the executive branch of what is known as "the administration."* (143, emphasis added)

We submit that anyone reading Article I of the Constitution would have difficulty concluding that the President "*is the only person who under the Constitution is responsible for the acts of executive branch.*" Article I gives Congress an extensive and explicit role in administration (Dudley and Wamsley, 1998, 340).

Perhaps the move toward overhead democracy and a managerial presidency can be seen most clearly in the Brownlow Committees Report, which took what we consider breathtaking license with the Constitution in their recommendations. We do not know their intention and cannot attribute willful disregard of the Constitution to the committee and its staff. After all the principal models of a government executive with which they were familiar were the city manager within the council-manager form of government, a form of government, which Dwight Waldo has correctly referred to as the only unitary form of government in

America, and which is vastly different from the shared powers of the U.S. Constitution. It would be quite natural, however, for them to try to make the President the focal point of responsibility, which they were unable to locate in a Congress that they saw as a major source of waste, inefficiency, and corruption. Brownlow himself was a city manager and the council-manager form of government has been a mainstay in urban reform and nascent public administration of which the three-committee members and much of their staff had been a part. Perhaps they felt they could not be explicit about using the city manager as their model for a responsive executive so they felt compelled to try to draw upon and use the British government to make their point about fixing responsibility on the executive. But while it was drawing on a national government rather than the council-manager form of government in order to make a point about their recommended changes in their own national government, their logic is, to say the least, tortured. They could only do it by verbal sleight of hand. No doubt what they admired in the British system was the focus of responsibility in the Prime Minister and they wanted to see such a fixing of responsibility (and concomitant power) in the presidency. Therefore, they began with a statement that strains reason to the utmost: "Constitutionally, the President is the Prime Minister of the United States." After acknowledging that the President and Prime Minister are elected differently, a most important distinction for they are stunningly different, the report then slides to the point it wants to make by concluding that:

> The mere difference in the method of choosing the President on the one hand and the prime minister on the other does not warrant the conclusion, therefore, that the executive branch of our Government cannot be made responsible. (Brownlow, 1937)

The final outcome was a reorganization of the government that went further than anyone had imagined possible toward creating a managerial presidency and nurturing the concept of overhead democracy. The reorganization created the Executive Office of the President and moved the Bureau of the Budget to it from Treasury. It called for the establishment of "12 great departments directly responsible in administration to *the chief executive*" (Ibid., 34).

The trend to the managerial presidency is also clear in the report of the 1949 Hoover Commission that followed the same path of distortion:

> We must reorganize the executive branch to give it simplicity of structure, the unity of purpose, and the clear line of executive authority *originally intended—with a "clear line of command from top to bottom."* (Hoover, 1949, 3, emphasis added)

The Heineman task force (1967) appointed by President Lyndon Johnson almost two decades later hewed to the same line. Not until 1974 was there the slightest wavering in the doctrine of the president as CEO, and that was slight indeed and largely in reaction to Watergate and President Nixon's plans to centralize powers even further (NAPA, 1974).

And still decades later we find Ron C. Moe (1994) referring to these words approvingly and saying:

> This terminology was deliberately chosen to indicate that the commission accepted the theory of governmental administration first expounded by the Founding Fathers in 1787 and was concerned to reemphasize its essential validity for contemporary times. (112)

It is true, of course, that Article II, section I, states that "executive power shall be vested in a president," but the specific meaning of this sweeping phrase is left unclear and has been the subject of decades of struggle between presidents and congress. Congress has seized the opportunity to create positions of cabinet rank and below and to assign them statutory powers rather than the president, and of course they are as much or more subject to the pressures from congress as they are to those emanating from the White House. He may nominate persons to those offices but the Senate must confirm them. He may review and shape their budget request, but congress will do as it wishes with that request. He may try to influence and persuade such persons and their agencies, but congress can probably do this more effectively by hearings, investigations, and legislation. In the final analysis the grant of executive power to the president in Article II is, in the words of presidential scholar Edwin Corwin (1957) "a term of uncertain content"(3). As we have seen, however, this ambiguity has not deterred generations of scholars and practitioners from seeking to make the president the chief executive officer. All this by way of making the point that in our estimation Redford was not nearly as critical in his presentation of the "overhead democracy" concept as we believe he could and should have been. In fairness, however, it must be said that although he viewed overhead democracy as an important rationale for the American regime, he did criticize the concept as overly simplistic, suggesting that the influences on bureaucratic action bear in upon it from a variety of directions, thus making it seem more at the center of a web than a point at the end of a vertical line descending solely from the chief executive (72–80; Held, 1979).

Notwithstanding Redford's attempt to sketch a more complex and sophisticated model, overhead democracy's power as a normative theory in-use remained potent enough so that two decades later Lane and Wolf (1990) could state:

> [overhead democracy] is a powerful normative theory which satisfies the need for establishing political control over the bureaucratic administrative establishment. The fact that the theory takes an overly simplistic view does not diminish its significance as a powerful influence on public organizational cultures. (100)

For most of the 20th century, and most intensely in the past three decades, the concept and the practice of overhead democracy has been steadily transformed so as to mean the career officials are to be responsible and responsive largely, if not solely, to the president, who has been conceptualized in theory as the "chief executive officer" and spoken of in political rhetoric "as the only official elected by all the people" (Lane and Wamsley, 1998). "All the people" is of course a functional myth, but that need not detain us at this point. This transformation, some would say this distortion of the Constitution, has been possible, indeed inevitable, because of the failure of political elites generally, and political scientists and scholars of public administration in particular, to either fully understand or successfully convey to others, that "separation of power" is a misnomer in describing our government and therefore the managerial presidency or the president as "chief executive" is a serious distortion of the Constitution. Richard Neustadt was the notable exception to these lapses. As he put it, separation of powers would be more accurately described as constitutionally "shared powers—shared grudgingly" (Neustadt, 1960).

THE ADMINISTRATIVE PRESIDENCY MORPHS INTO THE POLITICAL PRESIDENCY

The Nixon administration was a critical turning point in the "morphing" of our conception of our government from one of shared powers in which administrators were responsible to both the president and the congress, to one derived from overhead democracy in which the president was the chief executive to whom administrators reported first and foremost. The Congress had come to be seen as simply part of the environment of the White House, alien and irritating, but not to be taken seriously.

As Richard Nathan (1983) has shown us, Nixon began his first term committed to keeping the White House staff small and finding the best people to be his cabinet secretaries. He was trying, in other words, to operate a "strong cabinet government," but found the results frustrating and disappointing. Nixon and his advisers felt that sending prominent persons who were "qualified" by dint of occupation or association with the interests concerned with the operation of particular departments led only to their pursuing their natural proclivity to act independently while "marrying the natives"; that is, allying themselves with the career administrators in the departments and its interest groups and becoming program advocates besieging or gaming the White House in general and him in particular.

By the beginning of his second year he had abandoned earlier ideas in favor of what Nathan calls a "counter bureaucracy" strategy, though it could just as well have been called a "counter prominent secretary" or "counter strong cabinet" strategy. Convinced that career administrators brought into government during Johnson's Great Society effort were a major part of the obstacles to his efforts to cut back government, Nixon set about systematically trying to wrest policy initiative from them as well as the prominent cabinet secretaries. He expanded the White House staff and sought through structures like the Domestic Council and other "working groups" to bypass the secretaries by bringing together White

House staffers and "working level" departmental executives below the secretaries to develop policy initiatives (35).

He also sought to exile, isolate, or get rid of career staffers perceived to be obstacles. A variety of means were used to this end but one infamous example was the Malek Manual, developed by Fred Malek when he was with the Department of Health Education and Welfare (HEW) (Malek, 1971; U.S. Senate, 1974). It was copied and circulated widely outside formal channels. The message according to Paul Light (1995) was "You cannot achieve management, policy or program control unless you have established control," and this meant "placement in all key positions of substantively qualified and politically reliable officials" (50). It did not take long for substantively qualified to be equated with "politically reliable." The manual noted that the administration had inherited a legacy of "disloyalty and obstruction at high levels while those incumbents rest comfortably on career civil service status" (9006–9007). It went on to spell out strategies for "neutralizing" such persons. Regardless of how much or how little it was used, or how much career administrators actually were obstacles to White House policy, no one doubts that the Malek Manual reflected the administration's outlook.

The result of this struggle by Nixon to gain better control of policy can be said to have resulted in the morphing of the administrative presidency into political presidency in which it was assumed that the only path to better control of policy was to appoint partisan loyalists to ever lower levels of administration. For example, the Nixon administration used the report of the second Hoover Commission to justify making the position of Assistant Secretary for Administration, which had traditionally been held by a high-ranking civil servant, a political appointment throughout the departments. This position had been an essential ingredient in providing continuity across changing administrations and providing appointees new to government or Washington with valuable information concerning the politics of government.

The essential role of the position can be seen in the experiences of one incumbent of that position in the Department of Labor.[5] He recounted how he was told by the incoming secretary that he should expect to "be gone in a few months." The secretary had no government experience and proceeded to commit one gaffe after another against the advice of the assistant secretary for administration. Gradually the secretary began to follow the advice of the assistant secretary and a few months stretched into years. Of course there is no long-term happy ending to this episode because a later secretary converted the position to a political appointment, but it illustrates the value of the position being held by a career officer. The politicization of this critical position throughout the government has probably diminished the general competence of departments and has also added a fourth layer of political appointees to the traditional Secretary, Deputy Secretary, and Undersecretary. Moreover, political appointees now have proliferated both above and below the Assistant Secretary positions, and resulted in a bewildering array of titles and levels.

Jimmy Carter's campaign and presidency was the final step in the "morphing" of the overhead democracy concept into a conception in which the political presidency is complemented by the dual conception of it as plebiscitary (Lowi, 1979). Now being seen as "popularly elected" (the electoral college notwithstanding), the words of the 1912 Taft Commission have come to full fruition. The president, who is seen as the "only officer of government elected by all the people" is now expected to be the CEO of the executive branch (Lowi, 1979). This change in conception also marked the emergence of bureaucrat-bashing as a bipartisan campaign tactic and made antagonism between the president and the bureaucracy a more or less permanent feature of our political culture and philosophy of governing. President Carter saw himself as a "people's candidate" who won in the wake of Watergate by running his campaign outside of the normal channels, and perhaps even in spite of the established party and government elites. He believed that bureaucrat-bashing struck a resonant note with the electorate, but once in office he found that the issue had less purchase. It paralleled and was linked to his experience with government reorganization, which he assumed was a concomitant of bureaucrat-bashing. Although reorganization of the "bureaucracy made for engaging rhetoric on the campaign trail, it did not resonate on Capitol Hill. Not because congress harbored any positive feeling for bureaucrats, but rather because Congress was not ready to roll over and serve as part of the scenery of the "chief executive." It let it be known that it did not want the government reorganized by the president. It would unsettle interest groups and their relationships with committees, and necessitate restructuring committee jurisdictions, which is always an extremely delicate and difficult thing for congress to do. If there were to be any reorganizing done, Congress preferred to take the initiative.

Most of Carter's reorganization plans therefore went nowhere or achieved only minimal results. Eventually and ironically, however, his Presidential Reorganization Project (PRP) was able to produce a plan for reforming the civil service, which later would prove to be a more effective instrument of bureaucrat bashing than anyone could have imagined: the Civil Service Reform Act of 1978. The act was only passed by committing to making 10 percent of the new Senior Executive Service political appointees (discussed at length in Chapter 3). This was to have significant repercussions for the relations between civil servants and political appointees and for presidential transitions.

The poisoning of the relationship between the presidency and career public administrators reached its zenith, however, during the election campaigns and administrations of Ronald Reagan. Events of those years may have made it unlikely that the relationship will ever return to something like the alliance that existed in the Roosevelt and Truman years. This followed naturally from Reagan's simple but strongly held ideology and was captured in his famous sound bite—"government is not the answer to our problems; government *is* the problem."

The theory and practice of the Reagan administration's efforts at politicizing the civil service are forthrightly described and enthusiastically defended in Butler et al. (1984).

They centered on appointing to both cabinet and subcabinet levels loyal ideologues, or "Reaganites," whose qualifications were first and foremost loyalty to the president and his ideology. As John Ehrlichman explained:

> The three criteria we followed were, was he a Reagan man? Two, a Republican? And three, a Conservative? Probably our most critical concern was to ensure that conservative ideology was properly represented. (Newland, 1987, 45)

These appointees were not necessarily expected to know a great deal about the departments to which they were appointed. They were expected to know, or be eager to divine how President Reagan felt toward those departments and their programs. First and foremost they were expected to dominate and control career officials by preventing their access to "policy sensitive information" and participating in any activities perceived to have policy implications (Sanera, 1984, 13; Carroll, 1985, 169).

What needs to be said about this approach, which places policy control by the President and his party above all, and ranks ideological purity over substantive knowledge or astuteness in the politics of governance, is that it is more efficacious when the intent is to reduce government and its effectiveness, that is, ratcheting government and policy down or back, than it can be when trying to define problems and solve them through effective government action. To do the latter requires more input and participation of knowledgeable career officials who know government, the politics of governance, and the details of programs and their effective management. Indeed such knowledge and participation is essential in such a mode, whereas it is useful but marginally so in disassembling, destroying, or incapacitating government action through programs.

And to be fair, Reagan's critique of the federal government struck at just that point of vulnerability. Government as problem definer and effective solver had become a joke to Americans fed a steady news media diet of government goofs, ineffectiveness, and chicanery. Few understood that many of the problems government was stuck with were what Michael Harmon (1995) calls "wicked problems"—difficult problems nested or entangled in other difficult problems— and that American public administration had not lived up to even its own expectations in dealing with such problems. The fact that it had done better than was recognized or might reasonably have been expected, and that it had done so under difficult conditions, and in the face of ever-tougher problems, was unfortunately beside the point. The Reagan critique found a receptive audience.

Given the Reagan Administration's intentions toward government, the poisoned relationship created between the president and career administrators was effective and functional to the president's intentions or "mandate" (Sanera, 1984). Viewed from outside the Administration and from the perspective of history, these efforts may be collectively described as a continuation and elaboration of overhead democracy with a plebiscitary, administrative/managerial, political CEO president supreme in the realm of administration by means of an army of ideologically committed political appointees (Lane and Wamsley, 1998; Moe, 1985).

THE COMPLICIT ROLE OF POLITICAL SCIENCE AND PUBLIC ADMINISTRATION IN THIS DISTORTION

The Reagan Administration did not, of course, invent the overhead democracy, the plebiscitary and managerial president and the drive to establish political and policy control by the layering of political appointees. As we have seen, all this has been evolving steadily for many decades. As far back as the founding debate between the Federalists and the anti-Federalists there have been differing views of what the presidency should be. No less a figure than Alexander Hamilton is often presumed to have been favorably disposed to a stronger presidency because he called for "energy in the executive."[6] In more contemporary times, Herbert Kaufman (1956, 1073) identified the conflict within the study and practice of public administration between the doctrines of executive leadership and neutral competence. Kaufman felt the focus on executive leadership by public administration had played a part in transforming that focus into a quest for executive supremacy on the part of Presidents.

A constant theme used to justify this quest has been an appeal to long-standing democratic values embodied in Jacksonian representativeness and manifested in the form of loyal political appointees under the direction of a "popularly elected president." We think, however, that public administration has been all too ready and willing to see political appointees as the necessary means of assuring managerial control for a "popularly elected" president. We conveniently forget or overlook partisan redistricting, the winner-take-all nature of single-member constituencies, the electoral college, the impact of campaign financing that relies on powerful interest groups, and other unsavory aspects that lurk beneath the surface and of the mythic "popular election" and "presidential mandates." Public administration has been all too ready to accept the assumptions behind overhead democracy, the plebiscitary, managerial, and political presidency and to accept the assumption that such a president must have loyal political appointees (Kaufman, 1956, 1057). Students and practitioners of public administration have unwittingly abetted this presidential aggrandizement by: (1) talking, writing, and acting in the early decades of the field as though policy or politics *should be and could be separated* from administration or management; (2) in more recent decades by talking, and writing as though the two *could not be separated*; (3) our eager willingness, when called upon for recommendations and consulting to serve the purposes of plebiscitary and managerial presidents under the rubric of "reinventing government" or "the new public management"; and (4) often writing and acting as though politics and "management" *can and should be separated*. Is there any wonder that public administration has a legitimacy deficit? Of course, politics and administration cannot be separated now or ever, but we have not performed the difficult task therefore required of us as students and practitioners of public administration: of either making them *seem* distinguishable in some way, or making their inseparability functional and legitimate for our system of government.

Obviously, both political executives and career executives are part of the political process in the fuller sense of the term. The role of the former has a decidedly partisan dimension and more likely involvement in that end of the political process that includes campaigns and elections, that is, who shall hold state offices and with what agenda; and the latter has a decidedly nonpartisan dimension and involvement in that end of the political process that includes management or administration, that is, state action upon the agenda that emerges from the electoral and governance processes, which is not necessarily synonymous with the agenda for which a successful candidate(s) campaigned.[7] The two sets of role incumbents are thus thrown together in that part of the political process that we could usefully call governance, which is a convergence of the politics of elections and the politics of administration. We have not, however, developed a conceptualization that makes this clear. Instead we have come to *deny* that politics and administration are dichotomous, while continuing to talk and behave as though they are. In so doing we have clung to a role of faithful servant to the president as CEO, which has only continued to exacerbate expectations of a plebiscitary, managerial, and inevitably a political president, which then leads inexorably to an aggrandized presidency (Pfiffner, 1991, 172–174).[8]

In spite of the way the constitution reads and in spite of Neustadt's aphorism that the President's power can largely be summarized as "the power to persuade" (1960), public administration, has maintained (with concurrence from political science) that the President is *the* manager, the CEO of the executive branch, and has generally assumed that many problems of governance could be ameliorated by giving greater power to the President (Brownlow, 1937; Heineman, 1967; Nathan, 1983; Willoughby, 1927). This has been an inevitable outcome of the field's largely unconscious desire for a way to turn a government of shared powers into a hierarchy of monocentric power in which policy direction would be clear and specific (or so we have wanted to believe) and career officials would simply implement policy by efficiently "managing" (or so we have too often defined what we do). With this kind of ambivalent role conception, and yet a desire to take part in shaping events we have been complicit in creating our own problems. The term "shooting oneself in the foot" comes to mind.

As a prime example, the intellectual force behind the 1978 Civil Service Reform Act was a leading figure of public administration, no less than a former dean of the Maxwell School of Citizenship and Public Administration at Syracuse University, Alan "Scotty"Campbell. Indeed, Campbell made the enhancement of the President's ability to control "unelected bureaucrats," one of the central selling points for the CSRA in his efforts to get the bill through Congress. This was done by making it possible for political appointees (up to 10 percent) to be part of the proposed Senior Executive Service (the noncareer SES appointments discussed earlier in this chapter and widely described to this day as "all carrot and no stick"). It also made it possible for political appointees to "reassign SES personnel with the beginning of a new administration."

We have singled out the role of scholars and practitioners of public administration and their complicity in transforming American conceptions of "shared power" into "separation of powers," and the presidency (governorship, and strong mayorship) into plebiscitory "chief executive officers." Their role has been important and perhaps one of the least recognized by them and others, but it is only one of several contributing factors. The transformation of the office has been seen as only natural, a part of a necessary and ineluctable evolutionary trend—a combination of our displacement of fears, hopes, and anxieties against it, our increasing expectations of the office in a world of depressions, crises, terrorism, and emergencies, and a perceived need to better manage a government of increasing complexity.

Lester Salamon has said, "between the 1930s and 50s the presidency emerged as the legitimating center of the national political order, the primary repository of national hopes and ambitions" (1981, 287). The evolutionary result has been described succinctly by presidential scholar Edward Corwin: "Taken by and large, the history of the presidency has been a history of aggrandizement" (Corwin, 1957, 57).[9] Interestingly, Corwin wrote these words before the two most arguably "imperial" presidencies of this half-century, those of Johnson (1963–1969) and Nixon (1969–1974). However, he added the admonition that is key for our purposes in this chapter that the presidency's history of aggrandizement has not made it a more effective institution. And Schuhmann (n.d.) asks wryly:

> Is it any wonder that a branch of government expected to act as savior has turned out, in recent years, to behave so much like Sampson? (1987)

Notwithstanding the decidedly mixed legacy of efforts to expand presidential control, Presidents have continued in the last two decades to attempt to assert more political control over the bureaucracy. A preferred method of doing this is increased use of political appointees, particularly the phenomenon of "layering" political appointees more deeply into the ranks of executive agencies, what Light (1995) characterizes as "thickening" government. Unfortunately, however, there have been counter intuitive and dysfunctional results. In fact, we would argue that the presidency has been substantially weakened in its ability to lead during the past 20 years, setting aside for the moment the contention that the President's leadership capacity has always been more theoretical than actual (Schlesinger, 1989, 420–499).

This means that a more politicized, yet weakened presidency has attempted to assert more control over "the bureaucracy" even as its ability to lead it has been diminished. These same patterns have been echoed in many state houses and city halls throughout America.

As Lane (1994) argues, the President's attempt to control the bureaucracy has manifested itself by substituting political responsiveness as a qualification for career officials for the more traditional qualification of neutral competence of civil servants first established in 1883. As noted previously, however, public administration, because it has been unable to conceive of its own role as something more than managerial, has always allowed itself to be complicit in this because civil service reforms, executive budgeting, and government reorganizations have been portrayed as managerial means of creating more honest, effective, and efficient government, an arguable but rebuttable presumption. They also, however, have been vehicles for altering or distorting the constitutional role of the presidency by reconceptualizing the president as CEO after the manner of a city manager or corporate CEO. This has had the effect of giving the institutional presidency a claim to rival or surpass the congress's constitutionally specified power over the "bureaucracy" and importantly to forestall or trump any effort of public administration to conceptualize a legitimate role for itself in governance beyond that of the president's loyal instrument (Dudley and Wamsley, 1998; and Lane and Wamsley, 1998). Lane observes, however, that as presidents have inevitably sought to solidify, if not aggrandize, the power that flows from this reconceptualization of the presidency as managerial, they have just as inevitably sought to assert more control over the bureaucracy—the kind of power seeking that logically follows from the conceptualization of the president as CEO.

But the constitutionally mandated, shared powers nature of our government has always militated against: (1) a CEO conception of the presidency and (2) a role as "faithful instrument of the president's will" on the part of the bureaucracy. Nonetheless, political science and public administration have persisted in trying to make a system of polycentric power one of monocentric power, and that simply is not possible without causing dysfunction in the many forms we have discussed above.

Lane (1994) maintains that this struggle of the president to control bureaucracy has *not* resulted in more effective management of the bureaucracy, because "size, scope, and complexity of government organizations" militate against effective presidential control through political appointees and in fact through any agents (20, Salamon and Lund, 1982). Although civil service reform, the executive budget, and reorganizations fostered the emergence of the president as CEO or manager of the executive branch, and have given the presidency executive powers not specified in the constitution, these have *not* given presidents the kind of control they have felt they needed in light of mushrooming expectations.

POLITICAL APPOINTEES AREN'T THE SOLUTION; POLITICAL APPOINTEES ARE THE PROBLEM

But it is equally important to say that political appointees have done little to bring about a more effective managerial presidency. Indeed, it can be said they have also militated against it (Campbell, 1986, 14). Nevertheless, as Ingraham, Thompson, and Eisenberg (1993) note:

for much of this century, but most notably for the past 25 years, political/career relationships in Washington have been marked by presidential efforts to direct and control the permanent bureaucracy better. The key players in this relationship are the political executives appointed by the President . . . and the top career management cadre. (263)

Ingraham et al. found that, while the number of political appointees remained relatively stable during the Bush and Clinton administrations, the overall number of political appointees had grown dramatically in the last quarter century. A similar phenomenon exists at the state level, with increased layering of political appointees but, at best, uncertain results from this layering.

In addition to being ineffective as an instrument of political control, increased use of political appointees causes other problems. The proliferation of political appointees has led to considerable conflict between career and political executives (Lorentzen, 1985; Durant, 1990; Colvard, 1995). Colvard succinctly captures the problem of career-appointee relations even in the best of times in stating:

> Political officials come into an agency without detailed knowledge of the discipline of the agency and are suspicious of the career civil servants who have the knowledge they need. The career civil servants who have been developed as experts in their field, do not have a full appreciation of the legitimate role of the political official. Eventually they gain respect for each other, trust develops, and they understand their respective roles. (However) with the average tenure of political appointees being roughly two years, this process often takes a good deal of the time they have to work together. (34)

In addition to problems caused by the inexperience, short tenure in office, and hostility toward career bureaucrats found in political appointees, Aberbach and Rockman (1988) and Terry Moe (1985), suggest that politicization of the federal executive branch may lead to congressional retaliation. They speculate that congressional retaliation could take the form of more statutory restrictions on presidential personnel authority. We would hypothesize that it also is, and will, take the forms of increased congressional demands for investigations and studies. As the constitutional logic of *Federalist 51* suggests, none of the three branches of government will forever tolerate efforts by another branch of government to usurp its constitutional prerogatives. It is therefore certainly reasonable to expect an eventual congressional reaction to presidential usurpation of control over administration.[10]

We have reviewed alarming growth of appointees and the problems they create, as well as what has happened to the presidency and the complicity of political science and public administration in its distortion. We hope we have thus shown where we are and how we got to our present unhappy state in terms of political appointees and career executives. We are not arguing for congressional domination of the constitutional system, or even for efforts to diminish presidential power. Rather we argue for searching for ways we might move to some more useful relationship.

A MODEST PROPOSAL

We propose that the position of Assistant Secretary for Administration and their equivalents in all smaller agencies be returned to career status, thus making it the pinnacle position for Senior Executives. We further propose the elimination of all noncareer SES positions and all Schedule C appointments with exception of a few special assistants to political executives.

Noncareer SES appointments add yet another layer (or layers) between the career staff and the PAS appointees. The intended purpose of the entire SES corps, which was to create an elite group of nonpartisan senior administrators, has been blunted by the proliferation of PAS appointments and the layering of these appointments above the SES level of the organization, and it has in no way been advanced by making 10 percent of that corps political appointees. The most justifiable uses of political appointees, the so-called "heavy lifting" in public agencies—bringing political clout and high level political connections to an agency, providing varied private sector experiences, and the ability to have phone calls returned from the White House—are less likely to be found in someone who is selected for a noncareer SES slot, given the large number of PAS slots that remain vacant at any given time. In other words, if a person has settled for a noncareer SES appointment, it can be presumed (fairly or not) that in the pecking order of Washington he or she were not well-connected enough to obtain something higher, that is to say a PAS slot.

The Volcker Commission warned that "the more positions are opened up to political appointees at lower levels, the harder it is to recruit high-quality people to fill them" (Volcker, 1989, 224). Scotty Campbell's original intention for the SES (Campbell, 1978), to create an elite corps of senior career administrators with mobility across agencies failed for a variety of reasons. Space does not allow a full recounting of those reasons here, but among them were: pay compression caused by being linked to relatively static congressional pay, institutional cultures that buttress a long tradition that weighs against moving among agencies, and abuse of the transfer provisions of the SES to punish suspected or anticipated disloyalty. One of the principal reasons for the failure of the SES, however, was that most SES slots have now been pressed too low organizationally to interest political appointees of executive caliber. As the Volcker Commission (1989) and Light (1995) found, the downward penetration of political appointees has pushed SES slots ever lower in the organization. We feel it is imperative that all the roughly 700 SES positions be open only to career officials. A cadre of career administrators at the Assistant Secretary level would provide a corps of truly senior administrators, provided that there was also a concomitant pruning of the bloated ranks of PAS slots and elimination of the 10 percent of appointees within the SES.

Such a pruning as our "modest proposal" would entail is in order, if for no other reason than the simple fact that it has become increasingly difficult to fill all of the PAS slots available. PAS slots, by their very nature of requiring Senate confirmation, run directly into what David Broder termed in the *Washington Post* a "pipeline problem" with significant backlogs of presidential nominees awaiting Senate confirmation. As ideological partisanship has intensified and the legislative and executive branches have often been in different hands the confirmation process has become much more difficult, perilous and protracted. G. Calvin MacKenzie (1994) has conducted a study documenting the average length of the appointment/confirmation process over 30 years. He finds that it has quadrupled from 2.4 months under Kennedy to 8.5 months under Clinton.

For 20 of the past 32 years, the Senate has been controlled by a different political party from the one occupying the White House. This fact, combined with reduced deference to presidential selections (probably sparked by Reagan's nomination of Robert Bork to the Supreme Court and John Tower to Secretary of Defense) have significantly complicated the process of confirmation for appointees. More than half of the appointees confirmed between 1984 and 1999 waited 5 months or more to be confirmed. As the pipeline problem has grown worse because of factors on the legislative side it has also worsened on the executive side. Two-fifths of those finally appointed felt the process was confusing and one-fourth said it was embarrassing. Nearly half felt the Senate made the process frustrating, and a third felt the same about the White House (Barr, 2000). Increasing numbers of potential appointees are simply not willing to endure the probing and disruption of their lives and careers that is entailed in accepting a high-level appointment. Paul Light sums up the situation—"it is no exaggeration to say that the appoinmtment process is broken—as it stands now Mother Teresa would have trouble getting confirmed" (Barr, 2000). Nor does it appear likely to improve soon. Future administrations will likely be even more cautious and slow. As Paul Light says, "A bad appointment can hurt you a lot more than a good appointment can help you" (Barr, 2000).

Perhaps there is no better place to seek support for our "modest proposal" than to turn again to David Cohen, the retired SESer and his forty-six-page tightly reasoned polemic against amateur government. Cohen sums up his argument this way:

> While the 3,000 political appointees at the top cannot be blamed for all the ills of the federal government, but they are a large part of the problem. They make the job of the civil servant harder, draining his energy and dampening his creativity and initiative. They comprise whole layers of unnecessary bureaucracy and impede communications and work flow. They often have fish other than their management duties to fry, and some of those fish have a bad smell. They also cost us a lot of money. (1998, 494)

Cohen goes on to point out that it would be futile to try to require qualifications and standards for political appointees because it would prevent politicians from rewarding supporters—the right political resume seldom has the right managerial credentials as well. Even if that rarity occurs, Cohen points out that the government is not improved by a manager new to government service, distrustful or hostile toward career staff (and perhaps government generally), and who will not stay long enough to become fully effective (494).

Cohen also makes a convincing case for the assistant secretary ranks being filled by careerists, "nearly three-quarter of all Executive Schedule positions are in this category of officials who oversee major program or functional areas and report directly to the department or agency head." This he says is the "level" at which career professional managers with long-term commitment to program and institutional needs are so critical.

Finally it should be obvious by now that this "modest proposal" is neither modest, nor is it simply about reducing salary costs. Although there would be millions of dollars saved by eliminating about 2,400 of the approximately 3,000 appointees (Cohen estimates $350 million in salaries and $150 million in processing annually [479]), the real savings would be less visible but more valuable beyond calculation in terms of greater effectiveness and perceived legitimacy of our government—a vast reduction in: the long-term vacancies, delays in refilling them and the resultant treading of water by the career staff; the extensive head-hunting and recruitment efforts, the excruciating long and detailed background checks; the agonizing confirmation proceedings, in-processing of the survivors, the disruptions and delays that go with vetting them into the organizational structure; the time lost absorbing and orienting the new appointees into organizational processes, the lost time that comes with dealing with their mistakes and misunderstandings; and finally, coping with their early and often abrupt departures. All these things are more prevalent at the beginning of an administration, but because of the rapid turnover are *annual, ongoing, and continuous.* The costs of this continuous dysfunction, whether measured in cost effectiveness or dollars, is staggering.

Nor should we forget that our "modest proposal" would also reduce political faux pas, scandals, foul-ups, wasted motion, and meaningless iterations that now accompany the accommodation of the patronage army. As things stand now, political appointees not only fail to give chief executives the control they wish, but they are also a major source of political difficulties and costs. They are perhaps most analogous to unexploded munitions that can be expected to go off at any moment. It is time to face this fact, to drastically reduce their ranks and expand those of the SES, and to seek in a variety of ways to develop trust and a working relationship between the remaining political appointees and the career executives.

CONCLUSION

It is a principle bordering on a cliché of sound communication that less is sometimes more. The objectives for which political appointees exist, including managing the career service, are best served not by a large volume of political appointees but instead by a small number of higher quality appointees. In an era of divided government, lessened career interest in the federal service, and weakened political parties, continued proliferation of political appointee slots, many of which will remain vacant for long periods of time, is a recipe for an ineffective government at a time when it is called upon to do more and more with less and less. If there has ever been a time since the end of the 19th century for scholarly concern, and even outrage, over the growth of political appointees and the threat they pose for effective politics *and* administration, this is it. And if the problems of filling these political appointments with qualified people gets any worse our government will not be one of "strangers" in Heclo's memorable phrase, but instead a government of ineptitude and vacancies.

NOTES

1. Deborah Gore Dean is the former barmaid and erstwhile socialite who was an assistant to the Secretary of Housing and Urban Development in the Reagan Administration. She was indicted on several felony counts and some of the charges are still being appealed at this writing. Craig Livingston is the former bouncer and campaign advance man who requested background files of nominees for office of the F.B.I. The files delivered included many of prominent Republicans thus setting off a minor scandal quickly labeled "filegate" that dogged the Clinton Administration for two terms. Gifford Pinchot was the famed naturalist and conservationist who became the first director of the U.S. Forest Service whose political and administrative skills are legendary. James Lee Witt is the was appointed director of FEMA by President Clinton when the agency was close to collapse and threatened with extinction. His political and administrative skills are credited with dramatically turning the agency around.

2. Although it hardly qualifies as outrage and did not focus simply on patronage, the tone of the report of the National Commission on the Public Service chaired by Paul Volcker was certainly one of deep concern.

3. One of the nine was never filled during the time of the study.

4. The evidence of a lack of confidence was clear enough in the wake of Hurricane Andrew. The president sent his own personal representative to supervise the relief efforts, thus leaving an embarrassed director playing second fiddle. Even more telling was the fact that the director was a protégé of Edwin Meese who was one of the president's closest advisers.

5. Conversation with Mr. Al Zuck.

6. Though it is not at all clear that Hamilton would have equated "energy" with expansion of the constitutional powers of the president, that is nonetheless widely assumed.

7. Politics, of course, is the art of creating a "mandate" from an agenda comprised largely of campaign slogans and then getting something through legislative and administrative processes that can plausibly be claimed to resemble that agenda in some way. Or alternatively, taking events originating in the legislative and administrative processes and by selective rhetoric and symbol manipulation creating something that could be perceived of as an agenda.

8. Scholar Terry Moe avoids the use of the term aggrandizement, no doubt finding a certain pejorative tone in it. He speaks instead of "centralization" and politicization." We think it can be argued that these are synonymous with aggrandizement but it is an arguable

point. Moe sees public administration scholars as being critical for "deinstitutionalizing" the presidency but offering little proof of deleterious effects. He also assumes that other institutions such as Congress will act to offset the trends of centralization and politicization. We think there is sufficient evidence of such negative effects and that he is being incorrect in his prediction (1991, 157, fn 36).

9. Much of the aggrandizement Corwin identifies is a result of national security issues, though expansion of presidential power to address these issues also leads to expansion of the powers of the domestic and managerial president.

10. The 104th Congress has been mixed in this regard, attempting to assert more control over some aspects of administration but also approving an enhanced recission authority that shifts power in budget making, the lifeblood of administration, more toward the President.

REFERENCES

Aberbach, Joel D., and Bert A. Rockman. (1988). Mandates or Mandarins: Control and Discretion in the Modern Administrative State. In James P. Pfiffner (Ed.) (1987). *The Managerial Presidency*. Belmont, CA: Wadsworth.

Ban, Carolyn. (1987). The Crisis of Morale and Federal Senior Executives. *Public Productivity Review*, 11, 1(43): 31–49.

Barr, Stephen. (2000). The Federal Page, Washington, DC, *Washington Post*.

Brownlow, Louis. (1937). *U.S. President's Commission on Administrative Management*. Washington, DC: U.S. Government Printing Office.

Butler, Stuart M., Michael Sanera, and Bruce Weinrod (Eds.) (1984). *Mandate for Leadership II*, Washington, DC: Heritage Foundation.

Campbell, Alan K. (1978, March/April). Civil Service Reform: A New Commitment. *Public Administration Review*, 38(2): 99–103.

Campbell, Colin. (1986). *Managing the Presidency: Carter, Reagan, and the Search for Executive Harmony*. Pittsburgh, PA: University of Pittsburgh Press.

Carroll, James D., A. Lee Fritschler, and Bruce L.R. Smith. (1985). Supply-Side Management in the Reagan Administration. *Public Administration Review*, 45(6): 805–814.

Cohen, David M. (1998). Amateur Government. *Journal of Public Administration Research and Theory*, 4: 450–497

Colvard, James E. (1995, Spring). Clear Air Turbulence in the Careerist/Political Appointee Zone. *The Public Manager: The New Bureaucrat*, 24: 34–36.

Corwin, Edward S. (1957). *The President, Office, and Powers, 1787–1957*. New York: New York University Press.

Dudley, Larkin S., and Gary L. Wamsley. (1998). From Reorganizing to Reinventing: Sixty Years and We Still Don't Get It. *International Journal of Public Administration*, 21(2–4): 323–374.

Durant, Robert. (1990, May/June). Beyond Fear or Favor: Appointee-Careerist Relations in the Post-Reagan Era. *Public Administrative Review*, 50: 319–331.

Durant, Robert, Charles T. Goodsell, Jack H. Knott, and William L. Murray. (1998). Responses to Robet Maranto's "Thinking the Unthinkable in Public Administration." *Administration and Society*, 29(6).

Harmon, M.M. (1995). *Responsibility as Paradox: A Critique of Rational Discourse on Government*. Thousand Oaks, CA: Sage Publications.

Heclo, Hugh. (1977). *A Government of Strangers.* Washington, DC: The Brookings Institution.

Heineman, Ben W. (1967). Final Report of the President's Task Force on Governmental Organization, the Organization and Management of Great Society Programs, June 1967. Administratively confidential. Washington, DC, unpublished.

Held, Walter G. (1979). *Decisionmaking in the Federal Government: The Wallace S. Sayre Model.* Washington, DC: The Brookings Institution.

Holden, Matthew, Jr. (1991). Why Entourage Politics Is Volatile. In James P. Pfiffner (Ed.), *The Managerial Presidency.* Pacific Grove, CA: Brooks/Cole Publishing.

Hoover, Herbert. (1949). *Commission on the Executive Branch of Government, General Management of the Executive Branch.* Washington, DC: U.S. Government Printing Office.

Ingraham, Patricia W. (1987, September/October). Building Bridges or Burning Them? The President, the Appointees, and the Bureaucracy. *The Public Administration Review,* 47: 425–435.

Ingraham, Patricia W., Elliot F. Eisenberg, and James R. Thompson. (1993, September). Pollitical Management Strategies and Political/Career Relationships: Where Are We Now in the Federal Government? Paper prepared for delivery at the annual meeting of the American Political Science Association, p. 16.

Kaufman, Herbert. (1956). Emerging Conflicts in the Doctrines of Public Administration. *American Political Science Review,* 50(4): 1057–1073.

Knott, Jack H., and Gary J. Miller. (1987). *Reforming Bureaucracy.* Englewood Cliffs, NJ: Prentice-Hall.

Lane, Larry M. (1994). Public Administration and the Problem of the Presidency. Paper prepared for the National Training Conference of the American Society for Public Administration, Kansas City, Missouri.

Lane, Larry M. and Gary L. Wamsley. (1998). Gulick and the American Presidency: Vision, Reality, and Consequences. *International Journal of Public Administration,* 21(2–4): 323–374.

Lane, Larry M., and James F. Wolf. (1990). *The Human Resource Crisis in the Public Sector: Rebuilding the Capacity to Govern.* New York: Quorum Books.

Light, Paul. (1997). When Worlds Collide: The Political-Career Nexus. In G. Calvin Mackenzie (Ed.), *The In-and-Outers: Presidential Appointees and Transient Government in Washington.* Baltimore, MD: Johns Hopkins University Press.

———. (1995). *Thickening Government: Federal Hierarchy and the Diffusion of Accountability.* Washington, DC: The Brookings Institution.

Lowi, Theodore J. (1979). *The End of Liberalism.* New York: Norton.

Mackenzie, G. Calvin. (1981). *The Politics of Presidential Appointments.* New York: Macmillan.

———. (Ed.) (1997). *The In-and-Outers: Presidential Appointees and Transient Government in Washington.* Baltimore, MD: Johns Hopkins University Press.

Malek, Frederick. (1971). Management of Non-Career Personnel: Summary of Recommendations for the White House Personnel Office, Washington. Mimeograph in Frank Thompson (Ed.), *Public Personnel Administration.* Oak Park, IL: Moore Publishing.

Maranto, Robert. (1993). *Politics and Bureaucracy in the Modern Presidency.* Westport, CT: Greenwood Press.

———. (1998a). Thinking the Unthinkable in Public Administration. *Administration and Society,* 29(6):623–642.

———. (1998b). Rethinking the Unthinkable. *Administration and Society*, 30(1): Newbury Park, CA: Sage Publications.

Moe, Ronald C. (March/April 1994) The Reinventing Government Exercises: Misinterpreting the Problem, Misjudging the Consequences. *Public Administration Review*.

Moe, Terry M. (1985). The Politicized Presidency. In John Chubb, and Paul Peterson (Eds.), *The New Direction in American Politics, pp. 235–271*. Washington, DC: The Brookings Institution.

NAPA. (1974). *Implications for Responsible Government*. Report of the National Academy of Public Administration prepared for the Senate Select Committee on Presidential Campaign Activities, Washington, DC.

Nathan, Richard P. (1983). *The Administrative President*. New York: John Wiley & Sons.

———. (1985). Political Administration is Legitimate. In Lester M. Salamon, and Michael S. Lund (Eds.), *The Reagan Presidency and the Governing of America*. Washington, DC: Urban Institute Press.

Neustadt, Richard E. (1960). *Presidential Power*. New York: Wiley.

Newland, C. A. (1987). Public Executives: Imperium, Sacerdotum, Collegium? Bicentennial Leadership Challenges. Public Administration Review. 47(1): 45–56.

Pfiffner, James P. (Ed.) (1987). *The Managerial Presidency*. Belmont, CA: Wadsworth.

Redford, Emmette S. (1969). *Democracy in the Administrative State*. New York: Oxford University Press.

Reich, Robert. (1997). *Locked in the Cabinet*. New York: Knopf.

Salamon, Lester M. (1981). Beyond the Presidential Illusion—Toward a Constitutional President. In Hugh Heclo and Lester M. Salamon (Eds.), *The Illusion of Presidential Government, pp. 287–295*. Boulder, CO: Westview Press.

Salamon, Lester M. and Michael S. Lund (Eds.) (1982). *The Reagan Presidency and the Governing of America*. Washington, DC: Urban Institute Press.

Sanera, Michael. (1984). Implementing the Mandate. In Michael Butler et al. (Eds.), *Mandate for Leadership II, pp. 457–560*. Washington, DC: Heritage Foundation.

Schlesinger, Arthur M. (1989). *The Imperial Presidency*. Boston, MA: Houghton Mifflin.

U.S. Senate. (1974). *Presidential Campaign Activities of 1972: Senate Resolution 60, Hearings before the Senate Select Committee on Presidential Campaign Activities*, 93 Cong., 2 sess., vol. 19. Washington, DC: GPO.

Van Riper, Paul P. (1958). *History of the United States Civil Service*. Evanston, IL: Row, Peterson and Company.

Volcker, Paul. (1989, 1990). *Leadership for America: Rebuilding the Public Service*. Lexington, MA: Lexington Books.

Willoughby, W.F. (1927). *Principles of Public Administration*. Baltimore, MD: Johns Hopkins University Press.

12

Civil Service Reform in the United States: A Strategic Analysis of Past, Present, and Future

ALI FARAZMAND

Civil service systems have played a major role in governments and public administration systems since ancient times. The great civilizations of ancient Persia, China, Rome, and Egypt benefited from and developed civil service along with the massive military forces they had at their disposal. Similarly, reform of the civil service systems has been a frequent activity governments and politicians have undertaken to streamline, modernize, and improve their administrative systems. Darius the Great's comprehensive administrative reforms around 500 B.C. included, among other features, promotion of a civil service system with an emphasis on merit and in-service training throughout the vast Achamenid World State Empire of Persia that extended from India and central Asia in the east to north Africa and south Europe in the west; the largest empire the ancient world had ever known. Chinese utilized competitive examinations for service entry. These and other historical civil service experiences were studied and seriously considered in the debates for civil service reform in the late-19th-century American government and public administration (see Van Riper, in this volume).

Contrary to the popular belief and the current general mode of anticivil service and antibureaucracy in the United States and around the world, both the civil service and bureaucracy are alive and well and indeed play a key role in the smooth operation of the American government and public administration. The nature, character, and role of these public organizations have, however, changed significantly. Any analysis of the bureaucracy and civil service system in this context must take into account a political economy perspective as well, in order to paint a clear and holistic picture of the American system of public personnel management and public administration. This can only be done from a strategic point of view, utilizing a macrolevel analysis with a political economy approach, because any isolationist, microlevel analysis and atomistic discussion of the civil service reform become meaningless. Any reform has gainers and losers; Pareto optimality rarely exists.

This chapter provides a strategic analysis of the American civil service reform from an historical perspective, with future directions and policy implications. Due to space limitations, the chapter focuses only on the major civil service reforms that are considered by the mainstream experts as the landmark reform events in American administrative history. What follows is divided into five sections: First, the issue of civil service reform is presented briefly in a theoretical context. Second, a theoretical discussion of the rationales and models of reform is provided. This is followed by an analysis in Section 3 of the 19th-century Civil Service Reform Act of 1883 with a historical background to its inception. Forth, the developments in the 1930s through 1960s are discussed for a better understanding of the conditions leading to the later strategic civil service reform in the 1970s. Fifth, the Civil Service Reform Act of 1978 is analyzed with its implications for the later time. Finally, further reform acts are considered as part of a strategic, long-term policy goal of the corporate administrative state now in control of the public sphere in the United States with significant implications for not only the public personnel system at home but also for governance and public administration around the globe.

THEORETICAL CONTEXT OF CIVIL SERVICE REFORMS

One of the fundamental functions of any government machinery in the world, whether democratic or autocratic, capitalist or socialist, involves a twofold strategic task: (1) to facilitate the smooth operation of the functions and responsibilities of the temporal government, that is to perform public affairs functions; and (2) to provide an effective mechanism of organizational control over the complex of governmental organizations involved in the functions of maintenance and enhancement of the dominant economic and social system, either in capitalism or socialism. The function of service delivery, including security, stability, and problem-solving and development is an implicit component of these two broad functions.

Civil service system oils the machinery of the ruling governance system in place; it provides administrative continuity, stability and order, and professional competence with partisan political neutrality that protects administrative behavior from the rushes and abuses of political sentiments of the time. Civil service systems, as opposed to military personnel, are composed of civilian career-oriented personnel whose actions and inactions are governed by structural and process laws, rules, procedures, and values. While civil service systems have a heavy emphasis on career-oriented merit systems with seniority-based organizational behavior, their strategic leadership positions are most often occupied by political appointees as executive representatives of the governing political party and ideology.

In essence, civil service systems provide (a) managerial, (b) political, and (c) legal bases of administrative behavior in government, with an ethical safeguard against potential abuses of partisan politics. Yet, history of governments, including the American governments, is full of stories of partisan, political, and personal abuses of career civil servants by political bosses. While these three functional roles of the civil service systems can potentially work together in harmony (especially in parliamentary government systems and to some degree in presidential systems like the United States), the managerial and legal functions can, and often do, conflict with the political functions of system maintenance.

This issue has been a key scholarly concern in public administration and bureaucratic politics, with scholars emphasizing the three approaches of *law, management, and politics* in the study and practice of the field (see Rosenbloom, 1993). To Rosenbloom, there is an inherent conflict between these three dimensions of, and approaches to, public administration, yet there is no clear answer to the potential problem. Dwight Waldo (1992) further explores the dilemma of reconciling the values of bureaucracy and civil service on the one hand, and those values of democracy and political system maintenance, on the other; his answer seems to be a need for both, with a "strive" to achieve the goals of the latter. It is extremely difficult, if not impossible, to conceive of democracy without bureaucracy (Waldo, 1992). This is a great scholarly debate beyond the scope and limit of this short essay.

What is important to note, therefore, is that civil service systems serve as a key instrument of rationalizing and implementing political, economic, administrative, and ideological goals and objectives, but away from the rushing and emotional characters of temporal political forces. They also serve many other functions and purposes, such as providing public employment, professionalizing the administrative system, providing technical expertise, establishing history and records, providing stability and continuity in government systems, promoting institutional memory through knowledge of expertise and experience, and offering structural guidance to political as well as administrative leadership.

These strategic instrumentalities of civil service system are a key to effective governance and to political leadership in pursuit of specific governmental or partisan goals and missions. As such, strategic civil service system is an integral part of governing and governance systems, and certainly instrumental to different political and governmental systems. Therefore, in both theory and practice, civil service systems (there are different systems of civil service orientations and applications) are key instruments to strategic public personnel administration in building and managing human capital in all times, especially in the 21st century.

Civil service systems by design, like any institutional system, have three fundamental features: structure, process, and culture. *Structure* consists of organizational hierarchy, decision authorities and levels, rules and regulations governing organizational actions, power relationships, and the linking pins to external as well as internal organizational environmental centers or points of interests, significance, and influence. For example, knowing their limits of organizational domains, a higher civil servant in a particular government organizational system may interact—either by necessity, functional duty and requirement, or personal desire—with key outside officials, policymakers, other civil servants, and citizens for the sake of organizational and professional purposes or both. Yet, structural requirements or rules may forbid direct personal interaction or communication between lower level civil servants with senior career servants, or vice versa, and similarly between mid-level civil servants with political executives of an agency. Structure, therefore, provides guidance and roadmaps, and defines the scope and limits of "what" is to be done; and structuration is a key organizational and leadership activity (Farazmand, 2004, 2005).

Process, on the other hand, defines "how" things are to be done, "what" a structure has allowed, and it provides the means by which the roadmaps are followed and the destination is reached. Processes help get things done, with or without efficiency, effectiveness, fairness, accountability, and transparency. Organizations and governments may be efficient yet secretive, unaccountable, and lack transparency, and indeed in violation of laws and regulations that serve to protect individual, constitutional, and other democratic rights of citizens and others.

Culture reflects the values, attitudes, perceptions, and beliefs of people or employees who do the work of the organization; they shape the culture of the system. The culture in turn is both formal and informal. The former represents the formal rules, regulations, and procedures hierarchically dictated and communicated for task implementation and goal achievement, while informal culture represents the grapevine, ideas and information originated and communicated by employees and workers through "conversations" and nonorganizational means. Once formed, informational culture can be a potent force to deal with; it can serve as either a catalyst or barrier to organizational change. Thus, institutional and cultural approaches to change and reform are considered more desirable to organizational and system change and transformation (Peters, 2002).

RATIONALES AND MODELS OF REFORM

Rationales for Reform

The need to reform a civil service system arises when these central features—structure, process, and culture or values—are either outdated, have become sluggish and inefficient and lack vibrant dynamics, are inflicted by corruption, or are resistant to changes that are demanded or imposed by external as well as internal forces, pressures, and expectations. The inability to adapt by a civil service system to changing conditions of governance and administration—both internally and externally—raises an urgent need for reform and transformation in the system, so as to respond to the dynamics of change of the time. Thus, adaptability and flexibility constitute one key rationale for civil service reforms. Civil service systems are generally structured by laws, rules, regulations, and procedures emanated from constitutional, legislative, judicial, executive, and agency sources and decisions. Civil servants are expected to observe these legal bases of actions within organizations that perform government functions within the rule of law and constitutional democracy.

By tradition, merit-based career civil servants also enjoy a degree of professional independence and are protected from potential partisan influences and politicians' preferential dictates or abuses. While independent professional expertise with legal protection may serve against corruption and partisan or personal abuses, the system may be viewed as resistant to political changes demanding higher values of efficiency, political responsiveness, and popular accountability. Balancing these two sets of legal/organizational and political values is a delicate issue that has been the subject of all administrative reforms, democratic governance, and bureaucratic politics for at least over a century.

A problem arises when external changes demanding civil service reform and transformation are viewed—rather accurately—as against the broad public interests and in such situations a civil service system resistance may be needed to protect universalistic public interests and values against particularistic private group or class interests. As will be seen later, this was a subject of professional debate during Ronald Reagan's presidency in the 1980s, when Donald Devine took extreme political measures to restructure and reform the civil service system— actually destroyed it—to achieve partisan political goals, measures that many professional civil servants objected to and resisted, but lost the battle (Newland, 1983). Similar political measures have been adopted by George W. Bush during his reorganization and consolidation of the security, intelligence, and immigration organizations into the Department of Homeland Security staffed with political appointees and nontenure civil servants, appointees at will (not to be confused with employees at will).

By far the most often noted and professed rationale for civil service reforms has been the elimination of corruption and building professional competency in the administrative and government system. Other rationales for reform include political reorganization and reforms that would restructure the system more in line with the rest of the governance system, modernization of the system processes and procedures, professionalization and institutional capacity building, and flexibility of the system to respond, to revive and perform more efficiently, effectively, and accountably in times of major socioeconomic changes. Still, sometimes reforms are adopted for the sake of reform, or simply to follow the trends set by others. For developing and less developed nations, the choice is limited, as reforms have demanded, as a condition, by powerful "external forces of policy change" such as the United Nations (UN), the World Bank (WB), the International Monetary Fund (IMF), the World Trade Organization (WTO), and other donor governments like the United States, European governments, and Japan. They tend to reshape the economic and political landscape of the world in the age of capitalist globalization with an antisocialist ideology (Farazmand, 1999).

Thus, civil service reforms have always been a key strategic policy instrument in public administration, and essential to strategic changes in governments, directly or indirectly. All changes have consequences with political economy implications for those who benefit and those who lose in the process, and civil service reforms are no exceptions.

Models of Reform and Change

Models of reform and change are in two categories, one dealing with the substance and consequences, and the other with the forms and directions.

Substantive reforms explain what entails and what is included in the civil service, how the new system is to perform, as well as who benefits and loses. Substantive civil service reforms also give policy priority signals of the administration in charge. They contain structural, process, and value features. For example, the Pendleton Civil Service Reform of 1883 established a merit system and signaled a strategic professionalization of public administration and government in the United States. Similarly, the 1978 Civil Service Reform Act strategically positioned the U.S. civil service toward a "businesslike" system of personnel management with extensive managerial flexibility and political executive discretion in employee-management relations; it also paved the way for privatization and contracting out schemes of the 1980s and beyond.

Formative models of reform include origins or forces behind reforms as well as directions of reform decision authorities. Guy Peters (2002) identifies three models of reform: top-down, bottom-up, and institutional models. *Top-down reforms* are elitist models of reforms decided and dictated by political and administrative elites; organizational elites take charge of implementing top-down reforms throughout agency and departmental systems. Organizational members have no say in the reform process but are affected by its consequences. *Bottom-up reforms* are considered *environmentally* induced or pressured reforms that reflect popular demands for change, with presumed responses by organizational elite's adaptability to change. *Institutional reforms* are considered more holistic and inclusive models of change that involve institutional culture and values as well as people or members of the system being affected by the reforms. The institutional model is therefore viewed as more desirable as it offers the advantages of both top-down and bottom-up models with additional features of cultural acceptability of the people being affected (Farazmand, 2005).

Most civil service reforms have been of top-down types, with few on institutional basis. Elites respond to popular citizen pressures or demands for change as long as the changes do not disturb the status quo system, or enhances the system with new directions. The sweeping privatization and contracting out or outsourcing of governments in the United States and around the world since the 1980s have been of the latter form and direction, toward market-based and corporatist governance systems promoting the goals of globalization of corporate capitalism in America.

THE CIVIL SERVICE REFORM ACT OF 1883

Also known as the Pendleton Act, the Civil Service Reform Act of 1883 was the first comprehensive civil service reform legislation in the United States. It was a pioneering act of legislation that had transcending effects on the national, state, and local governments across America. States and localities also adopted similar reform programs at the turn of the 20th century, commonly known as the progressive era characterized with professionalization of public management, council-management system, and merit-based competitive examination systems (Cayer, 1995). The 1883 civil service reform was a major part of a series of administrative, economic, and political reforms that were carried out as a result of many socioeconomic and political changes, upheavals, and events that took place in the latter half of the 19th-century American history.

The political economy issues of this period included, among others, the civil war and abolishment of slavery, the rise of large-scale industrialization and its corresponding monopolistic economic enterprises or corporations across the states, the farmers movement, the labor movement, the expansionist wars for land acquisition to the far west and south forcing Native Americans into confined "reservations," and the massive corruption that had swept the governance and administrative systems of the United States at all levels of government since the early part of the century.

In brief, the Civil War ended with the supply of a large number of freed slave-labor force moving into the industrial base of the North, and with the expansion of railroad west and southward, industrialization of the south emerged also. Industrialization created a new challenge of labor organization, an issue that demanded government attention. Similarly, interstate commerce expanded and in turn required some sort of government regulations as different states practiced differential treatments concerning labor, transportation, and public communication. In a growing economy and society, social problems also rose as immigration and population growth expanded into town and westward territories.

Northern industries and cities attracted freed black slaves and absorbed them with differential and low wages, creating more challenges of discrimination, managerial abuse, and corresponding rise of labor movement organizations such as the Knights of Labor and American Federal of Labor (AFL) to demand better working conditions, reduction of working hours, and abolition of child labor, among others. Other changes and corresponding challenges demanding reforms and government actions characterized 19th-century America. However, for the purpose of this chapter, the most important reform movement of the second half of 19th-century America was the administrative reform to manage the machinery of the government and public affairs (Skowronek, 1982).

The "government by gentlemen" of the early 19th century had already given way to the Jeffersonian and Jacksonian "spoils system" by which partisan and personal loyalties would serve as bases of employment into public office. While the government by the gentlemen "elites" was modified by the government by the "common nonelites" in the administration, the personnel system of government was replete of moneyed office seekers and corruption began to sweep the government administration throughout the entire United States of America. Sale of office for favor and money was common, and the well-intentioned Jacksonian "office rotation" system of personnel management was abused to scandalous levels. This and other forms of corruption reached the highest level of concern during the Lincoln administration engaged in the civil war and in dire need of politically and personally loyal people to carry out public policy decisions.

The rising corruptions in the governing institutions and the administrative system rose a massive popular protest that called for major reforms aimed at abolishing the spoils system and public office corruption, and protecting civil rights and other constitutional rights of citizens. Similar callings were made for reforms in social and economic areas of interstate commerce, market performance, and public-private sector relations. The result was the beginning of the rise of what Dwight Waldo (1948) has dubbed the "administrative state" or the government bureaucracy composed of a complex of legislation, laws, rules and institutions in the executive branch of government to regulate the private economy, monitor market activities, promote free interstate commerce, and streamline the government administrative system as demanded by the changing socioeconomic and political conditions of the time.

The growing in size and functions of the American federal government, rising from a nation-state to a fast industrializing regional and international power, became more complex and sophisticated beyond the capacity of a government staffed by "common-men." It required a far more competent, efficient, and specialized organizational and personnel system with technical expertise, functional skills, and professional knowledge to run this rising international government. The Pendleton Act of 1883 was the "strategic answer" to this rising need challenge of the time. It aimed at modernizing the government system by building capacity in its personnel administration through creation of a modern civil service system that would meet the challenges of the new time beyond the 19th century.

The Reform Act aimed at abolishing corruption by introducing a "merit system" replaced the runaway "spoils system" and created several *structural* features, such as the collective governing body of the Civil Service Commission (CSC), to promote and protect the merit system and handle its violation cases. The purpose was to create a professional civil service system highlighted by efficiency, fairness, and good government; more importantly, its mission was to provide a "check and balance" system, to be the "ethical watchdog, the moral guardian of governmental decision making" (Thayer, 1997, 95). *The process* of accomplishing the goals included mechanisms of a competitive examination system for entry positions, with a grade system that would allow promotion based on merit performance and job related qualifications with a career path to raise cadres of civil servants to highest possible levels so they would serve different political masters with the same institutional and professional knowledge, skills, and competence.

The emerging institutional *culture* emanating from this new system of civil service and personnel administration was based on the cardinal values of professionalism, technical expertise, knowledge and skills, efficiency and effectiveness in the management of public affairs, regardless of political bosses' orientations or preferences. The result was increasing professionalization of public personnel administration with a growing self-conscious civil service system that managed the functions of a modern government. The political emphasis of separating administration from politics, that is the "politics-administration dichotomy" as the administrative doctrine of the time espoused by Woodrow Wilson's (1887) essay "The Study of Administration," was clearly interpreted as a "political neutrality" and "neutral competence." These values of administration away from politics shaped, rather erroneously, the "first orthodoxy doctrine" in the American history of public administration as we all know it.

Thus, government by the "spoils and corrupt" was replaced by the "government by good and efficient." These characterizations, explanatory as they may be as far as the professionalization of the personnel system is concerned, can promote a misunderstanding and false representation of governance systems both politically and economically. Poignantly speaking, the government by "the elites" remained unchanged, and indeed was reinforced by new institutional developments, but the new government was managed by professionally trained and efficient civil servants whose employment was considered a "privilege, not a right." That meant that good and efficient public employees could be dismissed and politically abused at any time, even though civil service protection mechanisms had enjoyed some degree of independency via "neutral competency" afforded them. Thus, the new governing elites representing the powerful economic interest groups, that is the new industrial corporate elites and other commercial and financial elites, along with the rising military elites, formed the new power structure elites of the nation in search of regional and global expansion through wars, diplomacy, and economic instrumentalities.

Therefore, Mosher's (1968) characterization of the history of American public personnel and civil service system from "government by gentleman" to government by "professionals," "professional state," or "labor unions" of the 1960s should not be mistaken and taken with face value; government by elites, especially the "corporate business-military-political elites" has indeed been enhanced and strengthened. Professionalization of civil service and public administration has actually meant a reduction of discretionary power for political governing elites representing the real power structure, and de-professionalization and de-civilization of public service and administration enhance those arbitrary and discretionary powers and authority in administration and governance, as we have witnessed since the 1980s.

The professionalization of the civil service and personnel system, therefore, placed in government a modernizing strategic instrument of governance and administration capable of responding to the challenges of the "modern times," and of meeting the demands of the new "industrial state" with national, regional, and global programs and policies. This was done along with a strong "patronage" system allowing in the bureaucracy key political executives carefully selected based on personal, political, and partisan loyalty as well as financial campaign contributions, that is "money."

Thus, spoils system never left the personnel and civil system. This was the trend that continued—the dual career civil service and patronage systems—throughout the first half of the 20th century and during the two world wars, which increased the demands for more professioalization of public service and administration, and of the growing American bureaucracy. It was further enhanced during the global ideological cold war following World War II, served the globalizing government and transworld corporations worldwide, and through judicial intervention (court cases on employees constitutional rights) and political executive orders (for example, Kennedy's executive orders on government employees right to unionization and Johnson's on Affirmative Action) and civil rights movements from below gained a number of rights and privileges, including antidiscrimination civil rights laws and replacement of the "doctrine of privilege" with the doctrine of "substantial rights" granting public employees some degree of protection through due process of law against arbitrary managerial actions.

However, these developments were accompanied by a growing uneasiness, and even hostility, among a vide range of opponents of the growing "administrative state" that became even larger during and after the Great Depression induced New Deal programs and post-war turbulent decades of the 1950s and 1960s. Critics of the growing largess of the civil service and bureaucracy in the United States came from left or right and from business elites to academics whose cries for reclaiming democratic powers away from unelected discretionary bureaucrats were recorded and heard everywhere in late 20th century (Sayer, 1948).

The popular media, also owned by the elites, joined the band wagons and the result was preparation and mobilization of citizen publics to wage a war of bureaucracy-bashing and to get rid of the now "inefficient" and slow moving "monster" bureaucracy that only feeds itself and the "entitled welfare recipients" of the country. This rhetoric became the slogan of the 1980s and 1990s, and beyond. Elsewhere (Farazmand, 1989) I have discussed this major development beyond the scope of this short chapter. Other scholars have also done a great job (see, for example, Goodsell, 1995; Peters, 2001). Suffice it to say that the antibureaucracy, antiadministrative state, anticivil service, and now antipublic service began to prepare a political agenda for a new "civil service reform" that would solve the purported problems and streamline the government-corporate business relations in America.

THE CIVIL SERVICE REFORM OF 1978

The late 1970s was the beginning of a new era of bureaucracy-bashing and anticivil service systems in the United States. It also ushered a resurgence of the old "spoils system" under partisan political bosses in government. Having served its strategic role of enhancing a globalizing system of government and corporate capitalism, the increasingly self-assertive, broad public interests-oriented civil service and bureaucracy with high professional and partisan neutral administrative "standards" had by the 1970s become a rival competitor to the corporate business sector and its representative legislative elites in Congress who viewed competent administrative state a threat to their political discretionary power. Thus, the bureaucracy became the target of attacks, on the ground of democratic principles, from almost every direction, but mostly from the corporate business-funded think tank organizations, scholars, and politicians.

Almost every presidential candidate in 20th-century America campaigned against the federal bureaucracy and promised to destroy it. None did so after election to office; indeed, almost all left office with an even larger bureaucracy behind. All presidents have used the bureaucracy as a strategic instrument of change, policy, management, and all have benefited from its civil service system (Heclo, 1977). The legal and managerial foundations of the professional civil service system had provided a safeguard against abusive and unethical partisan and interest group-oriented policy and administrative actions for many decades. Now these foundations were considered by the conservative Right—politicians, business elites, and their academic counterparts—as a threat to flexible managerialism of the businesslike political executives and ideological politicians whose ultra conservative agendas were also directed by the conservative evangelist religious right with over 70 million church memberships under influence as time marched into the 1990s and the new millennium.

A series of antiproperty tax propositions adopted by various states paved the impetus for serious government cutbacks and civil service reforms that altered the character of the federal civil service and bureaucracy. Right after election to office, Jimmy Carter proposed—and received unanimous approval from his democratic Congress in 1978 for—a Civil Service Reform Act that changed the 1883 Reform Act's provisions in both form and substance. It was the second most comprehensive reform measure since the 1883 Pendleton Act. It moved the country's century-long established professional civil service with competent administrative standards toward a businesslike corporate personnel system at the discretionary disposal of partisan-motivated political bosses. According to its architect, Allan Campbell (1978), the act put the "personnel management...among the top priorities of the federal government" and replaced a "nonsystem" (Campbell, 1980) in pursuance of Carter's bureaucratic reform agenda, which turned into a "bureaucratic-bashing" strategy "that painted all civil servants with a common—and negative—brush" (Ingraham and Thompson, 1995, 56).

The Carter's CSRA was both *formative and substantive.* The formative changes included several *structural* arrangements, such as the replacement of the collective

Civil Service Commission (CSC) with an Office of Personnel Management (OPM) headed by a single director, a Merit System Protection Board (MSPB), a Federal Labor-Relations Authority (FLRA), a General Counsel for merit system protection, and a few others. The legislation also provided a whistle-blowing protection measure aimed at preventing corruption and promoting accountability and ethical behavior in public service, a measure that has failed the test of four presidents. But the most important features of the legislation were the threefold *substantive* changes that altered the spirit of civil service system in the federal government.

The first and most important feature of the reform Act was the *flexibilization doctrine* in dealing with the higher civil servants (and all others). The former supergrades who were now renamed as "senior executive servants" (SES) were given the option of getting out of the civil service protection and to perform as "generalist executives" for higher pay and bonus systems similar to corporate executives in the private sector, subject to a new "performance evaluation" requirement. Flexibilization was also developed through the SES *mobility and rotation* system, the ability to move or transfer to other agencies in need of managerial capacity. These two features of flexibilization were supplemented by appointment of 10 percent of SES positions with political executives at the top, plus similar provisions at other levels of the civil service system, allowing more discretionary patronage appointments on political and personal bases. Similar to the British elitist model, this feature of the civil service reform was a strategic change making a large number of "generalists" available to various agencies of the government under control of the political leadership.

The second substantive change was reform of the public sector labor-management relations through creation of a federal "Authority" acting like the private sector National Labor Management Board (NLRB). The Authority's empowerment to handle public employee relations limited unions' power and employees' ability to take cases to courts by referring matters of disputes to administrative judges or "agency adjudication." This change was consonant with the conservative Supreme Court's new doctrine of "agencification" of public employee relations in the last two decades, empowering administrative judges and agencies in matters of constitutional individual rights.

The third substantive change involved measures urging innovation and experimentation with new managerial techniques to find means of increasing efficiency and improving productivity in government organizations. These measures empowered agency executives to exercise private business techniques, approaches, and methods of organization and management with great flexibilities. Together, these three sets of substantive changes moved the federal civil service system closer to the private sector businesslike personnel management, subject to almost unlimited political pressures, influence, and discretionary authority. The flexibilization doctrine provided strategic instruments to public personnel *processes* of government and public administration.

The Civil Service Reform Act of 1978 has received a great deal of scholarly attention. While its supporters have praised it as "a remedy for bureaucratic ills"

(Campbell, 1980), critics have been many from various walks of life, calling its provisions a major "gift" to Ronald Reagan who used it as a key political instrument to reward partisan friends and punish unwanted civil servants, destroy the spirit of civil service system, and to cause a "crisis" in the federal government (Farazmand, 1989; Levine and Kleeman, 1986; Rosen, 1986; Thayer, 1987).

Perhaps a key matter of the fact is that Carter's reform *strategically* positioned the civil service system as a political management tool toward a businesslike personnel administration with great opportunity for political and organizational use and abuse of power, subjecting career employees to partisan political pressures, and destroying a century-long established system of professionalized safeguard that had served as a watchdog system against political corruption in the federal government. The Civil Service Reform Act of 1978 led to the "death" of an independent civil service system that had by spirit served as "an ethical watchdog, the moral guardian of governmental decision making," with the Pendleton Act of 1883 actually being "the full equivalent of a constitutional amendment" (Thayer, 1997, 95). It contributed to political abuse, as "easy firing" of career appointees by political bosses was made possible, along with increasing corruptions that occurred in various departments of government throughout the 1980s and 1990s.

However, the political economy of the Reform explains the strategic instrumentality it was intended to serve in the rapidly changing socioeconomic environment of corporate globalization with a need for a *flexible and subservient* federal bureaucracy under total political control. As noted earlier, historically, the federal civil service system was concerned with the "progressive era" managerial and legal values of efficiency and fairness in managing an expanding federal government with increasing domestic and global responsibilities. The political values of democratic responsiveness, responsibility, and representativeness were considered an inherently embedded component of the political and administrative arrangements within the administrative state under elected officials and their political appointees. But the relatively independent civil service system, especially since the two Hatch Acts of 1939 and 1940 protecting public employees from partisan political activities, was a professional body of neutral competence that had served against political bosses and their potential abuse of authority in government decision making.

This notion of embedded accountability and political control of the bureaucracy came under severe questions from various sources in the 1970s. The key concerns seemed to focus on democratic representation to citizens, as espoused by the conservative right politicians and scholars of "public or rational choice" theory (see, for example, Buchanan and Tullock, 1962; Niskanen, 1971). Their bureaucracy-bashing was followed with a call for massive privatization of government functions, dismantlement of the administrative state, and reduction of the civil service and bureaucracy into an instrument of law and order for social control. The subsequent reorganizations, reforms, and treatments of the federal civil service and bureaucracy under Reagan, who had viewed "government as problem, not a solution," proved how wrong or naive even the good-intentioned supporters of the 1978 Civil Service Reform were. Indeed, it was a powerful gift to Reagan's director of OPM, Donald Devine, who viewed OPM as a "political management institution," politicized the civil service, abolished the examination systems for career recruitments, and placed ideologically oriented right wing partisans in strategic positions of the system. He caused a virtual disintegration of the SES as well as demoralization of the entire federal civil service, and transformed it into a powerful instrument of "political management" (Ingraham, Thompson and Rosenbloom, 1993; Newland, 1992).

More civil service reforms were followed under the Clinton administration, with a further comprehensive aim at its flexibilization, and productivity-oriented goals to be achieved through downsizing, privatization, and other mechanisms similar to private sector business operations. Indeed, Clinton's vice president Al Gore's National Performance Review (NPR 1993) program of reform was a more comprehensive step beyond Reagan's and toward sweeping privatization, outsourcing, and changes, both substantive and formative. This was in line with the so-called "reinventing government" with business-entrepreneurial ideological concepts as prescribed by the White House consultants Osborne and Gaebler (1991). As a result, a new *culture of political entrepreneurship, spoils, and businesslike personnel management* was established by the time George W. Bush took the White House away—through the Supreme Court intervention—from his rival presidential candidate, Al Gore, in the year 2000.

Thus was placed the strategic position of the federal civil service and bureaucracy to serve the globalization functions of corporate America through sweeping privatization, a one-size-fits-all businesslike "new public management," and other measures that George W. Bush's administration has aggressively expanded on. The end result has been the rise of a new business-oriented managerial "orthodoxy" of "new public management" as we all know it. Elsewhere (Farazmand, 1999, 2002, forthcoming), I have argued that both sweeping global privatization and the spread of "new public management" in public administration theory and practice have served as *strategic instruments* in accomplishing the goals of corporate globalization and reducing the role of government and public administration into servants of the particularistic private big-business elites.

CONCLUSION: FUTURE OF THE CIVIL SERVICE

What then is the future of the civil service? What would be expected of the fate of the bureaucracy? Different perspectives may offer different responses to these questions. Mine is as follows: First, bureaucracy has survived millennia of political masters changing over time. As an institution of power instrumental to rule—whether democratic or authoritarian, elected or hereditary—bureaucracy has been and will continue to serve as a strategic instrument of power of the first order. This is a reality that all political statesmen and thinkers of the left and right from the ancient times have realized and lived with.

Bureaucracy may be changed in character to suit particular political and economic interests, but as an institution bureaucracy has a tendency to outlive all political and economic institutions and masters, and at times to "overtower" the society (Weber, 1947). Even the most vocal bureaucracy-bashers, from Jimmy Carter to Ronald Reagan and Margaret Thatcher and now George W. Bush have not only not abolished the bureaucracy, but also found it politically instrumental to their governance and administration, used it to their advantage, and made it even larger. The only differences are the orientations, character, and functions of the bureaucracy that have changed with changes in political masters or bosses. Jimmy Carter changed the character of the bureaucracy away from the welfare administrative state and toward a businesslike corporate governing system demanded by the globalizing corporate elites he represented.

Carter's Civil Service reform Act of 1978 was the prescription for the alteration of the bureaucracy and the "death" of the relatively independent professional civil service in the United States. That prescription was filled rigorously and quickly by the Reagan administration and the U.S. Civil Service, after experiencing severe crises—both institutional and identity, and theoretical and practical (Levine and Kleeman, 1986; Rosen, 1986)—in the 1980s, was buried in the grave, with the remainder to be further lashed in the 1990s. The "direct political control over the federal civil service" established by presidents Reagan and Clinton (Newland, 1992, 87) and through politicization (Farazmand, 1989), the federal government bureaucracy was strategically positioned—both in structure and process—to serve the strategic interests of the accelerated process of "globalization of corporate capitalism" now in its full swing (Farazmand, 1999, 2004).

The new bureaucracy under Reagan was significantly enlarged in both size and budget, rather than shrunken, but its orientations and functional characters were sharply changed toward military and security purposes, while the social welfare and service delivery capacities of the bureaucracy were drastically paralyzed. The end result was a two-fold crisis of both legitimacy and institutional capacity (Farazmand, 1989), both contributing to the often-mentioned slogans of antibureaucracy, anti-civil service, and antigovernment. They have justified the newly designed strategic policy of privatizing, outsourcing, contracting out, and dismantling the welfare administrative state in favor of the globalizing corporate sector. Economic institutionalists are currently happy with these developments (Williamson, 1985).

The sweeping policies of privatization and its ideological-intellectual twin of "new public management" that followed during Reagan and Clinton were designed to transfer governmental functions of the bureaucracy to globalizing corporations and to transform the bureaucracy and civil service—whatever remained of it—to perform strategically the interests of the private business corporations, hence serving the globalization process. Thus took place, one may argue, the death of the civil service—from Carter to Clinton. The character of the bureaucracy and civil service was profoundly changed—in structure, process, and culture—to reflect and serve the interests and goals of private sector globalizing elites at home and abroad, reducing the role of the bureaucracy to maintenance of law and order and social control through security and policing functions by enlarging, like his predecessor Reagan who expanded the military-security policing expenditures, and expanded the policing bureaucracy with size and expenditure. Both Reagan and Clinton, along with senior George Bush, engaged in promoting globalization not only by peaceful means, but also by violence of military action—in Granada, Nicaragua, El Salvador, Kuwait, and Iraq in the first Persian Gulf War against Saddam and later the Balkan war to dismantle Yugoslavia into fragmented small nations easy to control.

Globalization by violence was more aggressively pursued by George W. Bush's "extreme" government administration policy of globalization and global empire building that is well exposed domestically and globally. The tragic terrorist incident of 9/11/2001 gave him the perfect excuse for waging a global war on Muslims, nation-states, and governments, not following Washington's dictates, and political opponents with a powerful policy instrument of fighting "terrorism." The "pretext for war" has been set by false information, lying, and deception, extreme secrecy, lack of transparency, accountability, and more. He has invaded Iraq and Afghanistan, and has threatened, with different pretexts, wars of aggression against North Korea, Iran, and Syria—countries with sovereign governments outside of Washington's global realm of direct influence or manipulation. In serving such a global mission, new generations of security-intelligence-military personnel—in civil as well as military clothes—with different cultural and linguistic knowledge and skills will be needed to staff the rapidly growing global bureaucracy of the federal government in the United States and around the world.

The bureaucracy under the extremist style of the self-assumed "unitary presidency" under Bush has not been diminished; indeed, it has even been enlarged, and turned into a strategic institutional power of serving big business corporate elites as well as of militarization of the world and turning the domestic front into a "secret policing state" for security and "war-on terror" purposes. The bureaucracy has been inflicted with extreme secrecy, staffed with unqualified political appointees on patronage-spoils system basis, temporary and disposable employees, contracted-out services, contractual employees, and political bosses with business interests and personal association in mind. The professional civil service, whatever remained of it, has been transformed into employees and workers at the mercy of their political bosses, and the professional competence of the bureaucracy is paralyzed by the partisan political fears, with the incapacity and scandalous failure to respond to the major crises and emergencies, such as the Hurricane Katrina crisis in New Orleans during September 2005.

Today, the world's largest bureaucracy is composed of the direct military-security bureaucracies of the United States federal government (the Pentagon and the recently reorganized Homeland Security Department), with over 2 million personnel outside of the civil service protection system, professional employees, and workers who work under the personal whims of their political bosses. This figure does not include the security and contractual personnel working as covert agents in government and corporate business organizations in the United States and all over the world. Adding these figures together, plus the 18 million state and local government employees, a rough estimate might put the true figure of the American civilian, military, and security bureaucracy at well over 25 million in size. This figure may even be an understatement, because it does not include the national guards and reserve personnel, as well as the "secret full-time and part-time agents" operating worldwide. In this highly politicized environment, organizational members quickly learn that questioning or challenging political bosses' decisions means a downward foolish act of losing the job. "Patronage-driven political machines always have thrived on poverty and destitution, when people who need jobs will do whatever they are told to do, and businesses without business will do whatever they can to secure government contracts" (Thayer, 1997, 96).

The future of the American federal civil service and bureaucracy will continue to follow the recent trends of demolition, deinstitutioalization, deprofessionliza-tion, corporatization, and marketization, and deregulation to serve the new era of globalization and the challenges it poses to economy, governance, and public management. It will be:

(1) Depoliticized as far as civil servants' political activities are considered, hence limiting or denying public employees basic human rights to express themselves in matters of professional and organizational concerns.

(2) Politicized by partisan bosses who have turned the system into patronage-driven political machines for particularistic and corporate interests and global ideological agendas.

(3) Subjected to further downsizing and corporate takeover for profit maximizing purposes.

(4) Targeted for attacks from all directions for inefficiency and ineffectiveness.

(5) Subjected to further bureaucratic politics, meaning to be used as a strategic instrument for particularistic private business interests.

(6) Subjected deprofessionlization and deinstitutionalization for political patronage purposes. Yet, the latter two phenomena may require some qualifications, as even the globalizing corporatist state of America will need a knowledge-based economy and management system, and knowledge management cannot be done without a good degree of professionalization. However, deinstitutionalization reflects the new *ideological market culture* so pervading the entire governance and public administration with the "new public management." While proponents of this new ideological culture present a good picture of governance and administration (Barzelay, 2001; Donohue and Nye, 2000; Lindblom, 2001), its opponents warn against many serious problems it tends to inflict on broad public interests, governance, accountability, and erosion of institutional legitimacy of public administration organizations. There is a profound cultural change that has questioned the "basic assumptions" of the long-established administrative state with a relatively independent civil service that used to serve the nation—and most other nations as well—for almost a century.

The bureaucracy and civil service have already been extended into global areas to perform the globalization functions of American global superpower agendas, and this trend will most likely continue with great expansion in both scope and size in the 21st century. Thus, the bureaucracy-bashing slogans of the past might continue but the actual and substantive role of the bureaucracy and civil service will continue to expand under different languages and semantics. In fact, the sheer reality of historical impossibility of abolishing bureaucracy—reality or myth—makes it also difficult to dismantle the federal bureaucracy and civil service, especially when it is functional to system maintenance and expansion. However, the age of an independent professional civil service is over in the United States, and any future reforms of the civil service to restore its previous status will be an unlikely event in the age of globalization of corporate capitalism. Will the bureaucracy persist? Yes, but with a new character and function of serving the corporatist state charged with the globalization of corporate capitalism, through both peace and violence.

In conclusion, despite the above observations, several key elements of the civil service and bureaucracy need to be kept in mind; they might serve as a catalyst of incremental change agents for possible realignment of political-administrative forces in the federal government. These include a host of critical and enduring issues—for example, race, color, gender, religion, ethnicity, class, and age (Guy, 1995)—that tend to inevitably embrace legal and constitutional intervention though judicial processes as a last resort. Of these issues, gender, race, color, and religion as well as individual rights (citizens as well as civil servants) will likely raise from time to time concerns of legal and constitutional protection against abuse, arbitrary action, and violation of constitutional rights inviting judicial interventions in administrative matters; hence an increase in judicialization of the civil service, bureaucracy, and public administration (Rohr, 2002).

It may be a truism that a "civil service that cannot question is almost dead," but a host of "other" legal and constitutional bases of challenging the political administration of the bureaucracy can and will serve to a degree the survivability of the professional civil service and prepare the grounds for yet another possibility of reforming the patronage-based corrupt system of administration in the future. It, therefore, is, appropriate to end this chapter by a statement of caution that reforms may solve "problems existing at one time, often in the process creating a new set of problems that may generate subsequent reforms" (Kaufman, 1956; Peters, 2001, 4).

REFERENCES

Barzelay, Michael. (2001). *The New Public Management*. Berkeley, CA: University of California Press.

Buchanan, James M., and Gordon Tullock. (1962). *The Calculus of Consent*. Ann Arbor, MI: University of Michigan Press.

Campbell, Allan K. (1980). Civil Service Reform as a Remedy for Bureaucratic Ills. In C. H. Weiss and A.H. Barton (Eds.), *Making Bureaucracies Work*. Beverly Hills, CA: Sage Publications.

————. (1978). Civil Service Reform: A New Commitment. *Public Administration Review*, 38(2): 99–103.

Cayer, Joseph N. (1995). Merit System Reform in the States. In Steven Hays and Richard Kearney (Eds.), *Public Personnel Administration*, 3rd ed., pp. 291–305. San Francisco, CA: Jossey-Bass.

Donahue, John, and Joseph Nye (2000) (Eds.), *Market-Based Governance*. Washington, DC: Brookings Institution Press.

Farazmand, Ali. (forthcoming-a). *Public Administration in the Age of Globalization.*

————. (forthcoming-b). *Revitalizing Public Service and Administration.*

————. (forthcoming-c). *Globalization, Governance, and Administration.*

————. (2005). "Public Sector Reforms and Transformation: Implications for Development Administration." Ahmed Shafiqul Haque and in Habib Zafarullah (Eds.), *Handbook of International Development Governance, pp.* 545–560. New York: Taylor and Francis.

————. (2004). *Sound Governance: Policy and Administrative Innovations*. Westport, CT: Praeger.

————. (2002). Privatization and Globalization: A Critical Analysis with Implications for Public Management Education and Training. *International Review of Administrative-Science* 68(3): 355–371.

————. (1999, November–December). Globalization and Public Administration. *Public Administration Review.* 59(6): 509–522.

————. (1989). Crisis in the U.S. Administrative State. *Administration and Society*, 21(2): 173–199.

Goodsell, Charles. (1995). *The Case for Bureaucracy*, 3rd ed. Chatham, NJ: Chatham House.

Guy, Mary E. (1995). Women, Public Administration, and the Personnel Function. In Steven W. Hays, and Richard C. Kearney (Eds.), *Public Personnel Administration*, 3rd ed., pp. 232–246. Englewood Cliffs, NJ: Prentice-Hall.

Heclo, Hugh. (1977). *A Government of Strangers*. Washington, DC: Brookings Institution.

Ingraham, Patricia W., James R. Thompson, and David H. Rosenbloom. (1993). *The Promise And Paradox of Civil Service Reform*. Pittsburgh, PA: University of Pittsburgh Press.

Ingraham, Patricia W., and James R. Thompson. (1995). The Civil Service Reform Act of 1978 and Its Progeny: The Promise and the Dilemma. In Steven W. Hays and Richard C. Kearney (Eds.), *Public Personnel Administration*, 32nd ed., pp. 54–69. Englewood Cliffs, NJ: Prentice-Hall.

Kaufman, Herbert. (1956). Emerging Doctrines of Public Administration. *American Political Science Review*, 50: 1059–1073.

Levine, Charles H., and R. S. Kleeman. (1986). The Quiet Crisis of the Civil Service: The Federal Personnel System at the Crossroads. Occasional paper, National Academy of Public Administration.

Lindblom, Charles. (2001). *The Market Systems*. New Haven, CT: Yale University Press.

Mosher, Frederick. (1968). *Democracy and the Public Service*, 2nd ed., 1982. New York: Oxford University Press.

National Performance Review. (1993). *From Red Tape to Results: Creating A Government That Works Better and Costs Less*. Washington, DC: Government Printing Office.

Newfond, Chester A. (1992). The Politics of Civil Service Reform. In Patricia Ingraham and David Rosenbloom (Eds.), *The Promise And Paradox of Civil Service Reform*. Pittsburgh, PA: University of Pittsburgh Press.

Newland, Chester A. (1983, January–February). A Mid-Term Appraisal—A Reagan Presidency: Limited Government and Political Administration. *Public Administration Review*, 43: 1–21.

Niskanen, William, Jr. (1971). *Bureaucracy and Representative Government.* Chicago, IL: Aldine Atherton.

Osborne, D., and T. Gaebler. (1991). *Reinventing Government: How the Entrepreneurial Spirit Is Transforming the Public Sector.* Reading, MA: Addison-Wesley.

Peters, B. Guy. (2002). Government Reorganization: Theory and Practice. In Ali Farazmand (Ed.), *Modern Organizations: Theory and Practice*, 2nd ed., pp. 159–189. Westport, CT: Praeger.

———. (2001). *The Future of Governing*, 2nd ed., Laurence, KS: University Press of Kansas.

Rohr, John A. (2002). *Civil Servants And Their Constitutions.* Lawrence, KS: University Press of Kansas.

Rosen, Bernard. (1986). Crisis in the U.S. Civil Service. *Public Administration Review*, 46: 207–214.

Rosenbloom, David. (1993). *Public Administration: Understanding Management, Politics, and Law In The Public Sector*, 2nd ed. New York: Random House.

Sayer, W. (1948, Spring). The Triumph of Techniques over Purpose. *Public Administration Review*, 8: 134–137.

Skowronek, S. (1982). *Building a New American State: The Expansion of National Administrative Capacity, 1877–1920.* Cambridge, UK: Cambridge University Press.

Thayer, Frederick. (1997). The U.S. Civil Service: 1883–1993 (R.I.P.). In Ali Farazmand (Ed.), *Modern Systems of Government: Exploring The Role of Bureaucrats and Politicians*, pp. 95–124. Thousand Oaks, CA: Sage.

———. (1987). Performance Appraisal and Merit Pay Systems: The Disasters Multiply. *Review of Public Personnel Administration*, 7(2): 36–53.

Waldo, Dwight. (1992). *The Enterprise of Public Administration*, 2nd ed. Novato, CA: Chandler & Sharp.

———. (1948). *The Administrative State.* New York: Ronald; 2nd ed., New York: Chandler & Sharp.

Weber, Max. (1947). *From Max Weber: Essays in Sociology.* H. H. Girth and C. Wright Mills (Trans. and Eds.), New York: Oxford University Press.

Williamson, Oliver E. (1985). *The Economic Institutions of Capitalism: Firms, Markets, and Relational Contracting.* New York: Free Press.

Wilson, Woodrow. (1941, December) [1887]. The Study Of Administration. *Political Science Quarterly*, 56: 481–506.